W9-DCH-921

SHOW ME THY WAYS

Gertrude Hoeksema

Grade 4

Reformed Free
Publishing Association

Copyright © 1988 by
Reformed Free Publishing Association
4949 Ivanrest Avenue
Grandville, MI 49418

All rights reserved. The book, or parts thereof, may not be reproduced in any form without permission in writing from the publisher.

ISBN 0-916206-35-1
Library of Congress Card Number 88-61905

Second Printing 1996

PRINTED IN THE UNITED STATES

TABLE OF CONTENTS

LESSON 1
Our God and His Revelation

BEFORE WE BEGIN the lessons in Old Testament history for this year, we will find it helpful in our first lesson to ask and answer some questions about our God Who gave us a record of both Old and New Testament history in His precious gift of the Bible.

God has given us wonderful minds, but they are human minds, suited for thinking and understanding the things of the world we see and know. How, then, can we say anything about the God Who is a Spirit and lives in the highest heaven, Who is the Maker and Ruler of heaven and earth? Can we describe God? Take a few minutes to discuss these questions in class.

LESSON OUTLINE

A. We will ask three questions about God, and find some amazing answers.

    1. Who is God?

        a. Because God is so far above us, so holy and pure, it may be easier to say what God is not than what God is. We cannot discover God. He lives in the highest heaven, and we live on His footstool, the earth. If we searched for Him with our earthly minds and eyes all our lives, we would not find Him, because He is not of our world. We can know only things which we can see and taste and touch: trees, our friends, things to eat, such as apples, or the motor of a car which we can take apart. We cannot even think of a world not made of materials which we can handle.

        b. We cannot picture God. We know at the same time that He is not just an idea in our minds, but He is a Spirit, without a body which we can see, for our eyes can see only earthly things. Because we can think only of earthly things, in our minds we often picture God as some kind of man, don't we? It is hard for us who live on the earth to understand what a Spirit is.

        c. We cannot understand God with our earthly minds. He is perfect, pure, and holy, and our sinful minds and hearts do not know what that is. We think we are very good when we can get through a day without a scolding (even when we know our thoughts are evil). But how can we, with our evil thoughts, imagine our God Who never had nor ever will have even one evil thought? He lives in pure holiness*.

1

d.   We cannot contain God in time or space. We can be in only one place at one time: either here in school or at home, but not both places at the same time. God lives in a spiritual world, a world we do not know, one without minutes or hours or days, and without inches or feet or miles. We live in the time and space God created for us.

e.   We cannot compare God with anything because God is not like any- thing we know. We cannot even say that God is greater or more powerful than anyone or anything. He is the only Great and Powerful One.

2.   How can we, His children, know God then?

a.   We know God through His revelation*. He told us about Himself. How did He do that? He "breathed" His words through men whom He specially prepared. We call it inspiration*. He spoke to earthly men in earthly speech and He told them to write down His words. What did He tell them? He told them about Himself and His plan and His works: that He created our world in six days; that He chose His own special people out of a world of sinners to be saved from their sins by the blood of Jesus. God gave us all the details of His plan in His revelation. We call God's revelation the Bible. Think of all the people in Bible history to whom God spoke in a voice, and often told them to write down His words: Adam, Noah, David, Isaiah, and Paul. We know that God has seen to it that His Bible has been kept safe from the beginning of the world and will be safe until the end of time.

b.   God also told us about Himself in His created world. All the things He made tell us about their creator. Discuss in class some of the wonders which show that only our great God created our world. The beauty and variety of God's creation is almost endless.

3.   In His revelation, what does God tell us about Himself?

a.   He is infinite (or eternal). God does not live in time, and is not ruled by beginnings or endings. God never says, "I was," or "I will be," but His name is "I Am." God can never say, as we do, "Pretty soon I will do it," or "I didn't have time for it."

b.   He is omnipresent (or everywhere present). God does not live in space. Space could not hold Him! Is that hard to understand? When God sits on His throne, He does not take up inches of space, as we do. It is hard for us to understand, because we live in space. But at the same time, we know that God is present everywhere: in the highest heaven, with

2

our parents at home or at work, and also here in this classroom with us.

c. He is omnipotent (all-powerful). Any power that we can imagine is in His hand: He holds the stars in their places, and He lets us move our right thumbs back and forth, and He lets the devil run through the earth with his wickedness.

d. He is all-knowing. Do you know why we say that God is all-knowing? Because He planned everything and He makes everything happen down to the last detail. In the beginning God knew there would be a heaven and earth — in fact, a whole universe* — because He planned it; and all He had to do was speak His powerful Word. He knows you, too, because He planned your personality, and the house you live in, and everything you will do in your life.

B. God Is One

1. Before we start the stories of creation in our next lessons, we must know that many people, in fact, most of the people on this earth do not believe the creation story God told us. They believe the evil theory of evolutionism: that our world and everything in it happened by chance, and developed all by itself. Most people, also those who say they believe that the Bible is God's infallible Word (a Word without error), say that everything we see in this world tells us that it is millions or billions of years old. They insist that rock formations and fossils give us a different story from the story of the Bible. They say that the history of creation in the Bible is only a story God told, to teach us how powerful He is. Others believe that the days of creation were millions of years long. In other words, they do not believe God's revelation about creation.

Discuss some of the wrong ideas of
evolutionism in class.

2. Yet these same people say that they do believe God's revelation about Jesus. They say that they believe the part of the Bible which tells us about Jesus dying for us. They say that it is important to know that they are saved by the blood of the cross. But they do not believe in the Jesus Who was busy creating the world. Is it possible to believe some parts of the Bible, but not others?

3. It is not possible. Why not? Those who say they do not believe in God's creation story forget that our God is one God in three Persons. They forget that we cannot separate God. The God Who created all things is the same

3

God Who saves His people. They forget that the same Father, Son, and Holy Spirit were at creation and at the cross of Jesus.

4. John 1:1 tells us that the Jesus Who saves us is the Word of creation. Read John 1:1-3 and discuss it in class.

DO NOT FORGET: Creation and salvation always go together. You cannot believe the one without believing the other.

WORD STUDIES:

1. holiness — freedom from sin, purity, cleanness
2. revelation — to make something known — God made Himself known by speaking
3. inspiration — God breathed into men His Words so they could speak and write His Words
4. universe — the whole creation and everything in it

LESSON 2
Days One and Two of Creation Week
Genesis 1:1-8

BEFORE WE BEGIN the lessons on God's creation, think about this beautiful text from Psalm 145:10: "All thy works shall praise thee, O Lord; and thy saints shall bless thee." Do you know that all God's works, from the fields and the woods, to the birds and the animals praise their Maker? We, His children, are the saints who bless our God every day for giving us His great creation.

LESSON OUTLINE

A. Day One

    1. In the beginning

        a. If we read the first three words of Genesis 1:1, "In the beginning," we will know what the word Genesis means. It means beginning. And verse 1 tells us that in the beginning there was only God. God always was. But Genesis 1:1 tells us that God also made a beginning, a beginning of what? A beginning of His earthly creation and a beginning of time and space.

        b. Verses 1 and 2 are the introduction to creation. If you read the rest of verse 1, you will find out that God called the heaven and the earth into being. They did not look the same as they do now, for they were in unfinished form. It is hard for us to imagine what the heaven and earth looked like, for this was only the first step in God's creation. Later He would separate the finished parts from the unfinished creation. That is what the word create means: to divide or to separate.

        c. What did God do when He created*? Sometimes we hear this definition: "He made something out of nothing." That is not a very good definition. The Bible says it better: God created by the Word of His mouth. Do you know that God's Word is His Son, our Lord Jesus? It is a beautiful thought that God made our world through His Son, the One Who died to save us.

Read Hebrews 11:3 in class
and discuss how God's creation is different from
the things we can invent.

2. Without form and void

    a. Verse 2 is still God's introduction to creation. God is telling us what the earth was like in its unfinished form. The earth was "without form." It was without finished form. When mother makes a cake, she has a runny, sticky batter in her bowl — a cake in unfinished form, quite unlike the frosted, decorated birthday cake.

    b. The cake batter is also "void." Void means empty — empty of finished parts. The cake batter is a small picture to help us understand what God's earth was like on day one. It was empty of finished parts. The solids, liquids, and gases of God's universe were not yet separated.

    c. The Spirit — the Holy Spirit — moved or fluttered over the unfinished waters of the earth and heaven. We could compare it to the warmth of a mother hen who sits on a nest and gives life to her hatching eggs. So the Spirit of God gave life to His creation.

Read Genesis 1:3-5

3. "Let there be light"

    a. Our all-wise God created light first. Why? Because nothing can live without light. No plants, animals, nor people could survive in total darkness. Total darkness is not darkness as we see it at night, but darkness so thick a ray of light cannot pass through it. Think what it would be like to live in thick, black, icy darkness. Do you know that the light God made is also heat, power, energy, electricity?

    b. Because the light in our world is God's gift of life to us, it is a picture of the perfect light and purity in which God lives, for God always lives in the light. It is also a picture of the light of His love by which He saves us.

    c. God separated the light, which is a picture of His holiness, from the awful darkness, the black darkness which was over the earth, the darkness which is a picture of the misery of hell.

    d. When God created light, He created time: days with seconds, minutes, and hours; and each of God's days started with a morning and ended with an evening. God, the only One Who knows what is good, called His light good. Do you think of God's light as a new gift every morning, sent to cheer you and help you live through the day? Do you thank Him that you do not have to stumble around in total darkness?

B. Day Two

1. The waters of the universe

a.   Our universe is the whole system of things God created. It includes
our earth, the heavens, planets, and outer space. The waters before day
two were not waters as we know them, but where still in the unfinished
form of God's creation. Then God spoke His Word to the waters.

Read Genesis 1:6, 7

b.   These verses tell us about two kinds of waters, the waters above and
the waters below. The waters above are the waters which hold the sun,
moon, stars, and planets in their places. The next time you look at the
stars, remember that God's "waters above" keep them right where they
are. These waters reach into what we call outer space.

c.   What, then, are the waters below? They are the waters we can see:
the bodies of water under the firmament, such as lakes and oceans, the
rain, dew, mist, and clouds.

2.   The separation of the waters

a.   What is between the waters above and the waters below? The firmament. Verse 7 tells us that God divided these waters by creating the
firmament. The word firmament means beaten or stretched out. When
we look up, we see it as a beautiful, soft, blue covering over us. Actually
it is a huge, finely-beaten ocean. How do we know? Read Psalm 104:2
and Job 37:18, and find out.

b.   The firmament is the beaten-out ocean in which all the heavenly
bodies, the stars, and the planets, float; and the waters keep them exactly
in their right places. The whole world floats in these waters, which we
often call outer space. God made these waters to hold the bodies of land
in place so they would not collide. We know that God made the waters
above and below the firmament so that light and sound could pass
through them. Do you realize that if God had not created these waters,
we could not see the sun, nor communicate by radio or satellite?

DO NOT FORGET that there is another heaven besides "the waters above." It
is the heaven of glory, not made in time or space.

WORD STUDIES

1.   create — God's act of forming all things by the Word of His power

LESSON 3
Days Three and Four of Creation Week
Genesis 1:9-19

BEFORE WE BEGIN, we will remember that in the first two creation days, God was separating the parts of His world, to finish it. To make it easier to understand the creation of the third and fourth days, we could compare God's creation to the building of a house. On days one and two God made the materials for His house. Now He is ready to finish His house, and make it liveable for men.

LESSON OUTLINE

Read Genesis 1:9, 10

A. Day Three

   1. Finishing His house

     a. Verse 9 tells us that God spoke to the waters under the heaven and told them to be gathered into one place. God told Job, in chapter 38:8, how He did it. Read this verse in class. He put doors on the seas and oceans and rivers! Not doors as we know them, of course, but God's doors, which said, "So far, and no farther." Then the dry land, the home of men and animals, was lifted above the seas.

     b. "God called the dry land Earth," verse 10. We know that the inside of our earth is very dense and heavy, to make it firm and stable. God in His wisdom made a heavy foundation (a core) for His earth, just as builders make a heavy foundation for a large building. On day three, God finished the kinds of dry land on His earth, the soil: clay, sand, stony ground. . . . We could call them the "building blocks" of God's house. He formed the mountains with their rocky sides, and the deep valleys below. God was shaping His earth. Inside the earth He planted treasures for the people who would live in His house (the earth) — gold, silver, copper, diamonds, coal, and precious stones.

     c. It is possible that at the time of the creation God created only one large piece of dry land. Verse 9 tells us that the waters were gathered to one place, and the dry land appeared. God probably did not make His first "house" very big, because His first family was not very big. It took time for Adam and Eve's family to become large and to spread over the

8

earth. When did God make His "house" bigger? At the time of the flood. Then God made a different world. He made the continents as we see them on our maps of today. Turn to II Peter 3:6, 7, and see that he calls the world before the flood "the world that then was," and the world after the flood "the world that now is." Look at a map or globe and see how much of our world is water, the water in which our continents float.

2. Furnishing His house

a. Now we will come back to the picture of God's house. We can say that on the rest of day three God filled the kitchen and cellar, and decorated His house. How did God do this? He created the plant life. Read verses 11 and 12. Plant life is the lowest form of life. Plants are tied to the earth. They cannot move about, nor think, nor act. They use God's air, light, and heat, to grow. And God made them so they will bring forth fruit after their own kind. Each plant has its own special seed, so that an apple tree will bear apples and apple seeds. God will never do anything foolish like having an apricot tree bear seeds for beans! God made three kinds of plants: the grasses, the herbs (small plants), and the trees. When God furnished His house, He never ran out of ideas for the good kinds of food and furnishings to put into His house. He gave food plants for our kitchens and freezers; and flowers, trees, and shrubs without number for decoration — to make His house beautiful — and trees for wood and shelter. He made far more than we need. Our God is never stingy with His gifts.

b. As plants grow, God makes them point to heaven; and as plants always reach upward toward the light, they tell us, "Look to the light, a picture of the Light of the world." When sin came into the world, plant life suffered. Heat and lack of rain withered them. Weeds and poisonous plants, pictures of sin, crept in. Our Lord Jesus loved to tell parables about plants. One of them was the parable of the four kinds of soil (or the sower). In class, try to think of more parables about plants.

Read verses 14-16

B. Day Four

1. The lamps of the house

a. God's world already had light. You remember that God created light on the first day. On day four He put His light into carriers, or light-

9

bearers: the sun, moon, and stars. If we want to use the figure of a house again, we may say that the Lord gave us lamps and reflectors. The sun and some stars have light in themselves (and could be compared with lamps). The moon, planets, and other stars only reflect the light of the sun.

b. Verses 17 to 19 tell us what the light-bearers do. They rule our world. Remember: nothing in God's creation stands still, even though it often seems that way to our eyes. All the light-bearers travel in the path God made for them. As they travel, they rule our lives. How do they do that? They measure the time that God created on the first day into minutes, hours, days, months, and years. They set our calendars. God's sun, the ruler of the day, also controls the winds, storms, heat, rain, and the growth of plants. God's moon, the ruler of the night, controls the tides of the oceans.

> Discuss in class how these light-bearers
> rule the details of our lives.

c. Our sun is a picture of the Sun. Read Malachi 4:2. Who is the Sun of righteousness? Revelation 22:16 tells of the Morning Star. Read it and tell who He is.

DO NOT FORGET: Light-bearers reflect light. We have no light in ourselves, but we reflect the light of God through Jesus Christ. We are light-bearers, too.

LESSON 4
Days Five and Six of Creation Week
Genesis 1:20-25

BEFORE WE BEGIN the story of God's creation on days five and six, we may want to ask: "How did God create the fish, birds, and animals? How did He bring them out of the earth?" The answer is that we can never fully understand, for it is a great wonder. All we can do is believe it by faith.

LESSON OUTLINE

A. Day Five

   1. God's orderly work

     a. Before we study how God created the fish and birds on the fifth day and the animals on the sixth, we will find out what the ungodly world thinks about the beginnings of the fish, birds, and animals. Not only do they say that our world just grew and developed by itself through millions of years (we learned that in Lesson 1), but they say that life just started — all by itself.

     b. They teach that all life came from one small cell, which developed into tiny forms of plants. Then plant life gradually developed into the tiniest of animals, and after millions of years these tiny animals in the seas became fish, those in the air developed wings and became birds. Of the land animals, the lower kinds became higher kinds, and finally the highest kind of animal (possibly the monkey) became a man.

     c. All of this took, not six creation days, but billions of years. What a horrid idea! These unbelievers will not receive God's Word by faith*, because God does not give them faith. They believe only what they see or think they see. God lets us figure out from His Word how old the earth really is: about 6,000 years old.

Discuss in class
these ungodly ideas of evil men.

     b. It is true that God did create the living things in His creation in the order of lower, simpler kinds to higher, more intelligent kinds. We could think back to yesterday's lesson and call the plants which God created on day three living beings: they can not move and cannot think or understand anything. On days five and six God created living souls.

11

The fish and the birds of day five could move: they swam and they flew. These creatures are higher than the plants. We often say that God gave them simple minds, but when we remember what they can do, we would do better to say that God gave them wonderful minds.

Read Genesis 1:20, 21

2. From the waters and from the ground

a. God spoke His powerful Word to the waters and they brought forth the fish, all the kinds of fish from whales (sea monsters) down to the lowly minnows. Fish are some of the lower kinds of creatures, farthest from people in looks. They are flat, without arms or legs. They are farthest away in their surroundings. They cannot live on land. God did not tell the fish to develop fins and gills for a million years so they could survive in the water. No, He made a rule for the fish: because He created them with fins and gills, they must stay in the water in order to live.

Read Genesis 1:20 and Genesis 2:19

b. Did you notice that God called the birds from the waters and from the ground? The meaning is that possibly God called them from both land and water. It teaches us that birds belong to the earth, to the land or to the water. Though they fly in the firmament, they are tied to the earth for getting their food and making their nests. God's rule for birds is that they do not swim under water, but live on the land and fly in the air, and some swim on the surface of the water. Birds are a little closer to people than fish are. In what ways?

Read Genesis 1:24 carefully,
noticing the kinds of animals.

B. Day Six

1. The creatures closest to man

a. Did you notice that God created three kinds, or classes, of animals?

1) The creeping things: insects and small creeping creatures such as lizards. These are the most unlike people.

2) The beasts of the earth: the wild animals, who are somewhat closer to people in shape and size.

3) Cattle is the word the Bible often uses for tame animals, especially those we have as pets, and those who live nearer to us.

b. Animals are higher forms of living souls: they can crawl, hop, jump, and run. They can also hear, smell, taste, touch, and respond to other animals and to people. They care for their own young, and often show love, anger, or faithfulness; not by instinct, which is a natural reaction, but by using the senses God gave them.

c. Once more, God furnished His house. He was not stingy, but gave us a wide variety of living souls for our use: for beauty, for pets, and for food.

2. God blessed His living creatures

a. He told them to multiply after their kind, verse 21. That means a mother robin will have a baby robin, not a baby hawk, or a baby cat. God's Word knows nothing of one animal developing into another.

Read Genesis 1:30

b. God gave plants for food for the animals He had made. Why not meat? Because in Paradise there was no death, no killing, and therefore no meat from dead animals. They ate grass and herbs in perfection, with no fighting, no killing, and no curse.

3. Animals as types

a. God created some of the animals to be pictures (types*) of Christ. Think of the lamb for sacrifice, a picture of the Lamb of God.

b. God tells us that the animal world will be represented in heaven. Read Isaiah 65:25 in class and tell how the animals will be different in heaven.

DO NOT FORGET that although the living souls are wonderful creations of God, they cannot know and understand God. Only His people, to whom our Father gave minds and hearts and wills to understand, and grace* to believe, can know Him.

WORD STUDIES

1. faith — to know and to trust and to believe with a whole heart
2. type — an Old Testament picture of a New Testament reality: for example, a lamb as a picture of Jesus.
3. grace — God's favor and goodness to us, while we do not deserve it

LESSON 5
The Creation of Man, the Seventh Day
Genesis 1:26; 2:1-7

BEFORE WE BEGIN, can you imagine the wonderful joy and surprise for Adam when he first opened his eyes in the perfect creation God had made? Think about the wonder of it: a perfect man in a perfect creation! God made Adam understand all of His wonderful works, and he must have said, "My God, how great Thou art!"

LESSON OUTLINE

Read Genesis 1:25, 26

A. Day Six (continued)

   1. God talks to Himself

     a. After God had created the animals on day six, He paused and talked to Himself. Why? Because He was about to create a special creature, a man. The Bible often uses the word man as a term for a person. This man was to be made in God's image — in the likeness of God! He would be a creature who could think, understand, and who could know God. Man would be the highest creature in God's creation.

     b. Notice that God said, in verse 26, "Let us make man in our image." Remember, God is not more than one God, but He tells us here that He is more than one Person (we know He is three) in one Being. We call it the trinity, the unity of Three in One. Therefore He can talk to Himself.

   2. God creates man

     a. When God created the animals, He simply called them from the earth. See verse 24. But God did not call man from the earth, because He wanted to make man in his image*. Man must come straight from the hand of God. God took dust from the ground and breathed into it the breath of life. Can we imagine how God did this? No, we cannot begin to understand it, nor can we make any pictures in our minds. Why not? Because it was a wonder, which belongs only to God. We are too weak and earthly to understand this great work of God.

     b. Man is a special creature in God's creation, because God breathed into man the breath of life. Of course, the animal world breathes, too; but to man God gave a special breath of life. It gave man (Adam) the

14

ability to think, to use his will, to know God, and to know good and evil. He gave us these gifts, too.

c.   God made Adam in His image — His likeness. God made Adam as a picture of Himself. This means that Adam was able to hear and understand and obey God's Word, to be God's friend, and to do His will perfectly in love. God and Adam had no secrets from one another. What a beautiful picture of the man God made!

Read Genesis 1:28

3.   Man's duties

a.   God told Adam to have children, grandchildren, and great-grandchildren, many of them, and to fill the earth with people.

b.   Next, Adam must subdue* the earth. That means he must discover the riches of the earth, develop them (think of finding gold and making lovely jewelry from it) and use them as God's gifts to him. God gives these same duties to us.

c.   Finally, Adam had dominion* over the earth. He ruled it and cared for it, under God, not to earn wages, but as God's friend-servant. Before Adam sinned, he was God's perfect friend-servant. He ruled over the earth and cared for it perfectly in love to God.

Read Genesis 2:19, 20

d.   Then God brought the animals to Adam to see what he would call them. Because he was perfect, Adam could see into the very nature of the animals, and called each one the name which truly fit. It was not like thinking up a nice name for a pet, like Muffet or Prince. No, the animals were God's "words" of creation, and Adam spoke those words to the animals. After Adam named the animals, he was very lonely because he saw that each animal had a companion, a male and a female, a husband and a wife; and Adam was all alone.

e.   So God made a help meet for him — a helper fit for him. God made a deep sleep come to Adam, not like an anesthetic for an operation in a hospital, but a sleep to hide from Adam the great wonder He would work. Adam could not take a part in God's wonder. While Adam slept, God took one of his ribs and made a woman, his help meet.

Read Genesis 2:1-3

B.   Day Seven

1.   God looked at His work of creation and it was very good. Everything

served the exact purpose for which God had created it. What was that purpose? That everything, hills and trees, birds and wild beasts, but especially God's highest creation, man, would praise His greatness.

2. When God rested, He was not idle, but enjoyed His perfect work. He sanctified the seventh day. It means that He set the seventh day apart, to make it holy. That is what we do on the sabbath, too. We set it apart as a holy day, to enjoy God's perfect work. How do we enjoy God's special day?

Discuss in class how we like to enjoy
God's works on His special day.

DO NOT FORGET that we as God's children are tied to the earth. We like our life here. But because Jesus has given us new hearts, we like the day of rest the best, because it is a picture of the perfect life of heaven. Then we will live in the perfect sabbath forever. The Bible also calls it the perfect "Day of the Lord."

WORD STUDIES

1. image — the likeness of something or someone else
2. subdue — to discover and to use the riches of the earth
3. dominion — to have the rule over someone or something

LESSON 6
The Fall
Genesis 2:8-17; 3:1-15

BEFORE WE BEGIN the sad history of Adam and Eve's fall into sin, we cannot help remembering what their fall did to us. Because of that first sin of Adam, we are all born sinners, and if we are left to ourselves, we love our sins and hate God. But thank the Lord: He promised to send a second Adam, our Lord Jesus Christ, Who would give His life for us, and by His Spirit give us new hearts to love Him.

LESSON OUTLINE

Read Genesis 2:8-10

A. Man's First Home

    1. We do not know how nor where God made the garden of Eden, but we know that He made a real garden, with rivers and precious stones and lovely trees. Adam and Eve's home was a place of perfect beauty and pleasantness.

    2. The trees of the garden

        a. Every tree in the garden was pleasant to the eye and good for food, verse 9.

        b. The tree of life was in the middle of the garden. It had power to continue to give Adam and Eve earthly life, not if they ate the fruit just once, but if they continued to eat the fruit. This tree was a picture of the gift of life which God gave to them. To come to the tree of life was to come to God, to be God's friend, and to live in His favor. God would bless them if they ate of it.

        c. The tree of knowledge of good and evil was also in the garden. It was a pleasant tree, with good fruit on it. It was not a tree with poisonous fruit. Now read Genesis 2:16, 17. God said to Adam and Eve, "Thou shalt not eat of it." God would bless them only if they did not eat of it.

B. God's Command

    1. Why did God give this command? Remember, God always has a reason. He wanted Adam and Eve to know that "man shall not live by bread alone" (Deuteronomy 8:3). God was teaching His friends that there is more to a man than his body and his stomach. God made Adam with a spiritual side,

which loves God, lives with God, and obeys Him. God was teaching Adam and Eve to obey Him in love. That is the only true life for Adam, for us, and for all God's children: to obey in love.

2. That is the reason the tree is called the tree of knowledge of good and evil. Remember, God is the only One Who knows what good and evil is. If Adam obeyed and did not eat, he would do what God does: love the good and hate the evil. If he disobeyed and ate, he would hate the good and love the evil.

3. God told His friends what the penalty* for disobedience would be: the day that thou eatest thereof thou shalt surely die.

Read Genesis 3:1

C. The Temptation by Satan

1. A real serpent came to Eve, and he was subtle. Subtle sometimes means "sneaky." Here it means "clever, intelligent." Possibly the serpent was one of the highest animals, closest to man, far different from the snake we know.

2. Chapter 3 does not tell us that the devil spoke through the serpent, but the rest of the Scriptures tell us that the devil is a tempter and a liar. John 8:44 says that "he is a liar, and the father of it." The devil was speaking through the serpent. Who is the devil? A fallen angel, who fell because he rebelled against God. He was so proud that he wanted to be God, and God had to throw him out of heaven.

3. Now that he was fallen from heaven, Satan could not attack God, so he did the next best thing: he attacked Adam, the head of God's creation. But he did not go to Adam first. He came to Eve, not because she was weaker, but because Adam was the head of all creation, and God had given the commands to him. Adam might be harder to tempt.

4. Satan asked a clever question in chapter 3:1. Read it again. The answer is "no." Satan asked Eve this question to make her think, "If we can eat of all the trees, why will this one make us die?" And it turned out just as Satan wished. He made Eve think his way. When she answered him in verse 3, she said, "God hath said, Ye shall not eat of it." Then she added something: "neither shall ye touch it." God did not say that, but Eve was starting to agree with the devil.

Read verses 4, 5, 6

5. Now Satan told an outright lie: "Ye shall not surely die." He went on: "Your eyes shall be opened and ye shall be as God" (not gods). Eve listened. She, too, was becoming proud. She would like to be as God.

18

6. Satan had planted the lie in Eve's soul. She saw the three things we just read in verse 6:

    a.   That the tree was good for food

    b.   That it was pleasant to the eyes

    c.   That it was desired to make one wise.

Discuss in class
what I John 2:16 calls the three things Eve saw.

D. The Fall

1. After she ate, Eve knew her misery. Now she could not live with her perfect husband, so she gave him some of the fruit. It seems as if she did not have to try hard to persuade him, for he, too, ate. Both of them knew they had died a spiritual death*: their hearts were evil now. What did that mean? That their hearts were dead to God: they could not love Him, and they could love only sin.

2. The result was that they lost God's image, the perfect image in which God had made them, and they became the image of the devil. Both of them hid when God came, because they knew how ugly with sin they were. They could not stand before God's holiness. Those fig leaves could not cover the sin in their hearts!

Read verses 8-14

3. Notice that God came to Adam and Eve. They had done the wrong, and should have gone to God, but the Righteous God came to them. Adam could not answer God's question in verse 9, because he was afraid. He blamed "the woman whom thou gavest to be with me." Do you see that Adam was trying to put the blame on God because God gave him his wife? Eve blamed the serpent, and God cursed the serpent, verse 14. In verse 15, God made His promise to them, which we will study in our next lesson.

DO NOT FORGET that God was right there in Paradise all the time. If we ask, "Could He not have stopped that first sin?" the answer is yes. But God's plan called for Adam and Eve to fall into sin, because God wanted a greater glory for His people: to save them through the wonder of Jesus' death on the cross and to take them to live in heaven with Him forever.

WORD STUDIES

1. penalty — punishment for breaking the law

2. death — to live apart from God

19

LESSON 7
Cain and Abel
Genesis 3:15-4:15

BEFORE WE BEGIN, we must know what happened when Adam and Eve fell into sin: when they sinned, they fell into the arms of Jesus. The first verse of our lesson tells us about it.

LESSON OUTLINE

A. The result of the Fall

    1. When God asked Adam and Eve all those questions in chapter 3, which we read in our last lesson, they must have felt totally hopeless. They knew they had sinned, and they told the Lord that they sinned, but they felt miserable, the way we do when our sins are found out.

        a. They did not know how to repent and be sorry for their sin, because they had not yet heard about their Savior; and they had not yet heard any words of forgiveness from the Lord for their sins.

Read Genesis 3:15

        b. Suddenly the bright light of God's Word shone into the darkness of their hearts. How? God put the light of His promise into their hearts. Because Adam and Eve were God's children, and He loved them, He made them to be His friends. He made a covenant* with them. A covenant is a relation of friendship. How do we know that? Because verse 15 promises that the seed of the woman, one of her children, will some day crush the devil's head. That Child is Jesus, their Savior, Who would take away the darkness of their sin. He is Jesus our Savior, too.

        c. The devil, who was the liar and the tempter, would never have a place in that friendship. God put enmity (hatred) between the devil and the woman, and between his seed* and her seed.

        d. God promised that from the line of Eve's children would be born the Child who would bruise the devil's head. That Child was Jesus, who on the cross took away all the devil's power by dying for the seed of Adam and Eve, and taking their punishment upon Himself. Who are their seed? All of God's chosen children, from every nation. We are that seed, too.

Read Genesis 3:16-19

    2. Because of Adam and Eve's fall, God sent His judgments into the world.

20

a.   Sin came into every part of God's world. He cursed the earth so that it sprouted thorns, thistles, and weeds. Our earth is still under that curse. Although God did not curse Adam and Eve (for they were His children), He told them they would have pain, sweat, and sorrow.

b.   God showed that He covered Adam and Eve's sin by making coats of animal skins for them. Why skins? God was showing them that there was no forgiveness or covering of sin without the shedding of blood. God killed an animal (a lamb?) so they would look forward to the sacrifice of the Lamb of God Who covers all of our sins with His garment of salvation.

Read Genesis 3:22-24

c.   God could not let Adam and Eve stay in Paradise, the place of perfect friendship with God. That life was gone forever. Notice that they might not eat of the tree of life, for they would keep on living their miserable lives of sin. Paradise remained, possibly until the time of the flood. The cherubim, angels who guard God's holiness, and who stood at the gate of Paradise, were reminders that Adam and Eve could no longer live in perfect friendship with God. Sometimes we say that in Paradise the sun went down, the sun of the perfect light of God's favor shining on His people, and it did not rise again until Jesus came and took away our sins. We can look forward to heaven when the sun of God's love will shine on us forever.

Discuss in class what you think the saying
the sun going down means.

Read Genesis 4:1-15

B. Cain and Abel

1.   The Bible does not tell us all the details of the lives of Adam and Eve after they were driven from Paradise. We do know that Eve had a baby boy, "a man from the Lord." Did she perhaps think that the Lord was already filling His promise of sending a Savior? We do not know. But it shows that Eve lived in the hope of the promise of God. Cain, her first son, seemed to have been stronger than their next son, Abel, whose name means "breath."

2.   There were more differences between the two boys.

a.   To be able to survive in the world which God had cursed, they needed to raise food. So Cain became a farmer, a task which took strong muscles and hard work. Abel chose the quiet life of a shepherd.

21

b.   Although both boys had the same upbringing and certainly knew all about the beauty of the perfect life in Paradise, the sorrow of their parents' fall into sin, and the proper way to offer sacrifices of repentance to God, there was a vast difference in the hearts of the two boys. Abel believed the words of salvation his parents taught him and loved them with all his heart, but Cain was not interested, and hated to talk about sin and forgiveness. The seed of the woman and the seed of the devil (which God told them about in Genesis 3:15) was right in their own family!

C.   Their Offering

1.   Verse 3 says, "In process of time," when they were grown up, probably married (to their own sisters), both boys brought an offering to the Lord. Remember, an offering is a gift, a picture of offering oneself in holiness to the Lord. Notice that Cain went through the motions of serving God.

a.   Cain brought gifts from his farm, the fruits of his own work, with a heart full of unbelief, in disobedience to God.

b.   Abel brought a lamb from his flock, a bloody sacrifice, as the Lord had commanded, and came with faith in his heart, by the grace of God, in obedience.

Read Hebrews 11:4

2.   The Lord was well-pleased with Abel and his offering and displeased with Cain and his offering. How did the brothers know this? Most likely God spoke to them in a voice, as He did so often in this early history of Bible times.

3.   Cain was angry, not with himself and his wickedness, but with the Lord; and the Lord had to scold him and tell him that sin, like a wild beast, was crouching at his door. If Cain did well, he would rule over that beast of sin; but if not, the beast of sin would devour him.

4.   Cain could not reach God with his anger, so he turned his anger with God toward his brother and killed him. Remember, this was the wicked seed of the devil killing the righteous seed of Christ.

Read I John 3:12

5.   God asked Cain all those questions which we read in Genesis 4 because He wanted Cain to tell Him about his wicked deed. But Cain had no repentance and no love in his heart. Even though Cain said his punishment would not work (verse 14), God drove him away and put a sign on him — the

Bible does not tell us what kind of sign it was — so that the punishment would work, and no one who saw him would kill him.

DO NOT FORGET that Cain walked around as a living sign that God takes His people's side in the battle between the seed of the woman and the seed of the serpent.

WORD STUDIES
1. covenant — God's relation of friendship with His people
2. seed — the line of descendants: children, grandchildren, etc.

LESSON 8
The Generations of Cain and Seth
Genesis 4:16-5:32

BEFORE WE BEGIN the interesting genealogies* (the histories of these two families), we should know that the Lord gave Adam and Eve another Godfearing son to take Abel's place on the earth. His name was Seth. In Bible history genealogies are very important. Why? Not because God is just interested in a history book of families, but because His Word is showing us the line of His chosen people and the line of the ungodly in the world. The Lord wants us to be interested in seeing His work in bringing God's people to the time of Jesus, Who brought them, and us, salvation.

LESSON OUTLINE

A. Two Lines of People from Adam to the Flood

    1. Have you ever wondered how many years went by from the time of Adam to the flood? Our lesson gives the answer, for we can figure it out from the genealogies: 1,656 years. Turn to the chart in your workbook and keep it handy.

    2. People lived very long lives, had many children, and the numbers of people on the earth increased very fast. In their long lives they also had time to become rich and to become mighty men.

B. The Line of Cain

Read Genesis 4:16-18 and
look at the chart of Cain's line.

    1. You will notice that in the line of Cain's children, grandchildren, and great-grandchildren — his descendants* — the Bible does not give the dates of their births or of their deaths.

    2. We know, by comparing them with Seth's descendants, that each descendant lived hundreds of years. These years gave them time to have many children. By the time of the flood, there were easily one million people on the earth, and probably many more.

    3. Let us take a close look at the descendants of Cain.

        a. Cain built a city. He was a great man, a leader, a mighty man in the world.

        b. He and his descendants were interested in one thing: to make this world a great and lovely place in which to live.

c. They were intelligent, gifted people. Read Genesis 6:4. The "giants" probably were more than giants in height: they were giants in cleverness and skillfulness.

d. If we move on to verses 20-22, we read of Lamech's sons.

1) Jabal was known for being rich. He had cattle. To have cattle in those days, and to move from place to place to find the best grazing for them, was to get more cattle and to be rich. Jabal worked hard to be a great and rich man on this earth.

2) Jubal was an artist, a musical artist. Music is a beautiful gift from God, Who created sounds and notes and harmonies for us to use to His glory. Verse 21 tells us that Jubal used strings (harps) and pipes (organs) to make music. But he did not use his sounds and his words to God's glory. He had a sinful heart, and a sinful heart always sings songs of hatred and rebellion* against God. He was an artist who made life pleasant for the wicked citizens of this world.

Discuss in class
what kinds of music Jubal would play if he lived today.

3) Tubal-cain was an inventor of tools, utensils, and instruments of iron and brass. He was a clever inventor, who was famous for making life easier for everyone in time of peace, and for making weapons for battles in time of war.

e. These men from Cain's line, the line of the serpent (who is the devil) rapidly increased their wickedness. Cain was a murderer; and Lamech was a murderer who boasted about it. Lamech also disobeyed God's command about marriage and took two wives. How do you think the Lord felt about all this evil?

Read Genesis 5:4-6

C. The Line of Seth

1. Even though Genesis 5 seems to be all names, it tells us the story of the line of the woman (Eve), the line of the people God had chosen (another word for chosen is elected) to be His own.

2. God tells us the times of their births and of their deaths, so that we can make a complete time-table from Seth through Noah. Study the time-table in your workbook, noting the long life-spans of these saints, and how their lives overlapped. Only one son of each father is mentioned in Genesis 5. He

was not the only son, for the verses keep repeating that "they begat sons and daughters." He was not necessarily the oldest son, either. What son was it, then? It was the son who was next in the covenant line of promise, of the seed of the woman, from whose line Jesus would be born. That is the beautiful and important idea in chapter 5. Jesus was coming!

3. What do we know about these saints? Read chapter 4:26. They met for worship. We would say that they all came to church. We know that Adam lived 930 years, and he could teach all his descendants down to Lamech, the father of Noah, what God had taught him in Paradise. The church of that time had no written Bible, but Adam, Seth, and all the rest, passed on the knowledge of the fear of the Lord. We call this oral tradition*. Oral means spoken.

4. We read of no great works of these men of God. They were weak men in the eyes of the ungodly world. Yet they had everything they wanted, for they loved the Lord and could call on His name.

D. Enoch

1. If you count from Adam in Seth's line, you will find Enoch to be the seventh. If you count from Adam in Cain's line, you will find Lamech to be the seventh. Enoch and Lamech lived at the same time.

2. By the time of Lamech and Enoch, wickedness had increased very greatly. God's people were few and weak, because even many of those born in the line of Seth went over to the evil ways of Cain's line.

Read Genesis 5:24

3. When Enoch walked with God, he preached against the evils around him. Lamech heard him preach, and must have persecuted him and tried to kill him. Read Hebrews 11:5. He was taken to heaven "that he should not see death." His life was in danger! What did Enoch preach? Read Jude 14-16. It was not easy for Enoch, nor any of God's children, to live on the earth at that time. God gave them faith, and through faith they won the victory.

DO NOT FORGET that often we act as if we think more of this world than of our Father and His promises. Do we walk with God? Do you wish you could be like Enoch? Ask God for His grace to help you walk with Him each day.

WORD STUDIES

1. genealogy — the tracing of the histories of families

2. descendants — the children, grandchildren, and great-grandchildren born from one set of parents
3. rebellion — to disobey or resist God's law
4. tradition — handing down of knowledge and history from father to son

LESSON 9
Preparation for the Flood
Genesis 6

BEFORE WE BEGIN to study how the Lord prepared for His flood, it seemed as if the people in Cain's line were becoming more powerful and famous; and the people in Seth's line were becoming fewer and weaker. But remember: God always works through His few, weak people to do His will. Cain's line was not really powerful at all.

LESSON OUTLINE

A. The Wickedness on the Earth

1. Our last lesson told us that the wickedness on the earth increased with each generation. To understand what was happening, we may use the example of a car. When the driver starts out, he goes slowly. Then he accelerates, and keeps going faster and faster until he reaches the speed limit. This is what the wickedness on the earth at the time of the flood did — it accelerated.

2. Wickedness accelerated so fast that at the time of Noah, only ten generations from Adam, there were only eight people of God left in the church, surrounded by millions of the wicked. How did this happen?

Read Genesis 6:1-6 and 11

B. How the Wickedness Accelerated

1. In verse 2 we read about the sons of God and the daughters of men. The daughters of men were the women born in the line of wicked Cain, the ungodly daughters of ungodly parents. By the sons of God, the Bible means sons born in the line of God-fearing Seth. Not all the sons born from the generations of Seth were God's true children. Some were church members without God's love and grace in their hearts, who did not care about God and His promises.

2. Verse 2 also tells us that the sons of God married the daughters of men. If a son of God, an outward member of the church in those days, married one of the daughters of men, he knew how God wanted him and his wife to live. They must have one kind of speech, one love, one goal, and one faith, all coming from hearts that loved their Lord.

3. But the sons of men — most of them — did not want wives with the grace

of God in their hearts. They married because the girls were "fair," according to verse 2. They were beautiful, attractive girls, with all their beauty and attraction on the outside. These young men wanted to move away from God and live in the good times of the wicked world of their day. They wanted no covenant blessings of friendship from God, and did not want to look ahead to Jesus. They had left the line of Seth and chosen the line of Cain.

Read verses 4 and 5

C. The Result

1. When the sons of God and the daughters of men had children, they were giants. We learned in our last lesson that they were probably not giants such as Goliath, but people with very strong, physically-fit bodies, and with strong, brilliant minds, inventors and builders of civilization. They were men of renown (that means famous).

2. God saw that the wickedness of men was great. Wickedness is always great before God's holy eyes — even the sins we think are little sins. But verse 5 means:

   a. that because these people were so powerful and did such great deeds with their physical and mental powers, they became leaders who could lead the whole world into more and worse kinds of sin.

   b. that no good thoughts ever came from their hearts. They tried to imagine and invent more evil. That is why verse 11 says the earth was corrupt (rotten) and filled with violence (fierce, rough force). They would not listen to any laws, least of all to God's laws.

Compare in class
the world of Noah's day and the world we live in.

Read verse 3

D. God's Judgment

1. In those days, shortly before the flood, when wickedness was speeding so fast it seemed to be out of control, remember that God was leading all of this evil to work out His plans, not the plans of evil men.

   a. Verse 3 tells us that His Spirit will not always strive (or contend) with man. To contend* means to disagree, to scold, to judge. Through all these generations of the wicked line of Cain, God was "striving" and "contending" with the wicked. How did He do that?

   b. Through His own speech. He may have scolded many times with His

29

powerful voice. We know that He spoke with men on the earth. He also contended through the voices of His prophets. Think of what Enoch said in Jude 14 and 15, or of the 120 years that Noah preached.

2. The evil citizens of the world would not listen. They rebelled against God and persecuted His prophets. Their hearts were hard. The measure of wickedness in God's cup was full. God had made the evil accelerate, so that His measure would be quickly full. Why this hurry? Because the wicked were swallowing up God's people. Soon there would be only eight God-fearing people left on the earth (see chapter 7:7). He would send His judgment in 120 years.

Read Genesis 6:8

E. The Man who Found Grace

1. Notice the but: but Noah found grace. What a contrast to the violence of the people all around him who hated God. Noah was searching to see whether there was any grace for him, and he found it. Where? In God's eyes. The eyes of God tell us what lives in His heart. Of course, we know that Noah could not look up into heaven into the eyes of God. How then did he find grace in God's eyes? When God looked down on Noah, there was grace in His eyes, and He put that grace into Noah's heart.

2. How else did Noah find grace? God spoke to Noah and told him that He is the Lord, Jehovah, the One Who does not change: God spoke to Noah as a friend speaks to a friend. He told Noah His secrets. What were those secrets?

    a. That He would establish His covenant of friendship with Noah and his sons, verse 18.

    b. That He would destroy the whole world by a great flood.

    c. That He would save Noah and his family in an ark.

DO NOT FORGET that once more in the history of this world, the measure of wickedness of evil men will be full. It will be at the time when the Antichrist rules the world, just before Jesus' second coming. We are close to that time now. Read Matthew 25:38, 39.

WORD STUDIES
contend — to disagree, argue, scold, judge

The Flood
Genesis 7:1-8:19

BEFORE WE BEGIN, if you had to stand alone before a world of unbelievers, as Noah did, and do a seemingly foolish thing like building a big ark on dry land, would you have been able to obey the Lord? No, not by yourself. You could only do it as Noah did. He found grace in the eyes of the Lord, and God gave him faith to believe His promises.

LESSON OUTLINE

A. The Ark

1. During the 120 years before the flood, Noah preached and built the ark. Do not think of the ark as a simple, primitive boat. God saw to it that it was an advanced engineering project.

a. Although we are not sure exactly how long a cubit in Noah's day was (it is mentioned in chapter 6:15), we can estimate that the ark was at least 450 feet long, 75 feet wide, and 45 feet high, as large as one of our modern ocean liners. It was three stories high, with a window and a door in one side.

b. God does not tell us about keel or mast or sail, for the ark was more a storage boat than a sailing ship.

2. The only way Noah could build this ark was by a strong faith in the promise of God.

Read Hebrews 11:7

a. He did not build the ark in a harbor, but on dry land.

b. For 120 years he had to listen to the mocking* of the whole world. II Peter 3:4, 5 says that they told Noah that since creation, which was 1,600 years before, nothing on the earth had changed, and nothing would ever change. Do you know that God had never yet sent rain, but only a mist to give water on the earth? The mockers asked, "Where is the promise of his coming?"

Read Genesis 7:1-4

B. The Contents of the Ark

1. In the last part of chapter 6, God had given Noah instructions about the numbers of animals Noah was to take into the ark. But seven days before He

sent the flood, God instructed Noah (who was now 600 years old), his wife, his three sons and their wives, to go into the ark.

2.   Then the Lord Himself brought the animals to Noah: seven pairs of each kind of clean animal and one pair of each kind of unclean animal. Noah did not have to look for them, count them, capture them, nor lead them to the ark.

3.   By a wonder, in the full sight of the unbelievers, God marched all the species of animals to the ark, and Noah took them in. Then they waited for seven days.

Discuss in class this amazing sight
and the reaction you think the world around them had.

Read Genesis 7:16

C.   The Wonder of the Flood

1.   Everything was ready. Eight people, the animals, food, and whatever else they needed were in the ark. Then God shut the door, not as we shut a door and then leave, but God stayed at their door and guarded it. His arm was around them during the violent upheaval that was coming.

2.   Although God sent the first rain the earth ever had, it was not like the rain we know. It was even more than torrents or cloud-bursts.

   a.   II Peter 2:6 tells us that the world that then was perished. During the flood, God made a whole new world.

   b.   The flood was not just a catastrophe*. It was a great miracle*; and a miracle is a wonder of God's grace as He reached down to save His people — His people in the ark.

Read Genesis 7:11

3.   Exactly what happened, then, during the forty days and nights of rain?

   a.   God opened the windows of heaven. These are the waters above the earth which hold the sun, moon, and planets in their places, which we studied in Lesson 2. During the flood, the Lord took their anchors loose and put these heavenly bodies in different positions.

   b.   When God broke up the fountains of the great deep, He cracked open the crust of the earth, deep underground, and at the bottoms of the oceans, to make other bodies of land with huge mountains and deep valleys — the continents as we know them today.

   c.   It is very possible that God tilted the earth and made it rest on a slant during this upheaval, so that after the flood we have our four seasons each year, which the world before the flood did not have. God promised that these seasons will continue until the end of time, Genesis 8:22.

4. Everything (except the ark) was covered by water.

   a. The flood waters covered all the land of the whole world, and they were so deep that verses 19 and 20 tell us that the waters were at least twenty-two feet above the tallest mountains.

   Read verses 21-23

   b. Every living thing outside the ark perished: all people and all animals. All the beauties of the earth, for which the evil men of Cain's line worked so hard, were all gone, too.

D. Inside the Ark

1. What was inside the ark? The church, a very small church of eight people, with God standing at the door to protect His precious ones. The animals were there, too; for God saved not only His church, but also His creation. Do you know that after the judgment at the end of the world God will have the animal world of our earth represented in heaven? He will save His creation at the end of the world, too.

2. Have you ever wondered how it was possible to have all these animals, plus the large quantities of food, and all the cleaning and housekeeping supplies in one ark for a year and ten days? Even if we grant that the ark was as big as about five hundred freight cars, what about the animals' care and their smells? We do not know. But we do know that the flood outside the ark was a great wonder. Couldn't our God of the wonder have made the animals hibernate, or couldn't He have made them very small (micro-animals) inside the ark? Even men today have learned how to make things, such as computer parts, very small. But we will leave that wonder to God.

E. Coming out of the Ark

1. The waters stayed on the earth one hundred fifty days and then the ark rested on Mount Ararat.

   a. Almost three months later the tops of the mountains could be seen.

   b. Forty days later Noah sent out a raven, a strong bird who could survive on dead carcasses. It did not return.

   c. Seven days later Noah sent out a dove, a weaker bird, and she returned. She could not yet find a place to live.

   d. Seven days later Noah sent out a dove again, and she came back with an olive leaf. Noah knew that the waters were going down.

e.   Seven days later Noah sent out a dove again, and this time she did not come back.

f.   Almost two months later, God let Noah and his family leave the ark. They had been in the ark a year and ten days.

2.   The powerful, brilliant, famous followers of Satan were in hell. The church, eight humble, prayerful people of God, were alone in the new world which God gave to them.

DO NOT FORGET that God always connects the judgment of the flood with the judgment at the end of the world. The flood is a picture of the last judgment. The difference between the two judgments is that the next time God comes, He will destroy the world by fire.

WORD STUDIES
1.   mockers — those who poke fun of holy things
2.   catastrophe — a great and sudden disaster
3.   miracle — a wonder, given by God's grace

LESSON 11
God's Covenant with Noah
Genesis 8:20-9:29

BEFORE WE BEGIN, it is important to know that in our last lesson we finished studying the first time period of Old Testament history, the period from creation to the flood. In this lesson, we start the second long time period: from Noah's life after the flood to the time that the Israelites entered the land of Canaan, a period of about nine hundred years.

LESSON OUTLINE

A. God's Pleasure with Noah

1. God's revelation to us in the Bible is a wonderful thing. He tells us about the first thing Noah did after he came out of the ark. He set up a church in this brand-new world: not a large building, but an altar. On it he offered blood sacrifices from the clean animals which came out of the ark. And God smelled the sweet smell of Noah's offerings.

2. Next, God does another wonderful thing: He allows us to look into His heart. Read verse 21 once more. God did not say these words to Noah — not yet. God said them in His heart, the deepest center of God (and of us). And He gave us a glimpse of His purpose to love, to bless, and to save His world.

3. We read in Genesis 6:6 that before the flood the terrible wickedness "grieved him at his heart." He had to destroy the earth because of the evil on it.

4. Now everything was different. God was pleased. In His heart God said three things:

   a. That He would not curse the ground any more. Remember, before the flood, the ground fought the farmers and they could hardly get enough food from it.

   b. That He would never again kill every living thing on the earth with a flood.

   c. That from Noah's time on, He would always send the four seasons to the earth.

5. Do we know why God was so pleased with Noah? Yes: when Noah, as head of the church, offered blood offerings, he was saying that he looked forward to the forgiveness of sins in Christ, the Lamb of God. And God

smelled that sweet smell of Noah's faith. He was promising a better earth to His people. That is what God thought in His heart.

Read Genesis 9:1-7

B. God's Blessing of Noah

1. Now God was ready to tell Noah what was in His heart. When God blessed Noah and his sons (verse 1), He was speaking to the church, with eight members in it. It was not a perfect church, as we will discover later in this lesson; but God's church on earth is never a perfect church. God gave the blessing to Noah, as head of His church.

2. God gave Noah control over the animal world. He gave the animals to Noah, and to us, to use for food and for skins. God made the animal world to fear people. Especially in Noah's time, when there were many, many more wild animals than people, it was necessary that the animals did not attack them, but that they feared and dreaded them.

3. In verse 6 we read that God gave Noah the law of the death penalty* for murder. God did not say, "You may put a murderer to death," but, "You must shed his blood. Do not put him in prison for murdering his neighbor. Kill him." Why? Verse 6 says, "For in the image of God made he man." We know that we lost God's image through Adam's fall, but it is still true that the first man was made in God's image. It is also true that God commanded that no one may take away a man's life. Now men must stand in God's place on the earth to see that justice is done, to see that the murderer is punished. How do men do that? They set up a government, with some men chosen to be rulers. Not just any person may kill the murderer, but the chosen rulers in the government must investigate, have a trial, and do justice. Noah was the first "governor" after the flood, and God passed on that authority to governments of all nations.

Discuss in class whether our government obeys Genesis 9:6.

Read Genesis 9:9-12

C. God's Covenant with Noah

1. God had more to tell Noah. He made a covenant, a relationship of friendship, with Noah, promising to be with him and his children — all his descendants. Notice that God did not make any kind of agreement with Noah, or ask Noah whether he wanted a covenant. No, God did it all. With whom did God make this covenant? With everyone who will ever be born in the world?

a. That cannot be. God was speaking to His church, His people. God can have friendship only with His people for whom Christ died, for no one else. Our pure and holy God has no friendship for the ungodly. We know, of course, that wicked men were born from the family of Noah, but God was not talking about them. He was talking to His chosen church.

b. God also blessed the animals for His people's sake. We cannot live without the animals on the earth. Have you ever thought about it that we and all creation belong together, and that God does not merely save people, but He saves a creation?

Read verses 13-17

2. The sign of God's covenant was the rainbow. Before the flood there was no rain, and consequently, no rainbow. What is a rainbow? It is one beam of white light, a symbol of God's pure light, reflected into its seven colors, which is a picture of His grace shining through His promises, His promises to be the Friend and Savior of His people: for seven is the number of God's covenant. A rainbow always shines against the background of a dark cloud, a sign of God's anger against our sin. But the rainbow of God's grace always shines through, and He promised never to send another flood over the whole world.

Read verses 20-29

D. Noah's Sin

1. Many years must have passed before Noah sinned. His sons already had grown-up children. Now, when Noah was old, he fell into a serious sin. He knew it was wrong, but he did it anyway. He became drunk.

2. His son Ham saw his father lying drunken and naked in his tent, and ran to tell his brothers. Ham did not feel sorry about his father's sin. He did not blush, but was glad to find out his father's sins and share the news with his brothers. Ham was disrespectful and rebellious toward his father. Laughing and mocking to his brothers, he showed that he hated his godly father, that he hated his father's preaching, and that he hated God.

3. Shem and Japheth did not enjoy their father's sin, but were sorry and ashamed, and reverently covered their father. Remember, these sons were not young boys. They were more than one hundred years old. They did what Isaiah 33:15 tells us all to do.

E. The Blessing and the Curse

1. Noah awoke and knew what Ham did, and cursed him. When Noah spoke, he prophesied*. God spoke through him. Noah did not curse Ham directly,

37

but he cursed Canaan, his son. Canaan must have showed the same ungodly traits as his father Ham. We know from Bible history that the Canaanites were cursed, for they served the Israelites, who were the descendants of Shem. 2. Noah had more words from God. He blessed Jehovah, the God of Shem. From Shem were born God's chosen people, the Israelites; and from the line of the Israelites the Savior was born. Japheth's children are the Gentiles, who share in Shem's blessings. Do you know that we are descendants of Japheth? We share in Shem's blessings, the blessings of our Savior.

DO NOT FORGET that God keeps repeating His blessings and cursings. Just as Adam first fell into sin and then heard God's curse on the serpent and His blessing on Seth's children, so Noah first fell into sin and then spoke the curse on Ham and the blessing on Shem and Japheth. Those curses and blessings will last until the end of the world.

WORD STUDIES
1. death penalty — punishment by death for a sin
2. prophesy — to speak God's Word through His Spirit, sometimes to foretell the future.

LESSON 12
The World at the Time of Babel
Genesis 10, 11

BEFORE WE BEGIN, we must know that God did what He said He would do. He gave Noah and his sons many children. Families, tribes, and nations* began to develop, and God told them to spread over the whole earth, like branches of a tree.

LESSON OUTLINE
A. The Descendants of Noah

1. Chapter 10 tells us that the descendants of Ham settled in the southern part of Asia and in Africa; the descendants of Shem settled in Asia near the Persian Gulf, and those of Japheth settled in Europe. Find these areas on your worksheet for Lessons 13 to 15.

2. In Old Testament times, we do not hear much about the line of Japheth, or the line of the Gentiles. We might say that God had sort of "put them on a shelf" until Jesus came. Today's lesson will include the lines of Shem and Ham.

Read Genesis 10:9, 10

3. Who was this Nimrod, grandson of Ham, and why was he so important?

a. Nimrod was a mighty man who began to build kingdoms, and he was the first man who thought of the idea of having a world empire, ruled by one man, Nimrod. Many men in the later history of the world copied him. Think of what you have heard about Nebuchadnezzar, or Caesar, or Napoleon, or Hitler. They all tried to copy Nimrod and rule the whole world.

b. Nimrod was a rebel. His name means "to disobey." God had told Noah and his descendants to have families, to multiply into tribes, and to spread over the earth. Nimrod thought he had a better idea: to keep all the people in one place, in one large kingdom, where Nimrod would be the only ruler. He did the opposite of what God had commanded.

c. Nimrod was a mighty hunter. After the flood, the wild animals multiplied and stayed near the areas where the people lived. Nimrod had the strength and the daring to hunt these beasts, and he made life safer for everyone. People followed him! He was a hero! And Nimrod hunted before the eyes of Jehovah, **verse 9.** This does not mean that the Lord was pleased with Nimrod, but that the Lord looked at wicked Nimrod and used him as His servant to do what He wanted him to do.

Read Genesis 11:1-4

B. The Kingdom of Nimrod

1. The people on the earth — most of them — traveled to the Plain of Shinar, where they found building materials, brick and mortar. There they built a strong city, with the best inventions of science and industry. In rebellion against God's command to spread over the earth, they stayed in the city, where it was easy to get their wicked heads together and plan more evil.

2. The tower (verse 4) was not really a brick tower trying to reach God's heaven physically*. These men were not fools. They did not want to go to heaven and (if it were possible) start a battle with the Most High God. No, they were terrified of God's holiness. They built the tower as a sign which would tell everyone what great things man can do.

3. Under Nimrod's leadership, they made for themselves a name (verse 4). What name? "We are gods." Also: "Anti-God and Antichrist." And, as gods, they could say, "We can reach to the heavens with all our abilities and inventions. We can do anything we wish. We will bring all the people of the world into one great kingdom. We will be the gods of this world." What did God in heaven do? He laughed at them. See Psalm 2:4.

Read Genesis 11:5-9

C. The Confusion of Languages

1. God came down and visited men in an appearance. We do not know what form He took. In verse 6, God is saying to Himself that if they are left to themselves, nothing will stop them from having a wicked world power, with Nimrod as the ruler. They all spoke the same language, possibly the language Adam spoke.

2. God suddenly changed the languages the people spoke, but He did more. He changed the people: their appearances, their feelings, their ideas. God made the races of people, at least a beginning of the great differences of the races, along with the differences of speech. He branched them out by His power. Now they wanted to spread because they could no longer agree. The name of the city was Babel, which means confusion.

Discuss in class what must happen
in our world before the Antichrist can come.

40

D. The Descendants of Shem

1. Genesis 11:10 to the end is important because it traces the line of God's people; and this line is important because it is God's covenant line which leads to the promise, the coming of Jesus. The line of Shem is the most important genealogy in the world.

>   a. Using the information from chapter 11, the chart traces the history from Shem to Abraham in exact numbers. We can figure that there are two hundred ninety years from the flood to Abraham.

>   b. The families in Shem's line had many more children than the one son who is mentioned in the genealogy. This one son was the one chosen to carry on the line of Christ.

>   c. This list of names is comforting. Why? Because God was blessing the families of His people, and He continued His promise to them through all the wickedness of Nimrod's world-power.

2. Notice the difference in the length of men's lives. Noah's life span was in the 900's, Shem's in the 600's, the next few in the 400's and 500's. Peleg's, at 239, was much shorter. Why? Genesis 10:25 says that the earth was divided (at Babel) during his life. Men born after the time of Babel lived shorter lives, about 200 years.

3. There was still no written Scripture — only oral tradition*, which we studied in Lesson 8. People learned the fear of the Lord from their ancestors. Notice that Noah was still living for the first 50 years of Abraham's life.

DO NOT FORGET that the Lord always does everything right for His purpose. He made His people with strong bodies, to live long lives, so that His truth could be handed down to several generations. Abraham could have heard from the mouth of Noah all about the wonder of the flood.

WORD STUDIES

1. nations — a group of people in one area, with one language, under one government
2. physically — using one's body or material things
3. oral tradition — the Word of God spoken from father to son for many generations

LESSON 13
God Calls Abram
Genesis 11:27-12:20

BEFORE WE BEGIN to study Abram, we must understand that when God gave His covenant promise to Abram, He was not making a new covenant with him. It was the same covenant which God had made with Adam (in Genesis 3:15), with Noah, and with Shem. With Abram, God would develop* His covenant by choosing a special nation from whom would be born The Promised Seed of His covenant, our Lord Jesus Christ. And Abram was the father of that special nation.

Read Genesis 11:27-32

Have your workbooks out.
As you read the next paragraph,
find Ur in the Plain of Shinar on your maps.

LESSON OUTLINE

A. The Call of Abram

1. Before Abram's call, he lived with his family in Ur, in the plain of Shinar, near the Persian Gulf. At first, most of the people who settled there feared and loved the Lord. They were the descendants of Shem. Slowly, evil crept in. Some descendants of Ham moved near, and many of Shem's seed joined them in their wickedness. The kingdom of Nimrod and the tower of Babel were not very far from Ur. After the Lord confused the languages, the people scattered, but Abram's family stayed in the same general area. Look at the chart of Shem's descendants from Serug to the end.

a. Notice that Nahor was the father of Terah; and Terah had three sons: Nahor, Haran, and Abram. Haran died in Ur, leaving his son Lot.

b. God's call to Abram came about twenty years after the building of the tower of Babel. God called Abram to leave Ur of the Chaldees. Genesis 11 does not tell us that. But Stephen, in the New Testament, does.

Read Acts 7:2, 3. Genesis 15:7 also tells us.

c. History books tell us that Ur was no longer in the hands of God-fearing people, but that idol worship, especially worship of the moon, had taken the place of the worship of Jehovah. Joshua 24:2 tells us that Abram's father Terah was an idol-worshipper.

42

d. When God called Abram to leave, his whole family traveled with him, until they came to Haran, where they stayed until the death of Terah (Acts 7:4). We do not know why they stayed in Haran. Abram may have been waiting for the Word of God to lead him on.

Read Genesis 12:1-9

2. We do not know how God called Abram at Haran: by a voice, a vision, a dream, an angel. . . ? He gave Abram a command which had two parts:

a. Get out of your country and leave your family and relatives behind.

b. Go to a land that I will show you. Where was it? Abram did not know.

3. God gave him a promise with four parts:

a. I will make of you a great nation.

b. I will bless you.

c. All families of the earth will be blessed in you.

d. I will give this land (Canaan) to your seed.

4. Taking his wife Sarai, who was also his half-sister, his nephew Lot, and his servants, Abram went by faith. With Jehovah leading him step by step, he came to the land of Canaan and stopped at the city of Sichem (or Shechem) and built an altar there. By building the altar, he was showing the people who already lived in Canaan that he was living by God's gift of faith. He showed that he believed God's promise that his descendants would some day possess this promised land.

Read verses 10-13

B. Abram's Stay in Egypt

1. Probably soon after Abram's arrival in Canaan, God sent a famine. Abram must have already had many trials: he and his family were alone as worshippers of Jehovah among thousands of idol-worshippers; he did not own an inch of the land, and he migrated from place to place to find food for his animals. Then God sent another trial: a famine. Abram's faith failed. It seemed as if he could not trust God anymore, so he began to plan his own life.

2. Genesis 20:13 tells us that before they left Haran, Abram and Sarai had agreed to tell a lie, or at least a half-truth: that Sarai was Abram's sister. She was his half-sister, but the truth was that she was his wife! Now as they left the land of promise and traveled to Egypt, Abram reminded her of their lie, and she agreed to tell the half-truth. The Bible tells us that Sarai was a beautiful woman. She was sixty-five years old already, but she lived to be one

43

hundred twenty-seven, so she did not seem as old as a woman of sixty-five is today. Why did they lie? Abram was afraid the Egyptians would take Sarai and kill him, verse 12. Abram had God's promise that his children would inherit Canaan. Yet he lied because he was afraid of being killed. Is that hard to understand?

Discuss in class the problem of telling half-truths.

3. When Pharaoh saw Sarai and took her into his house, Abram must have consented* to her going. Even when Pharaoh planned to make her his wife, Abram kept up his lie about her. Pharaoh thought that soon Abram would be his brother-in-law, and treated Abram royally, giving him riches of animals and servants. What was Abram really doing? He was trading Sarai his wife for sheep and oxen and camels.

4. This was a very serious sin, for Abram was helping the devil. The devil did not want Sarai to be the mother of Abram's children, because Abram's children would be the ancestors* of Jesus; and the devil was trying with all his might to prevent Jesus from being born. If Sarai married Pharaoh, the devil would succeed in his plans. At the same time, Abram knew in his heart that nothing could stop God's promise. Yet he traded earthly riches for Sarai, the covenant mother from whom Christ would be born. That was the seriousness of his sin.

5. But God always keeps His promises. By His goodness and grace, He rescued Abram.

   a. By sending plagues (sickness) to Pharaoh and his house.

   b. When Pharaoh discovered the lie they had told him, probably by asking Sarai, he called Abram and scolded him. Abram, the servant of Jehovah, the father of many nations in Jesus Christ, had to listen to a scolding from a godless king. Ashamed and humbled, he did not answer the king.

   c. Pharaoh sent him back to Canaan. Even when Abram sinned, the Lord had let him get riches from Pharaoh; and Abram went back to Canaan a rich man.

DO NOT FORGET that Abram and we are very much alike. We both have faith in God's promises, and we both love them more than anything in our lives, and yet we both easily stumble into great sins, and must hear stern words of scolding. But our God is always merciful and kind to us.

44

WORD STUDIES

1. develop — to unfold gradually, to grow
2. consent — to give permission, to agree to
3. ancestors — the parents of descendants; the people from whom Jesus was a descendant.

LESSON 14
Abram and Lot
Genesis 13:1-14:16

BEFORE WE BEGIN, in this lesson we will meet Lot, Abram's nephew. We already learned that he traveled with Abram from Ur of the Chaldees; and he probably was also with Abram and Sarai in Egypt.

Read Genesis 13:1-4

LESSON OUTLINE

A. Abram at Bethel

1.   After Abram and his family left Egypt, they traveled back to Bethel, and called on the name of the Lord there. What do you think Abram said to the Lord? He must have said, "Forgive our awful sins in Egypt." He repented and confessed his sin before the face of God. How do we know that? Because he went to the altar to sacrifice. When he sacrificed an animal, and saw its blood pour out, he was looking forward to Jesus, whose blood would make him and his wife clean from this sin. And God heard him for Jesus' sake.

2.   Abram could not really call on God in Egypt, because he had run away from God in disobedience, and God does not listen when His children purposely walk in disobedience. That was a serious sin. Now he was walking in the right way again.

Read verses 5-8

B. The Quarrel

1.   In our last lesson, we saw that the Lord, through Pharaoh, made Abram rich in cattle, silver, and gold. Lot shared in his riches. Lot, too, was one of God's children. We learn that from II Peter 2:7, 8. But when they came back from Egypt, Lot forgot something: that it was Abram who was being blessed by God with riches. In Old Testament times, God made earthly riches a sign of His blessings*. As Abram's nephew, Lot shared in those riches.

2.   But Lot wanted riches for himself. He liked those earthly treasures. He seemed to forget that they were only types of the riches of grace and blessing that God poured down on those He loved. Lot looked out for himself. Abram looked for God and the heavenly land. Soon there was trouble. Lot started it because there was not enough pasture land for all the flocks, and he

wanted the good pasture land. That led to the fighting between the herdmen of Lot and of Abram for the best lands.

3. Abram worried about the trouble, because, he said, "We be brethren." He did not mean that they were "blood relatives," but "brothers in the Lord;" and they could not worship at the altar together when trouble divided them. Besides, the Canaanites and the Perizzites, the idol-worshippers, were in the land. It would not be to God's glory to have His children fighting before the heathen of the land.

Read verses 9-13

C. The Solution

1. Abram said they must separate. He did not think of himself first, and even though God had given the land to him, he let Lot choose the part of the land he wanted. Think how wrong it was for Lot to choose: he might not leave Abram because where Abram was, there was the church and the altar of sacrifice; and it is always wrong to leave God's church. Besides, Lot was the weaker child of God, and he needed Abram's strength, his trust in God, and his example, to lead him.

2. Lot should have insisted that it was Abram's right to choose, because God had given him the land, but Lot was greedy and wanted the best. He saw only the lush, grassy valley toward the east. It reminded him of Egypt and of the garden of the Lord in the land far to the East they had left.

3. Worst of all, he looked toward Sodom and Gomorrah, the cities in that valley that were so evil they were almost ready to be destroyed by the judgment of the Lord. Even though the riches of the plain blinded his eyes, Lot knew what he was doing. He chose that land. He pitched his tent toward Sodom, and gradually crept closer to the sinful dangers there, as a moth does to a candle. At the same time, Lot was a righteous man, and God would save him from his foolishness and sin.

Read verses 14-18

4. Abram was alone again, the way God wanted it to be, for Abram had the promise. God repeated His promise, and Abram was content to walk through the land and settle to the south, in Hebron. See the map in your workbook.

D. The Wars of the Nine Kings

1. Shortly after Lot moved toward the cities of Sodom and Gomorrah, there was war. This is the history of the war:

    a. The four kings mentioned in chapter 14:1 lived in the Plain of Shinar, from which Abram and Lot had come. Chedorlaomer, according to verse 4, was the leader. The powerful army of these kings, still with some of the might from the days of the tower of Babel, was so strong that they forced all the other nations to pay them tribute money*.

b.   The kings of Sodom and Gomorrah and the other cities nearby paid the four kings money for twelve years. In the thirteenth year they rebelled, and said, "No more taxes." The next year, the fourteenth, the four powerful kings came with their armies for war.

Read Genesis 14:8-12

c.   These armies may have taken the same route to Canaan that Abram and Lot had taken. They came from the north and swept south through the nations which lived on the east side of the Jordan River, winning easy victories. Find the area on your map.

d.   The four kings from the East pushed south to the area of Sodom and Gomorrah and three smaller cities. The five kings of these cities fought the four invading kings and their invading armies in a dangerous battle-field, full of slime pits; and the four kings and their armies won a great victory. Many of the soldiers of Sodom and Gomorrah were killed. The rest fled to the mountains.

e.   The four victorious kings from the East plundered* Sodom and Gomorrah, taking prisoners, among them Lot, and all his possessions. Notice that Lot had not fought in the battle, but that he now lived in Sodom.

Discuss how Lot had come to live in Sodom at this time.

2.   Someone escaped and ran to tell Abram the Hebrew, who was living at Hebron. Why did they call him the "Hebrew?" It means "from the other side," and could mean that he came from the other side of the Jordan River. But it means more.

a.   It means that Abram was a stranger in the land, not a born Canaanite.

b.   This is not all it means. Abram's side was God's side; and he was on the other side — not on the side of the wicked of the land.

3.   Why did the messenger run to Abram? Abram was not an army captain. The messenger knew, and the people knew that the Lord of heaven and earth blessed him. The Lord had protected him and his riches from the four evil kings from the East.

48

E. The Rescue of Lot

1. Abram prepared for battle. He had three hundred eighteen trained servants and three chiefs of the Amorites to help him fight.

2. This small army, helped by the grace of God, won a victory over the four kings, freed the prisoners, also Lot, and captured the spoils. No one else had been able to win. Why did Abram win? God blessed and helped him and gave him the victory.

DO NOT FORGET that being called "a Hebrew" is a lovely name to be called. Try to think of yourself and everything you do as from "the other side, the Lord's side."

WORD STUDIES

1. blessings — God's favor and goodness
2. tribute money — money paid by one ruler to another ruler
3. plunder — to take by violence, to steal

LESSON 15
The Meeting with Melchizedek and the Covenant with Abram
Genesis 14:17-15:21

BEFORE WE BEGIN, we remember that Abram, with strength from his heavenly Father, freed his nephew Lot, along with the captives from Sodom. But Lot did not learn a lesson. He went back to that evil city. God had a more serious lesson to teach him.

Read Genesis 14:17-24

LESSON OUTLINE

A. The Meeting with Melchizedek

1. After the enemy armies were conquered, the king of Sodom and the other kings hiding in the mountains came out to greet Abram. And suddenly a new king entered the picture. His name was Melchizedek, and he was called the King of Salem (which means peace), and Priest of the Most High God.

2. We do not know the history of Melchizedek. He was not descended from the line of Abram, but probably from the line of Japheth, Noah's son, for some of Japheth's God-fearing descendants were still in the land of Canaan. Melchizedek ruled his people, who were a small God-fearing nation in the middle of the wicked Canaanites, as king-priest under God.

3. Melchizedek brought bread and wine to Abram; and as Priest of the Most High God, he blessed Abram. Verse 20 tells us that Abram gave Melchizedek tithes: that is, a tenth part of the spoils of the battle he had just fought. Why?

    a. Other passages in the Bible tell us that Melchizedek was a picture — a type — of Christ. In Hebrews 7 we read, "Thou art a priest forever after the order of Melchizedek;" and we read that Melchizedek was "made like unto the Son of God;" and "abideth a priest continually."

    b. So when Abram gave Melchizedek the tenth part of the spoils, he was saying that all the spoils of battle belonged to Melchizedek, because he was a type of Jesus, to whom everything in heaven and earth belong. Abram understood that Melchizedek was a type of Christ, and that Melchizedek was a greater priest-king than he was.

4. After a wonderful time with Melchizedek, Abram had to deal with the wicked king of Sodom. The king of Sodom offered to give him a big reward

for rescuing his city and winning a victory, but Abram would not take even a shoe lace, lest the king of Sodom would say, "I made Abram rich." He did not want the riches of evil men.

Read Genesis 15:1-6

B. God's Appearance to Abram

1. This appearance happened some years after the battle with the four kings from the East. Abram was nearly eighty-five years old when God came to him, and still the promise that his descendants would inherit the land of Canaan had not come true. Abram did not have even one son, and he was becoming very old, almost too old to have children.

2. The reason that Abram and Sarai had no son was not that they lived in sin. No, they had repented from their sin and weakness in Egypt, they had come back and lived as strangers in the land of Canaan; Abram had the faith and courage to fight the four kings, and he had built altars as a witness to the heathen people around him.

3. Now was the time for God to comfort him, and He came to Abram in a vision*. In this vision while Abram was awake, he was "in the spirit" and saw spiritual, heavenly things. But in the vision he also saw and handled real things.

    a. God first told Abram that He was his shield*, his protection, to keep all dangers from him. God was also his reward*, the gift of Himself God gave to Abram, the gift of forgiveness, peace, and all His blessings.

    b. Next, in the vision Abram talked with God about the problem which troubled him most in his life: he had no son. Maybe his servant Eliezer could be his son?

    c. God gave the answer. He took Abram outside to look at the stars, and promised that Abram's seed would be as many as the stars which he could not count. This seed would be born from Abram's son. Abram could not understand how God would do this, but he believed by faith.

Read verses 7-21

4. Abram asked the question you and I would ask: "How will I know?" He knew the Lord would do it all for him, but how will God keep His promise? In the vision, God showed him. This is what God told Abram to do:

    a. Take three animals, each three years old: a heifer*, a she-goat, and a ram. Abram must kill the animals, divide them in half, and lay the halves opposite one another, in rows. At the end of one row he must put a dove,

51

which he had killed, and at the end of the other, a pigeon. Remember that Abram did this all in a vision.

    b. When the birds of prey swept down on the carcasses, Abram drove them away.

5. Abram knew what this part of the vision meant. In those days, when people made agreements of friendship or of promises, they walked between the parts of the animals. And if they made promises to one another, they said they would rather die, as these animals had died, than break their promises.

6. Abram's vision must have lasted from the night before, when he saw the stars, through the next day, when he saw the animals, until sunset, verse 12. Then, when the sun went down, Abram saw a smoking furnace and a burning lamp.

C. The Meaning of Abram's Vision

1. What was God's meaning of these rows of dead animals? God was showing Abram that He had made a covenant of friendship and of promise with him, which would look forward to the promise of the birth of Jesus. He would send salvation. God alone made the covenant, and He made all the promises. And the vision meant that God would pass through the pieces of the dead animals to show that He would keep His promise; and that He would die rather than break His promise. How did God pass through the halves of the animals?

    a. In a smoking furnace which was a picture of God's anger as He burned the wicked with fire. That is the way God always treats the wicked — in anger.

    b. In a burning lamp which was a picture of the light of salvation He gives to His people.

2. What did all this mean? When God passed through the pieces, He showed Abram and us that He did have to die to save His people. When? At the cross, when the Son of God shed His blood for our sins. God was showing Abram the story of salvation.

3. The birds of prey which Abram chased away had a meaning, too. They were pictures of the power of sin and hell which try to take God's people away from God.

Discuss how we have to fight
the birds of evil each day.

52

For a while, Abram felt a horror and great darkness — a picture of the dark days ahead for all of God's people.

5.   At the end of the vision, God passed through the horror of darkness — a picture of the darkness of the cross, where Christ passed through death for us.

DO NOT FORGET that the vision God gave to Abram is for us, too. It is God's way of teaching us the beautiful truths and the happiness of our salvation.

WORD STUDIES

1.   vision — a revelation from God to someone while he is awake
2.   shield — a protection from danger
3.   reward — a gift
4.   heifer — a young cow

The Birth of Ishmael
Genesis 16, 17

BEFORE WE BEGIN this lesson, be prepared for a striking difference between our last lesson and this one. In our last lesson, when God made His covenant with Abram, he was on the mountain-tops of faith. Today we find Abram in the deep valley of weakness of faith, trying to run ahead of God.

Read Genesis 16:1-3

LESSON OUTLINE

A. The Impatience of Abram and Sarai

1. The events in this lesson happened rather soon after the promise in chapter 15. Abram and Sarai had problems deep down in their hearts. On the one hand, they both believed by faith the promise that God would make Abram the father of many nations, and that they would have a son. On the other hand, God was taking too long to keep His promise. They were impatient. Besides, they could not see how it was possible for God to give them a child anymore. Their trouble was that they looked around them at earthly reasons for solving their problem right now, instead of looking up to the God of the wonder. They decided to do something about their problem.

  a. Sarai started it. Not because of pride or rebellion against God, but because she wanted so badly to have the seed of the covenant, she decided they could have a child another way.

  b. It was a common practice in those days to give one's maid to her husband as another wife. It was not right, but it was done. Because her maid was her own possession, her maid's child would then be Sarai's child. Abram and Sarai decided that was probably the way God wanted them to have the child of promise, so Sarai gave Hagar, her Egyptian maid, to Abram as his wife.

2. Both Sarai and Abram ran ahead of God. They decided it was their work to help God establish His covenant.

Discuss in class how you have been impatient with God's ways,
and have tried to run ahead of Him.

Read verses 4-6

B. Hagar Runs Away

1. Abram took Hagar as his wife, his second wife. When Hagar, the proud, rebellious Egyptian, knew that she would have a child, she looked down on her mistress Sarai, and would not obey her. Hagar did not want her child to be Sarai's child, and Hagar did not want to be a servant to Sarai anymore. Do you think Sarai began to realize how wrong her plan had been?

2. Sarai, frustrated and unhappy, said to Abram, "My wrong be upon thee." It means, "The wrong done to me come upon you." They had to share their guilt. Yet we can understand their feelings, can't we? They wanted a covenant child, but their plan did not work. They got, not satisfaction, but vexation*. God was chastising* them. That means scolding and correcting His children for running ahead of Him.

3. Abram gave Sarai permission to do as she pleased with Hagar. To make her obey, Sarai was harsh, and she humbled and mistreated Hagar.

Read verses 7-16

C. The Promise to Hagar

1. Hagar ran away toward her homeland of Egypt. This was very wrong of Hagar, for her duty was to be obedient to her mistress. She traveled as far as Shur, in the desert. Find it on the map in your workbook. There the Angel of Jehovah found her. Do you remember that the Angel of Jehovah is the Old Testament revelation of the Christ, before He was born as Jesus, our Savior?

2. The Angel called her "Hagar, Sarai's maid." Why? Because Hagar forgot her place as Sarai's maid. She needed a reminder to be humble to her mistress, and the Angel told her to go back and obey.

3. The Angel of Jehovah promised, too, that Hagar would have a son, whose name was to be Ishmael, which means God hears. He and the nation born from him would be wild men, travelers of the desert, trouble-makers with their horses and spears, and independent of other nations.

4. Now Hagar knew that she could not run away from God. She said, "Thou God seest me," and she called the well where she had stopped Beer-lahai-roi, which means, "The well of Him that liveth and seeth me," verse 14.

5. Hagar went back to Sarai. After Ishmael was born, the baby was Hagar's, not Sarai's. Sarai had tried with her own plans to have a baby, and now she knew that by her own plans and her own strength she could not make God's covenant promise come true. But God had a reason (He always does) for having Ishmael born first. What was it? It was that God showed that He

rejected* Ishmael from His covenant and chose Isaac to be born only by a wonder of His grace. Abram, who was eighty-six years old already, would be his father.

Read chapter 17:1-5

D. God Appears to Abram

1. Thirteen years of silence went past. God did not come to speak to Abram nor to promise him anything. Abram must have been worried and disturbed by God's silence. He knew he had done wrong when he tried to help God along to get the child of the promise. He may have wondered whether, after all, Ishmael was the child God had chosen. Abram was now ninety-nine years old, and Sarai almost ninety. It was too late to have a son anymore. The Lord was silent, and there was unrest in Abram's soul.

2. Then God appeared to him and told him that He is the Almighty God, Who has all the power to make His promises come true.

   a. God changed Abram's name to Abraham, meaning father of many nations.

   b. In verse 7, He promises to be a God to Abraham. Abraham (and we) need more than just a friend and protector. He (and we) need an Almighty God.

   c. God reassured Abraham that this land of Canaan would be the land of Abraham and his seed.

3. Then God gave Abraham the sign of circumcision — for all the sons born in the line of the covenant — as a symbol of being clean from sin.

Read verses 15-17

4. God gave Sarai a promise, too. He changed her name to Sarah, which means princess. She would be the mother of the line of kings in Israel, and also the mother of the Royal King Jesus. Not only that, but she would be the mother of the children of promise in all nations, of all who belong to Jesus. We can say that Sarah is our spiritual mother.

5. What was the reaction of Abraham? He laughed. It was not a laughter of mocking or unbelief, but a laughter of wonder. God would give a baby to a hundred-year-old father and a ninety-year-old mother. He believed and was happy. Read Romans 4:18-21.

6. Yet Abraham wished that Ishmael could also live before God as one of His children (verse 18). Although we know that some of Ishmael's descendants were saved, Ishmael was not the chosen son. The chosen son was Isaac.

DO NOT FORGET that we have an intense interest in the coming birth of Isaac. Only by the wonder of the birth of Isaac could Jesus be born hundreds of years later. And the birth and death of Jesus is the most important interest in our lives, because if we have Jesus, we have everything.

WORD STUDIES
1. vexation — trouble, anger, frustration
2. chastise — God's correction of His children in love
3. reject — to cast away

LESSON 17
Three Visitors Come to Abraham
Genesis 18

BEFORE WE BEGIN, it will help us to know that the visit of the angels in this chapter happened less than a year after God's promise to give Abraham and Sarah a child the next year.

Read Genesis 18:1-8

LESSON OUTLINE
A. Abraham at Mamre

1. In your workbook for this lesson, find Mamre on the map. Now picture Abraham sitting in the door of his tent in the heat of the day, probably about two o'clock in the afternoon. Abraham looked like a stranger in the land. He had no house — just a tent; and he was sitting in the door of the tent, looking for a better country, a heavenly one, Hebrews 11:16.

2. Then he saw three men coming toward him. Did he know that they were special? They appeared to Abraham as real men in real bodies, which God had prepared for this special occasion.

3. It was the custom in that country to bow to newcomers, and that is what Abraham did. But Abraham had to notice something special about their faces because there was no sin reflected there. They were unusual visitors, who looked different.

> Discuss in class how our faces show our sinfulness.

4. Gradually it must have dawned on Abraham that the Lord had come to visit him in the form of a man. It was a picture of the birth of our Lord Jesus, Who was God born in a human body like ours, and Who took the form of a man.

5. As Abraham served his guests, he must have felt more and more that he was serving the Lord.

B. Abraham Entertains Three Visitors

1. The Lord gives us a glimpse into Abraham's feelings as he rushed about to serve his visitors.

    a. He was eager. He ran to meet them (even though he was one hundred years old) and bowed to the ground. He sensed that they were special guests, maybe royalty. They were: the King of heaven and earth was one of the guests, verse 2.

b. He was humble. He asked whether they would show him their favor, verse 3.

c. He was reverent. He called his guest "My Lord," verse 3.

d. He was kind. He gave them water to wash their hot, dusty feet, and invited them to rest in the shade of the tree, verse 4.

e. He was hospitable*. His "morsel of bread" became a feast of cakes, butter, milk, and tender calf's meat, verses 5-8.

f. He was helpful. He did not order his servants to do the work, but ran the errands himself.

g. He was joyful as he began to realize that he was serving the Lord.

h. All these verses breathe his love, for love is eagerness to serve, and love is friendship with God.

2. Hebrews 13:2 tells us that we must imitate Abraham, for when we entertain God's people, and when we help them, we are doing it to Jesus (Matthew 25:45). It is one way of serving our Lord.

Read verses 9-15

C. The Announcement

1. If Abraham had any doubts, the Lord's question in verse 9 told him that his visitor was the Lord. He knows all things. He knew Sarah's name. Now Abraham was sure!

2. Notice, in verse 10, that the Lord says, "I will return." The meaning is that the birth of the promised child is His work, and His promise. He will give the son.

3. Sarah, eager, interested, was eavesdropping at her tent's door, and she laughed inside herself when she heard the announcement. It was not a nice laughter, but the laughter of unbelief.

4. The Lord saw Sarah's laughter and scolded her, at the same time showing her that He is the Lord, and that giving her a son is not too hard for the Lord, verse 14. Sarah, frightened, added a lie to her laughter, and denied her sin.

D. Abraham Pleads for Sodom

1. When the heavenly visitors got up and began to walk toward Sodom, Abraham walked along with them. It is then that the Lord spoke to His two angels in the presence of Abraham.

a. He asked a question which answers itself. Read it in verse 17.

b. While the Lord was asking His two angels the question, He asked it so that Abraham, His friend, would hear the answer.

59

c. Why did God share His thoughts with Abraham? Because He had promised to be Abraham's friend, to bless him and to make a great nation from his seed, verse 18. There was another reason: the Lord knew that Abraham must teach his children and grandchildren and great grandchildren to walk in the Lord's ways. And Abraham could not teach them if he did not know the Lord's ways. Then the Lord told him what He was going to do: destroy Sodom and Gomorrah, verses 20, 21.

Read verses 20-23

2. Abraham had a problem with the Lord's announcement that He would destroy these wicked cities. Oh, he knew that the Lord's ways are right, and that the world before the flood had been destroyed because it was ready for God's judgment*, and that now Sodom and Gomorrah were ready, too.

   a. Abraham's problem was with the righteous (God's children) who lived in these cities, not only Lot, but all of them. He knew, and we also know, that God lets the wicked and the righteous live together in this world, although we cannot see on the outside what is in their hearts.

   b. Abraham wanted God to spare the cities for the sake of the righteous people in them, because he knew, and we know, that God never destroys the righteous with the wicked. God would never put His people into hell with the wicked. He knew that God could not destroy His own children, for whom Christ died.

Read verses 24-33

3. Abraham was not interested, either, in how many righteous men were in Sodom, but his great concern was this: "Shall not the Judge of all the earth do right?"

4. So he prayed a humble prayer, because he knew that he was dust and ashes, verse 27; and he also prayed a bold prayer when he said to the Lord, "That be far from Thee," in verse 25.

5. Abraham started asking whether there were fifty righteous in the city, and he must have become more and more disappointed as he went down to forty-five, forty, thirty-five, thirty, and twenty. He ended his pleading to the Lord with the number ten. What was the Lord's answer? There were no righteous people in Sodom. The Lord would take the only righteous man out of the cities, Genesis 19:29.

DO NOT FORGET that Abraham's concern for God's people at the time of the

60

destruction of the wicked is our concern, too. When the end of the world comes, what will be the end of the righteous? We do not know, but we are sure that God will be watching over them in His love.

WORD STUDIES
1. hospitable — being kind and generous to guests
2. judgment — a punishment for sin

LESSON 18
Sodom and Gomorrah Are Destroyed
Genesis 19

BEFORE WE BEGIN, we should know that while Abraham was talking with the Lord and begging Him that He would not destroy the righteous with the wicked, the two angels went on to Sodom.

Read Genesis 19:1-3

LESSON OUTLINE

A. The Angels and Lot

1. Lot was sitting at the gate of Sodom. Often an arch served as the entrance to a city in those days, an arch with deep alcoves and seats for people who wanted to sit and talk, do business, or hold a court hearing.

2. From his reverent greeting, Lot must have recognized the messengers as different, as special, even as heavenly messengers. Their faces were sinless, in stark contrast with the evil faces of the men of Sodom.

3. Although the angels said they would stay in the street all night, Lot kept urging them to be guests in his home; and like Abraham, he entertained them in great style, with a great feast. But he planned to let them go very early in the morning. Sodom was not a safe place.

Read verses 4-11

B. The Men of Sodom and Lot

1. The men, young and old, from all parts of Sodom, gathered at Lot's door. These men were terrible sinners. We know that all sins are terrible in the sight of our holy God, but the Bible tells us, especially in Romans 1, that the sins of ungodly men lead to worse and worse sins. As the men of Sodom thought of more and more dreadful sins, they had sunk into the lowest pit of sin.

   a. The law of God commands that a man shall find and love and marry a woman and establish a godly home and have a family of covenant children in His fear.

   b. The men of Sodom would not live in the natural way which God had created, but, instead, God gave them over to the worst kind of sin. They lived sinfully with other men, working evil, which Romans 1:26 calls "against nature."

2. Because the men of Sodom had sunk to the lowest of sins, God said

they were ready for judgment. Their cup of evil was full to the brim.

3. Before Lot and his holy visitors were ready for bed that night, the evil men were milling about Lot's house. Lot went outside to them, closing the door behind him to protect his family and his visitors inside, and he scolded them.

> a.   To protect his visitors, Lot made a very strange offer. He would bring out his two daughters to these crude, unholy men, who could hurt and humble them. Lot probably knew they would not accept his offer, but at the same time it was just as much of a sin for the evil men to hurt Lot's daughters as to hurt his visitors. It was wrong for Lot to offer them his daughters.
>
> b.   The Sodomites ridiculed* Lot. They called him a new-comer, a foreigner — and did Lot think he was their judge?
>
> c.   They began pushing, to surround him at the door.

4. The angels — sent as guards for God's people — pulled Lot in and shut the door.

5. By a wonder, the angels made the crowd of men blind, not with a blindness of their eyes, but with mental blindness, so that they could not understand where the door was. Their eyes saw, but not rightly, which was a picture of the blindness of sin.

C. The Angels' Announcement

1. Lot, his wife, and two daughters listened to the message of the angels. They asked if Lot had more family members — sons-in-law? These sons-in-law quite likely were men of Sodom, engaged but not as yet married to Lot's two daughters, because they were not living in the house with them.

2. The sons-in-law laughed and mocked, verse 14, as evil men always do when God talks to them.

Read verses 15-29

D. Sodom and Gomorrah are Destroyed

1. At dawn the next morning, the angels hurried Lot and his family out of the city. But the angels had trouble. Lot and his family, especially his wife, liked to live in Sodom. How do we know? They lingered, found excuses to stay in the den of sin a little longer. The angels had to put their hands on them to hurry them out. Lot and his family were dragged out of the filthy pit of evil. Why were the angels so patient with such slow obedience from Lot? Verse 16 has the answer: "the Lord being merciful to him." Lot was

63

God's child, although right now he was walking and living in sin, but he was righteous*, according to II Peter 2:8.

2. But Lot was a righteous man who was no example to us. He had eyes for the riches and luxuries of this world. He moved away from the church when he left Abraham, to get these riches. He let his daughters promise to marry men from Sodom. Yet he had God's grace in his heart. At the same time, God did not wink at his sin. He never does. But God chastised him. Lot soon lost his family and all his earthly goods, and became a wanderer on the earth.

3. The angels gave Lot further instruction. They must escape to the mountains. Once more Lot complained: "Oh, not so, my Lord," verse 18. He still could not cheerfully and thankfully obey, but begged to run to the little city — that is what Zoar means — and the angels granted him this, too. The angels hurried him the whole way: it was as if God had to chase him out of the fire of destruction. The sun had risen when Lot came to Zoar.

4. Then the Lord poured fire and brimstone (sulfur)* from heaven on those cities, killing everyone who had lived there. Until the minute of God's destruction, the Sodomites went about their duties, saying that their destruction could never happen. God's fire burned everything, even the soil, so that no one could ever live there again. What happened to the place where the cities had stood? God changed it into the Dead Sea. Find it on your map. Now the Dead Sea, with vapors of sulfur hanging over it, with no life possible, is a reminder of God's total destruction of the wicked.

Discuss in class what the Bible says about
the wicked at the end of the world.
Matthew 12:36-42 will help.

5. In verse 17 we read that the angels warned, "Look not behind thee." Why not? Because looking back meant that their hearts and their longings were in those cities, and that they wished they could go back! Lot's wife felt that way. She needed just one more look at the city she loved, she looked back, and she died on the spot. She was punished by becoming a pillar of salt, the same sulfur which destroyed the cities.

6. Abraham must have known that God would destroy the cities that morning, for he went to the place overlooking Sodom and Gomorrah, where he had pleaded with the Lord the day before; and he saw the smokey furnace of the cities. But God remembered Abraham and saved the one righteous

man Lot from the furnace of destruction. The righteous did not perish with the wicked.

DO NOT FORGET that when Jesus said, "Remember Lot's wife," He was saying that we cannot serve two masters. We will be destroyed if we serve Lot's wife's master, and we will be saved when we serve Lot's Master.

WORD STUDIES

1. ridicule — to make fun of
2. righteous — living according to God's holy will
3. sulfur — a pale yellow powder which burns

LESSON 19
Abraham and Abimelech
Genesis 20

BEFORE WE BEGIN, we will find out when Abraham visited Abimelech. When Abraham was ninety-nine years old, God promised him a son in one year. Shortly after that, the three heavenly visitors came to him in Mamre; and then Sodom and Gomorrah were destroyed. Very soon after that Abraham moved away from the Plains of Mamre. So Abraham was still ninety-nine years old.

Read Genesis 20:1, 2
Have the map for Lessons 19 to 22 on your desk.

LESSON OUTLINE

A. Abraham Goes to Gerar

1. Suddenly Abraham picked up his tents and left the area of the city of Hebron, where he lived on the Plains of Mamre, and traveled south. At first he settled somewhere between Kadesh and Shur. Find these places on your map. Do you remember that when Hagar ran away, she fled to Shur?

2. The Bible does not tell us why Abraham started to wander south toward Egypt. We can guess that he was looking for pasture land, but we do not know. Soon he went north to Gerar, in the land of the Philistines. Find it on your map.

3. When you read verse 2, where Abraham said about Sarah, "She is my sister," did it surprise you? Would you expect Abraham to fall into the same sin of lying so soon?

   a. It is hard to understand Abraham's thinking, for although he did not want to give up Sarah again, and although he may have been afraid, he knew that his lie to Pharaoh had not worked. Yet he tried it again.

   b. Now his lie was a more serious sin, because he was telling his second lie after he had learned a hard lesson from his first lie in Egypt. Once more Abraham's faith was weak; and not only Abraham's faith, but Sarah's also. They had not really left the sin of lying.

   c. To make matters worse, Abraham told this lie just a very short time after the Lord had come to him and promised that Sarah would surely have a son. And once again, when the Lord visited him in the form of a man, he heard the Lord's wonderful words that Sarah would be the covenant mother; and Sarah heard the Angel of Jehovah when she was listening at her tent door.

d. Abraham had been so happy. He was on the mountain-tops of faith. Now he fell very low, and his faith was very dim. Do you think we should judge Abraham? Before we do, shall we look inside ourselves to see whether we often go from the mountain-tops of faith and trust in God to deep pits of gloom and unbelief?

Read verses 3-7

B. God and Abimelech

1. Abimelech, whose name means "my father is king," took Sarah into his palace. Who was Abimelech? If we turn to Genesis 10 and read verse 6, we find that Mizraim was one of the sons of Ham. Now find Philistim in verse 14. Philistim was Mizraim's grandson; and from Philistim came the nation of the Philistines, with Abimelech as their king. Although the Philistines and their king came from the line of Ham, they were not the descendants of Ham's son Canaan, whom God had cursed. And some of the descendants of Ham had not left the fear of the Lord. Abimelech and his city of Gerar were some of the people who still worshipped God.

a. Abimelech took Sarah because she was beautiful and because he believed their lie that she was Abraham's sister. Then God came to him in a dream and warned him that he would soon be a dead man. Notice that God treated Abimelech very differently from the way He treated Pharaoh. He did not warn Pharaoh. But God let Abimelech know that he was in trouble.

b. When we read Abimelech's answer to the Lord, "Lord, wilt thou slay also a righteous nation?" he sounds shocked. Abimelech feared God. He did not know that he was sinning. He thought he was upright and innocent.

c. God's answer in verse 6 is important. God said that He knew Abimelech's integrity*, his honesty, and innocence. God is the only One Who knew what was in Abimelech's heart; and only God's children have integrity in their hearts. God was good to Abimelech. He kept him from sinning, from taking Sarah as his wife.

2. Even though God knew that Abimelech took Sarah ignorantly, He commanded him to give Sarah back to her husband; and if he did not, he would die. Abraham, even though he had sinned dreadfully, would pray for

Abimelech and his people. Why? Because Abraham was a prophet. He spoke God's Word and he made God's will known to men.

Read verses 8-18

C. Abraham and Abimelech

1. Early the next morning Abimelech called all his servants and told them the unhappy story. They were sore afraid (verse 8). Is it any wonder? They had done no wrong, and they could all be dead men. Then Abimelech called Abraham and scolded him. This is what he said:

    a. What have you done to us?

    b. How have I offended you that you brought such a great sin to my kingdom?

    c. You did things you should not have done.

    d. What did you see here in my kingdom that made you do this thing?

2. Would you have known how to answer Abimelech's questions? Abraham did not know what to say, either. He must have felt thoroughly ashamed, even as he tried to give Abimelech a weak answer: "I thought the fear of God was not in this place."

3. Abraham admitted that he and Sarah had agreed to this lie long ago when they left Ur of the Chaldees.

Discuss in class how God's child
feels when he must confess his sins.

4. Abimelech acted like an upright, God-fearing man, far differently from the way Pharaoh acted toward Abraham.

    a. He gave Sarah back.

    b. He gave Abraham sheep, oxen, and servants.

    c. He invited Abraham to live in his land (Pharaoh had chased Abraham out of Egypt).

    d. He told Sarah that he had given one thousand pieces of silver to her "brother." We would call that "rubbing in" the lie they had told.

5. Abraham prayed for Abimelech and his people, and God healed them.

DO NOT FORGET that Abraham learned a lesson from this righteous king. He learned that God cannot be served by telling lies, but that He is delighted when His child walks in integrity, as Abimelech did.

WORD STUDIES

integrity — honesty, innocence

LESSON 20
Isaac and Ishmael
Genesis 21:1-21

BEFORE WE BEGIN, think of the birth of Isaac as being a great wonder. The birth of any child — your birth — was a wonder. Have you ever asked yourself how God made you just as you are, different from everyone else? Isaac was a wonder in a special way, because God gave him to parents who were older than your oldest grandparents. We would say they were ready for the grave — not for a new baby! Our lesson will tell why God planned it exactly this way.

Read Genesis 21:1-7

LESSON OUTLINE

A. Isaac is Born

1. For many, many years already, the Lord had been promising Abraham and Sarah a special son, the son who had to be born so that from his descendants Jesus could come. Why didn't God give them their baby years ago when they were younger and stronger? Because God wanted them to trust, to have faith that God would give them a child, even though they were too old. Paul, in the New Testament (in Romans 4:18), said about Abraham: "Who against hope believed in hope, that he might be the father of many nations." He could not hope, and yet he did hope. Why? Because God would make the impossible become possible, by a wonder.

2. When Abraham was one hundred years old and Sarah was ninety, God gave them the promised baby. Just a year earlier, when she listened to the angels at her tent door, she had laughed the laughter of unbelief. Now she laughed in faith, and she wanted everyone who heard about it to laugh with her, to laugh in joy that a mother too old to have a son was the mother of the child of promise. God (in chapter 17:19) had already given the child a name: Isaac, which means laughter, the laughter of faith.

Read verses 8-13

B. Ishmael Mocks Isaac

1. Now there were two children in the family of Abraham. The problem was that one was the son of Abraham and Hagar, and was thirteen years old already. The other was the wonder-child, the son of Abraham and Sarah.

   a. Before we go on with the story, we will compare the two boys. It will be like looking in on the family for a few moments. If you could meet Ishmael and look at his outward appearance, you would see a strong, healthy boy, who liked to be outdoors especially with his bow and arrow. Isaac, even as a young child, would look weak and frail to you. He may have had weak eyes, because later in life he became blind.

b. We cannot look at the inside of the boys, but God can. He tells us what we would see. Ishmael was proud, rebellious, a mocker who hated God and His church. Isaac had a weak character. He did not have any "get-up-and-go," and was a follower, not a leader. He was submissive* he easily gave in and did as he was told. In his heart he had a powerful love for the Lord, and had grace to believe in His promises.

2. When Isaac was two or three years old, and not a baby anymore, his father made a great feast for him, to celebrate that he had left babyhood and was starting to grow up. Verse 6 tells us that it was a big event. But trouble came to the feast.

a. Sarah saw it first. That is not a surprise, is it? Mothers always see things first. But this mother and baby were very special, and Sarah had a reason for watching. She saw Ishmael, now fifteen or sixteen years old, mocking the young Isaac of two or three years old. We are not told how or why Ishmael mocked. He may have been jealous of the big feast for Isaac, or jealous that "all nations would be blessed in him," such a weak, puny, babyish child. Galatians 4:29 tells us that he persecuted* Isaac. He was mean. He showed hatred. He would like to see Isaac dead. Why? Because he had no love of God in his heart. Although he was ungodly, he wanted to be the firstborn, the child of the promise, so that he would inherit all of Abraham's earthly riches. He had no thoughts of the beautiful promise of the Savior. But Isaac was in his way to earthly riches and importance. Ishmael showed all of these things in his mocking.

Discuss in class whether you have ever been mocked
for believing God's promises and being obedient to Him.

b. Sarah saw something else. She saw that her servant Hagar (verse 10 calls her "the bondwoman") and her mocking son must be put out of the family and sent away. That sounds rather harsh, doesn't it? Abraham thought Sarah was too hard on Hagar and Ishmael. He was grieved.

3. God came to Abraham with the answer: Sarah is right. Cast him out. Ishmael's children belong to another nation. Why couldn't they all stay in

70

one happy family? Weren't they all in one church?

a. The answer is no. God was teaching Abraham that even though both boys were his sons, only Isaac was God's son. Ishmael was not the child of the promise. He was not one of God's children, but a wicked child of Satan, a mocker, and a hater of God's children. What, then, was God's answer? Separate them. Send Ishmael away.

b. In Galatians 4, God has told us that wicked Ishmael, living with Abraham's righteous family, is a picture of what always happens in God's church. Think of the nation of Israel, the nation of God's people. Inside the nation, living with God's people, were always the worshippers of idols, the disobedient, who made trouble. And God always worked to separate and destroy the wicked so that His people Israel would serve Him with a pure heart again.

c. Our churches are the same. Even in the church we have not only God's true children, but also rebellious sinners who will not repent.

C. Hagar and Ishmael Sent Away

a. Early in the morning Abraham sent Hagar and Ishmael away. Some people think that Abraham did not give them much water in their bottles, so that they would come back. We do not know. Hagar went toward Beersheba. Find it on your map. The sun was hot and all the water was gone. Ishmael needed water badly. Hagar let her son drop under one of the shrubs. There lay the sixteen-year-old young man, dying of thirst.

2. Hagar could not stand it, so she went a long way off, and cried. Ishmael cried, too. God heard Ishmael's voice, not a voice of humble prayer, but the cry of a young man dying for water, and God's angel showed Hagar a wonder: a well of water.

3. Why did God save wicked Ishmael? Why do we read that God was with him, in verse 20? God gives us His answer. Because some of Ishmael's children would be God's children, and God saved Ishmael's life for their sakes. He tells us in Isaiah 60:7 that Kedar and Nebaioth, sons of Ishmael, were His children, too.

DO NOT FORGET that we as the church (God's people) and the world (the devil's children) cannot live together. Sometimes we must shop at their stores or work for them, but we cannot live together and enjoy it, nor try to worship together, because we love opposite things. Thank God that He gives us grace to love and serve Him, and that He makes us happy when we do.

WORD STUDIES

1. submissive — to give in to the power or authority of someone else
2. persecute — to chase with cruel, hateful treatment

LESSON 21
Abraham Offers His Son
Genesis 22

BEFORE WE BEGIN, in this lesson the Bible does not merely tell us an interesting story about Isaac's life. The Bible is not a story book or a history book, but a book of salvation. God tells us this story about Isaac because we need to know it for our salvation.

Read Genesis 22:1, 2

LESSON OUTLINE

A. God Tests Abraham

1. We read in verse 1 that "God did tempt Abraham." What does that mean? It does not mean that God tempted Abraham to sin. Two other words the Lord uses for tempting are "trial"* and "testing." These words do not mean, either, that God gave Abraham a test or a trial to see whether he would pass it or not. God knew. He made Abraham and planned his whole life. He knows us, too; and sometimes He gives us tests and trials in our lives.

2. What does it mean, then, that God "tempted" or "tried" Abraham? It is more like testing gold, melting it down, taking out all the impurities, testing it some more, until finally it comes out of the fire as perfect, solid gold. God tested Abraham, and He tests us, to make us pure. And each time God tests, Abraham (and we) must use our faith in Him. That is the way God makes our faith solid, strong, and pure.

Read verses 3-10

B. A Test of Abraham's Love

1. God tested Abraham's love for Him by asking him to do the hardest thing imaginable: to offer his only son as a burnt offering to God. God did not test Abraham to see whether he loved the Lord, not even to see whether he loved the Lord more than he loved his son, but to make Abraham's love for God strong and deep: to show to Abraham, to Isaac, and to us, that the love of God is always first.

2. Remember that Abraham loved his God above everything. But, oh, how he loved Isaac! Did he love God so much that he could put a knife through the heart of his own son?

3. Remember, too, that Isaac was his only son. Abraham had waited until he

73

was one hundred years old for him, after all the years of hoping for the son of the promise.

4. Remember, finally, as Abraham took a donkey, two servants, wood for the offering, and his only son early in the morning, that the test of his love was not over. From Beersheba, where Abraham had pitched his tent, to Mt. Moriah took more than twenty hours of walking. They walked for three days.

    a. They must have been three days of torture in his heart, three days of thinking that he could turn back and go home again.

    b. Then the third day came, when Abraham left his donkey and his servants, and he and Isaac went the rest of the way alone. Isaac was not a small boy anymore, but a young man strong enough to carry the wood for the sacrifice. Isaac did not know that he was carrying the fuel that would burn him on the altar. But Abraham did, and it must have been hard for him to go on.

    c. When Isaac finally asked, "But where is the lamb for a burnt offering?" Abraham once more passed the test of love. When he said, in verse 8, that God would provide a lamb, was he thinking that the lamb would be Isaac?

C. A Test of Abraham's Faith

1. Twice before, God had put Abraham's faith to a test: in Egypt, with Pharaoh, and in Gerar, with Abimelech. And both times he had failed miserably. He lied. Now God was putting him to a much harder test. We might call it the supreme test.

2. He had the promises which God gave him, and which God had repeated to him. He had the promised son, and God had said, "In Isaac shall thy seed be called." Abraham had faith. He believed God's promises with all his heart.

3. Now what? Will God destroy Isaac? How then would Jesus be born? Abraham struggled between two impossible choices: to believe God and keep Isaac, or to believe God and destroy Isaac.

4. But he trusted. His faith held strong. How he must have wrestled with his problem as his feet dragged up the mountain. He knew that God would make a way out. If He did not give a lamb, maybe He would raise Isaac from the dead. (See Hebrews 11:19.)

D. A Test of Abraham's Obedience

1. Now it was time to lay his only son on the altar. The wood was all in order, and it was time to tie up his son and lay him on top of the wood. But

how could he? God had said it was wrong to kill. In Genesis 9:6 He said, "Whoso sheddeth man's blood, by man shall his blood be shed." He may not disobey God's commandment.

2. On the other hand, God had commanded him to kill his son. He may not disobey that command, either. Abraham was ready to obey God's command; for God, Who knows everything, had the right to take Isaac's life, and He had the right to tell Abraham to do it for Him. So Abraham obeyed.

E. The Offering

1. Abraham passed the three tests: of love, of faith, and of obedience. Everything was ready. Isaac was tied to the altar and Abraham had his knife raised, saying in his heart, "I am going to kill my son."

2. For in his heart Abraham obeyed. In his heart he had already offered him to God. When he stood there, it seemed as if the sacrifice were all finished. Hebrews 11:17 is a Word of God which looked into Abraham's heart and said that he had already offered Isaac. Read that verse.

3. What about Isaac? He did not fight. He let himself be bound and put on the altar in obedience.

4. Then the Angel of Jehovah called to Abraham: "Now I know that thou fearest God," verse 12. God knew it all the time, but He said it to reward Abraham and to strengthen his faith. He did it to show us Abraham's faith, too.

5. They needed one thing more: a ram, a type of Christ, a sign that Isaac did not have to die, because Christ would come to die for him. Isaac could not save himself by dying. Only the Lamb which God would provide could save him. Abraham could spare Isaac from dying; but God did not spare His only begotten Son. He gave His dearest possession for Isaac and for us.

DO NOT FORGET that Abraham called the place "Jehovah-Jireh," verse 14, which means "Jehovah will provide." He provided His Son, the Lamb, to die not on an altar, but on a cross. The story of our lesson is a picture of His death for all His people.

WORD STUDIES

trial — putting our faith to a test to make us pure.

LESSON 22
The Death of Sarah
Genesis 23-24:9

BEFORE WE BEGIN, do you know that the story of Abraham's faith when he offered up Isaac was the climax, the high point in his life, even though he lived more than fifty years longer? The Lord does not have much more to tell us about his life on earth, and in this lesson He is making the way for the history of Isaac.

Read Genesis 23:1, 2

LESSON OUTLINE

A. Sarah's Death

1. Verse two says that Sarah died in Kirjath-Arba. That was the name of the city in Abraham's time. The Book of Joshua tells us why: Kirjath means "city" and Arba was the name of a great man, a giant, who conquered it. Therefore Kirjath-Arba means the "city of Arba." Later its name was changed to Hebron. Abraham had moved there from Beersheba. Find it on the map for Lessons 22-24.

2. Abraham and Sarah had lived together for one hundred twenty-seven years: first as half-brother and sister in their father Terah's home, then as husband and wife. They had been very close together, especially when they lived as strangers in the land of Canaan. There is a more important reason why they were so close to one another: both had a strong faith in the promise of God.

3. Abraham came in from his fields to mourn for Sarah. He wept and was very sad.

4. God looked at Sarah as an important woman in Bible history. She is the only woman whose age when she died is told us: one hundred twenty-seven years. The Lord mentions her in Hebrews 11, the chapter of the heroes of faith; and He mentions her again in I Peter 3:6 as an example of a godly wife. The whole of chapter 23 tells us about her death and burial. Our lesson will help us understand why.

Read verses 3-9

B. Abraham and the Sons of Heth

1. When a member of our family dies, we think of a cemetery to bury him. Abraham thought about a burial place, too. His problem was that he did not

own an inch of the land of Canaan, although God had promised that his seed would inherit the whole land. But Abraham needed a burying place to bury his wife right now. He did not even think of going back to Haran or to Ur to bury Sarah. No, this was the land God showed them, the promised land, and here Sarah must rest in death. Abraham knew why: this land was a picture of resting in the heaven of glory, because Canaan was a picture of heaven. That is why it was so important for Abraham to bury Sarah in the earthly Canaan.

2. Abraham spoke to the sons of Heth. They were one of the tribes of the Canaanites, later called the Hittites. He asked them whether he might buy a plot of ground so that it would be his own possession, to bury Sarah. The sons of Heth knew Abraham. They said, "Thou art a mighty prince among us." Why did they say that? Abraham had no throne nor kingdom. The sons of Heth saw another kind of prince in Abraham: God's prince. They saw the godliness of his life, and his life as a stranger among them. They saw the miracle of the wealth God gave him, and the special birth of Isaac. They saw the grace of God in Abraham's life.

3. At first they offered to give Abraham a burying place. He could bury Sarah in their sepulchers* (graves). But Abraham refused. He and Sarah could not join the heathen sons of Heth during their lifetimes; and they must be separate in death, too. Abraham asked to buy the cave of Machpelah.

4. Once more they offered to give it to Abraham (verse 11) but Abraham insisted on buying it. Ephron, probably the ruler of the city, asked 400 shekels of silver, a high price in those days, and Abraham paid with the wealth God had given him.

Read verses 17-20

C. Sarah's Burial

1. Abraham bought Machpelah, which probably means "the separated place," with its field, cave, and trees.

2. Abraham insisted that he buy it at the gate of the city, where the court was, with the people as witnesses, so that it was legal*, and everyone knew he owned it.

3. Why was it so important for everyone to know? Was it not just a burial place for his wife? No, it was a sign of Abraham's faith, a picture of owning a place in heaven. When he and his children died and were buried there with Sarah, they knew that nothing else mattered: they had a place in the heavenly Canaan. And Sarah was the first to be buried there.

77

4. That is why Machpelah is so important: Abraham and Sarah were separate from the world in life and separate in death, too.

Read Genesis 24:1-9

D. Abraham and His Servant

1. The death and burial of Sarah reminded Abraham that it was high time for his only son to be married. Isaac was already forty years old. Abraham was an old man of one hundred forty years, and he thought he might die soon, too. He had one more important task in his life: to find a wife for Isaac. He had God's promise that his seed would be as many as the stars of the sky. And his only son was not married yet!

2. Why Abraham? Why did not Isaac find his own wife? Isaac was not a very strong character. He had been a "mother's boy." Three years after she died, he was still grieving for her. Isaac loved God and His promises, but he was slow. He lagged behind.

3. So Abraham took charge, and called his oldest servant, probably Eliezer, and told him to find a wife for Isaac. Abraham was afraid that Isaac would take the easy way out and find a wife from the Canaanites. But he trusted his old servant to find a godly wife for Isaac.

4. The servant must look for a godly wife for Isaac from the line of Shem's descendants. That was the line of promise in the Old Testament. Where would he look? In Haran, the place where Abraham and Sarah had lived, and where their relatives were.

5. Did you notice in verse 7 how sure Abraham was that Eliezer would bring back a wife for Isaac? God's angel would go with him to help him and keep him safe. God very really sends angels to take care of us, too. Read Hebrews 1:14.

Discuss in class how the angels care for us.

6. Abraham had one more reason for being so sure that Eliezer would bring back a wife: Isaac would have a wife and children because God had promised, "Unto thy seed will I give this land," verse 7. So he sent his servant away, and Isaac had nothing to do with it at all.

DO NOT FORGET that the Bible is always interested in the covenant line, the line of believers and their children. That is why God told us the stories of the burial of Sarah and the getting of a wife for Isaac — because the line of the covenant is the line of salvation.

WORD STUDIES

1. sepulcher — a burial place, often made in an opening of a rock
2. legal — done according to the law of the land

LESSON 23
A Wife for Isaac
Genesis 24:10-end

BEFORE WE BEGIN, the servant, probably Eliezer, did not go to Haran to choose a wife for Isaac, but to find her. He only went the way God led. Have you ever thought about the fact that God leads you to your friends — and to the person you will marry some day?

Read Genesis 24:10-21

LESSON OUTLINE

A. The Servant's Journey

1. If the servant left from Hebron, he traveled about seven hundred fifty miles before he arrived at Haran in Mesopotamia. The Bible sometimes calls it Padan-Aram, which means The Plain of Aram. Verse 10 calls it the "city of Nahor," the city where Nahor, Abraham's brother, lived.

2. How did he travel? With a caravan* of ten camels. Why so many camels?

    a. For the servants he took along. In those days a man would not be safe traveling alone.

    b. For carrying food and supplies.

    c. For the expensive gifts for Abraham's relatives, to show that Isaac was from a rich family, able to support a wife.

    d. Extra camels to take back the wife the Lord would give Isaac, and her maids.

3. If the loaded camels traveled fifty miles a day (which they probably did) how long would the trip take? When they arrived at Nahor's city, the servant rested the camels at the well. It was nearly evening, the time when the shepherds gave their flocks water. What must Eliezer do next? How would he find a girl he did not know? He knew that he had come here because he trusted the Lord, and the Lord would show him.

4. He also knew what to do. He prayed. Read verse 12 once more. He prayed for good speed, for success, because he was walking in the way the Lord told him to walk. The servant talked with God as we talk with a friend. He needed a sign because he had an impossible task. How could he know God's will? He knew that God had already chosen a certain special girl as Isaac's wife. Now Eliezer had to find her.

80

5. The servant chose a sign that would fit a special girl, one who was kind and hospitable, willing to serve a stranger, who would do extra chores with a cheerful and loving heart, and do it for God's sake.

6. Before he finished his prayer, the Lord answered him. Rebekah came. Who was she? She was the daughter of Bethuel the son of Nahor. Look at the chart on your worksheet for this lesson, and figure out her exact relationship to Isaac. Eliezer saw a fair — a beautiful — girl.

    a. She did exactly what the servant had prayed for. After she politely gave him a drink, she ran to do the back-breaking work of drawing huge amounts of water for the camels.

    b. The servant kept quiet. He did not yet know who she was. And he wondered at God's way of answering him so soon.

Read verses 22-32

B. At the Well

1. Eliezer had taken along jewelry, and he gave the girl two arm bracelets and an earring (or forehead jewel) of gold. When he asked her who she was, and she answered that she was the daughter of Bethuel, the servant knew she was the daughter of Isaac's cousin. But Rebekah did not know this stranger yet.

2. Maybe she suspected, because when Eliezer asked for a place to stay, she was excited, and ran home to tell the news. She came back with her brother Laban. What kind of man was Laban? He was eager to help Eliezer, and he even boasted (in verse 31) that "I have prepared the house." Notice, too, that he was especially eager to be kind to the servant when he saw the expensive golden jewelry.

C. At the House of Bethuel

1. The servant would not eat until he had told his story. In verse 33 Laban, not his father, says, "Speak on." Laban was taking the important place his father should have taken.

2. This was probably the first time these relatives had heard the story of Abraham and Sarah since they had moved away to Canaan. The servant told the beautiful story of Jehovah's care. He told:

    a. how God had blessed Abraham with riches

    b. about the wonder-birth of Isaac

    c. that Isaac, the child of the promise, needed a godly wife.

3. He ended his speech by asking them to let him take Rebekah home as a wife for Isaac.

4. Read verse 50. Once again Laban spoke first instead of his father Bethuel, and said they could not speak to him good or bad. It is not a very happy nor a very godly answer, is it?

Read verses 54-60

5. Then the servant brought out his jewels and gave them to Rebekah, her mother, and her brother. Her father is not mentioned. Why not? Are you getting a picture of the family? The servant was getting the picture. Laban was boss. His father was a weak man, and his mother did not have much to say. It was not a very strong, God-fearing home. From such a home Rebekah came.

D. Rebekah and the Servant Return Home

1. The next morning Eliezer made an astonishing statement: "Send me away to my master." He meant, of course, "Send Rebekah, the bride whom the Lord has chosen for Isaac, with me today." Was that not asking a lot of Rebekah? A bride wants showers, she must pack, say good-bye to her friends, especially when she goes far from home. And she would be marrying a stranger. Didn't she need time to think it over? Laban and her mother asked for ten days at the least.

2. But the servant was doing the Lord's business, and the Lord's business always comes first. Rebekah, with faith in her heart, said, "I will go." She would trust the God-fearing stranger, go to a faraway country, and marry another stranger — all because God had chosen her.

3. They left that day for their long trip home. At this time, Isaac was in the south country, near the well Lahai-roi. When their trip was almost over, Rebekah saw Isaac in the field, meditating*. She dismounted from her camel, and put on her veil, a sign of respect in those days. And the servant told Isaac everything that the Lord had done.

4. Isaac and Rebekah did not know one another yet. They married by faith. And Isaac loved her because the Lord had brought them together.

DO NOT FORGET that twice, in verses 27 and 48, the servant told Rebekah's family, "I being in the way, the Lord led me." That way was the right way, the way of faith, God's way.

Discuss how we as fourth graders can know God's way.

WORD STUDIES

1. caravan — a company of people traveling together through the desert
2. meditate — to think or to pray

LESSON 24
Jacob and Esau
Genesis 25

BEFORE WE BEGIN, Chapter 25 tells us that we have come to the end of Abraham's life. Once more he took a wife, Keturah, had six sons, and lived thirty-eight years longer. This is the last chapter in the history of Abraham.

LESSON OUTLINE
A. Abraham's Death

1. We will not read all the names in the first part of this chapter. These names tell us that Abraham had children and grandchildren from his marriage to Keturah and from the line of Ishmael. But these are not very important names in Bible history. God only mentions them.

2. The most important verses are 5 and 6. Read them. It was right for Abraham to give all his possessions to Isaac, for God had told him that Isaac was his heir*. Abraham gave his other sons gifts. He was a rich man and took care of them. Abraham was preparing for the day of his death, and he sent Isaac away from his other sons. He knew that Isaac had a weak character, and that this son of God's covenant must live separate from the people who do not love God and His promises, so that he would not be tempted to do evil.

3. When he was one hundred seventy-five years old, Abraham died, and Isaac and Ishmael buried him next to Sarah in the cave of Machpelah in the land of promise. After the death of Abraham, Isaac lived near the well Lahai-roi. Do you remember that God found Hagar there when she ran away from Sarah, and that she named the well? The name means, "The well of him that liveth and seeth me."

Read Genesis 25:19-23

B. Isaac's and Rebekah's Prayers

1. The Lord does not tell us anything about the first twenty years of their life together: only that they waited for a child. Isaac and Rebekah kept remembering the word of God to Abraham: "In Isaac shall thy seed be called."

2. Why did the Lord wait so long? To show Isaac and Rebekah that the promised child was not their child, but God's child; and this baby could be born only after they struggled with God and prayed hard for a baby, after

83

they had told God that only He could give them the child of the covenant.

3. Isaac and Rebekah did not do what Abraham and Sarah had done. They did not try another way to get the child of the promise, but Isaac entreated the Lord. He begged Him for a baby.

4. The Lord answered their prayer. When Rebekah knew she would have a baby, she felt a struggle inside her. She asked the Lord why this was happening to her, and God gave her a surprise. She and Isaac would be parents of twins!

    a. Not just ordinary twins, but each child would grow into a nation of people.

    b. The older twin would serve the younger twin.

5. What does that mean? Read Romans 9:11-13. God was teaching Isaac and Rebekah that not every child born from covenant parents is one of God's children. God showed to Rebekah election* and reprobation*. What do these big words mean? Election means chosen, and reprobation means rejected or hated. Before they were born, Rebekah knew that Esau, the older, was rejected, and that Jacob, the younger, was chosen by God to be His own child.

6. The older twin would serve the younger. It is a picture of the way the sinful world will serve God's church.

Read verses 24-26

C. The Birthright

1. If we could meet the twins and compare them, we would find that:

    a. Esau was a likeable, good-natured child, brave, strong, ready for physical exercise, a boy who loved hunting.

    b. Jacob was weaker, a sort of "sissy," a mother's boy, clever, and sneaky.

    c. If we saw the twins, we would choose Esau. But God chose Jacob. Esau was not willing or ready to talk about the promise or the love of God. Jacob's whole life centered on God's love, and His promise to His people.

    d. Father Isaac loved Esau most and mother Rebekah loved Jacob most. Do you think this was a happy, peaceful home?

2. God's rule for His people in Old Testament times was that the promises He had made went to the firstborn child. He had the right by birth, or the birthright. What was the birthright?

a. The promise that he would have possessions (his father's possessions) in the land of Canaan. It was a picture of having a place and possessions in heaven.

b. The promise that God would be his God and the God of his children.

c. In Isaac's family, it meant that he would be one of the ancestors of the special Seed of the promise, Jesus Christ, the Savior.

d. That he would rule over his brothers, a picture of Christ ruling His people.

Read verses 29-34

3. Esau, as the firstborn, had the birthright. Jacob wanted it. He may have purposely made some tasty pottage, or bean soup, in order to be ready to make a deal with his hungry brother when he came back from hunting.

4. Esau, famished, asked Jacob for some of that red bean soup, and Jacob was ready for him. He suggested a trade: the birthright (Esau's place in God's kingdom and the line of promise) for Jacob's bowl of red soup.

5. The trick worked. Esau traded his birthright for a bowl of soup. He was interested only in earthly things. He said, in verse 32, "I am going to die," not, "I am ready to die of hunger." He meant, "When I die, that is the end of everything."

6. Verse 34 tells us that Esau did four things: ate and drank, rose up, went his way, and despised* his birthright. Hebrews 12:16 calls him "a profane* person."

DO NOT FORGET that all ungodly people are profane people. They live for a good and comfortable life here on this earth. They despise the love of God, His promise of salvation, and the joys of heaven, which are dearest to the hearts of God's chosen children.

Discuss in class why Jacob bought the birthright from Esau,
and then discuss why it was wrong for him to buy it.

WORD STUDIES

1. heir — one who gets the possessions of a father after his death
2. election — those who are chosen by God before the world was
3. reprobation — those who are rejected by God before the world was
4. despise — to look down on, to scorn
5. profane — to treat holy things with disrespect; an ungodly person

85

LESSON 25
Isaac and Abimelech
Genesis 26

BEFORE WE BEGIN, we will find out how much time has passed between the beginning of yesterday's lesson and today's lesson. You will remember that Isaac was sixty years old when his twin sons were born. Now Jacob and Esau were young men of at least twenty years old, for Esau had already traded his birthright for a bowl of soup. That would make Isaac about eighty years old.

Read Genesis 26:1-5

LESSON OUTLINE

A. The Famine and the Blessing

    1. Once again the Lord sent a famine in the land. Do you remember that soon after Abraham and Sarah had come to the land of Canaan God sent a famine? What did Abraham do? We learned in chapter 12 that he went to Egypt.

        a. The Lord let Abraham go to Egypt. He did not stop him. And He let Abraham fall into the sin of lying about his wife.

        b. Verse 2 suggests to us that Isaac planned to follow his father's example, and go to Egypt; but the Lord stopped him. Why? Isaac's faith was not strong enough for him to go to a heathen land with its many temptations. Instead, the Lord chose to make Isaac's faith stronger.

    2. The Lord appeared to him. We do not know how: possibly in a dream or a vision. God told him, "Stay in this land, the promised land." Then God would bless him and give him many descendants, who would inherit the land. Isaac needed to stay in the land so God could help and strengthen his faith.

    3. Isaac obeyed God and stayed in what seemed to be a house of death instead of the land of promise. The famine was very bad. There were not enough crops for them and their herds. But Isaac trusted Jehovah. He stayed in Canaan and went to Abimelech in the city of Gerar. You remember that Abraham had also lived there for a time (chapter 20). You remember, too, that all the kings of Gerar had the title "Abimelech."

Read verses 6-11

B. Isaac's Lie

    1. Do your parents tell you things that have happened before you were

born? Probably all parents do. It is likely that Abraham and Sarah did, too, especially the stories about God's care and His promises. They were godly parents, just as our parents are; and as we learn from our parents, so Isaac must have learned about the results of his parents' lies to Pharaoh and Abimelech.

2. Did his parents' lessons keep Isaac from telling a lie? No. Abraham's lie to Abimelech was a half-truth. Isaac's lie in verse 7 was a total lie. There was no reason for the lie. No one was bothering him. No one was trying to take Rebekah from him. He and Rebekah must have lived with the lie for a long time, until one day when the king looked out of the window and saw them. They were not acting as brother and sister, but as loving husband and wife.

3. Abimelech called for Isaac. He was angry. Can you blame him? He scolded Isaac (verses 9 and 10) and Isaac had every bit of it coming. Abimelech found out their lie before anyone tried to marry the beautiful Rebekah. Why? The Lord knew Isaac's weakness of character and his weakness of faith. He did not let anyone touch his wife. It was a lesson to Isaac: God's protecting care was always with him.

Read verses 12-16

C. Isaac's Greatness

1. In verse 3, God had said, "Sojourn* in this land, and I will be with thee, and will bless thee." Now God's promise was coming true. When Isaac planted his fields, the Lord made his crops grow much better than they usually did. Verse 12 says that he reaped one hundredfold: that is probably one hundred times the amount of seed he planted. He had much better crops than his neighbors.

2. The blessings of crops, flocks, and herds were types of the blessings of salvation and of God's blessings in Old Testament times. God made Isaac a great and powerful man, with riches, animals, and servants because He loved Isaac.

3. The men of Gerar were jealous. Although there were still some godly men there, these jealous men had left the fear of Jehovah, and wandered away from His law. They were not only jealous. They were afraid. Wicked men are always afraid of the power of God's wonders.

Discuss what happens to people
whose hearts are filled with jealousy and fear.

Read verses 17-22

87

D. Trouble with the Men of Gerar

1. The first thing these evil men of Gerar (the Philistines) did was to stop up the wells which Abraham had dug many years ago. Without wells of water, animals and humans die. These men were trying to harm Isaac, to bring him down from his greatness.

2. Abimelech did not scold his wicked people, but asked Isaac to leave, because Isaac was too great. What should Isaac have done? He should have stood up to Abimelech as his father Abraham had done many years earlier. When Abimelech's servants had tried to do that to Abraham, he scolded, and refused to be friends with Abimelech until he promised not to stop up his wells. Chapter 21:25-30 tells about it.

3. Isaac meekly* moved away. He wanted no trouble, and went to live in the valley of Gerar. First, he opened all the wells which Abraham had dug.

    a. Then he began digging a new well. The Philistines promptly claimed that it belonged to them. Isaac hated fighting and arguing, and he moved on, letting the Philistines have it. He called the well Esek, which means contention (or argument).

    b. Isaac dug another well, and had the same problem. He left once more, calling the well Sitnah, which means enmity (or hatred).

    c. He dug a third well, and the men left him alone. Isaac named it Rehoboth. Find the meaning of this name in verse 22.

    d. Then he settled once more in Beersheba.

4. What must we think about Isaac? He traveled through the land by faith as God had commanded, but at the same time he was easy-going, peace-loving, hating trouble, and often slow and lagging behind the Lord.

DO NOT FORGET that God's children must be peacemakers. Jesus said, "Blessed are the peacemakers. . . ." But Jesus does not want us to make peace at any price. We must stand up and fight for the right, scold what is wrong, and at the same time, "as much as in you lieth, live peaceably with all men," Romans 12:18.

WORD STUDIES

1. sojourn — to live in a place for a time

2. meek — patient, gentle, lacking backbone

LESSON 26
Jacob Gets a Blessing
Genesis 27

BEFORE WE BEGIN, we have learned that in His revelation God does not tell us everything that happened in the lives of His saints, but only those things which teach us about the history of our salvation. At the same time, God lets us figure out some details by ourselves. By studying other passages from the Bible, we know that Isaac was an old man of one hundred thirty-seven years old now, and close to being blind.

Read Genesis 27:1-4

LESSON OUTLINE
A. Isaac's Plan

1. The last two verses of chapter 26 tell us that Esau married — not one — but two Canaanitish women, descendants of Canaan, the son of Ham, whom God had cursed for his sin. (We learned about it in Lesson 11.) This shows that Esau wanted to be wicked and rebellious, and wanted to show his parents, and God, that he did not care about serving Him. Isaac and Rebekah were very sad about it.

2. Yet Isaac loved Esau — not with the love of God, but with a natural, earthly love. He loved Esau for his pleasant personality and for the delicious food he cooked; and he wished that Esau had been the boy chosen by God for the promise of God's friendship.

    a. At the same time, he knew that before the twins were born, God had told Rebekah that He had chosen Jacob but had hated Esau.

    b. He knew, too, that Esau did not care about his birthright, but had sold it for a bowl of red soup.

    c. And he knew that Esau wanted to live a sinful life with two heathen wives.

3. Isaac was not happy with the Lord's plan. He wanted to bless Esau. And remember, in Old Testament times, God's saints were prophets. God spoke through them, and what they said would happen.

4. He knew that Rebekah loved Jacob because he was chosen by God; and he knew she was right, that Jacob must get the blessing. But he did not talk over his problem with her.

5.   Instead, he went ahead with his own plans. He called Esau to his tent and asked him to bring venison, not necessarily deer meat, but some wild game, and make him a tasty meal. Then Isaac promised to bless him before he died.

Read verses 15-17

B.   The Plans of Rebekah and Jacob

1.   Rebekah knew how much Isaac loved Esau. She was suspicious. She watched. And when she saw Esau going to his father's tent, she listened, and heard the details of Isaac's plans.

2.   What should Rebekah have done? She could have stopped Esau. She could have talked with her husband Isaac and showed him how terrible it was to disobey the Lord. She could have gotten the whole family together and talked about being blessed by God only in the way of obedience.

3.   Rebekah did none of these things. Instead, she chose a sneaky plan to deceive (fool) Isaac. Quickly she called Jacob; and immediately she started her plan to disguise him and cook tasty food for Isaac. She had every detail ready, even to putting skins of goat's hair on Jacob's smooth hands and neck to imitate Esau's skin. She found Esau's clothes with the smells of hunting on them for Jacob, the stay-at-home boy, to wear.

4.   Rebekah's motive* was right: for Jacob must have the blessing. Her method of sneaking and lying was all wrong.

5.   Remember that this was a godly family. Yet every member was ready to trick another member, all in the name of getting God's covenant blessing of friendship. They were all trying to run ahead of God.

Discuss in class how, when we know something is wrong,
we will find reasons to do the wrong anyway.

Read verses 18-26

C. Isaac and Jacob

1.   While Isaac was waiting for Esau, he had time, in the darkness of his blindness, to think. He knew he was doing wrong. Suddenly a voice burst in on the silence, and he asked a strange question: "Who art thou, my son?" The voice did not sound right to him, and he was too blind to see which son it was.

a.   He heard Jacob's answer: "I am Esau." But because he was guilty, and his conscience* was bothering him, and because the voice sounded like Jacob's, Isaac had to make sure.

b.   Only when Isaac touched his hands, covered with goat skins, was he convinced it was Esau.

90

2. Now we will look at Jacob. He was God's chosen child, and he wanted the covenant blessing more than anything in the world. But in trying to get it by himself, in his actions or words he lied to his father five times:

   a. when he disguised himself (verses 15, 16)

   b. when he said, "I am Esau" (verse 19)

   c. when he said, "The Lord thy God," which was Esau's way of talking (verse 20)

   d. when he said, "I am" to Isaac's question, "Art thou my very son Esau?" (verse 24)

   e. when he kissed his father, pretending to be Esau (verse 26).

3. Now Isaac was ready to bless him. He gave Jacob a blessing, but not the blessing. Remember that God was speaking through this blessing.

   a. Isaac told him he would have the blessings of the earth.

   b. And he would be ruler over his brothers, his relatives.

   c. Then Isaac stopped. He did not give Jacob the blessing of God's covenant friendship, nor the promise that all nations would be blessed in him.

4. Why not? Isaac did not dare to give those precious blessings of salvation to Esau. Don't forget: he thought he was blessing Esau! And God's hand kept him from doing it. The result was that Jacob, who wanted them so badly, did not get the blessings of God's friendship and salvation, either. God was ruling that, too. It was not time yet.

5. The result was that Isaac was disturbed and Jacob was sad and disappointed.

Read verses 30-40

D. Isaac and Esau

1. Jacob had barely left Isaac's tent when Esau entered. Father Isaac trembled badly. Why? He realized that in his stubbornness he tried, and almost succeeded to bless the wrong son.

2. When he knew that Jacob had already gotten the blessing, Esau cried bitter tears, and begged for a blessing. He wanted the blessings of his father's riches and possessions, but Isaac had no blessing from the Lord for him. Verse 39 should read, "Thy dwelling shall be away from the fatness of the earth. . . ." God never has a blessing for the ungodly.

Read verses 41-46

E. The Results of the Sins of This Family

1. The Lord never lets sins go without making His people feel the results. He made Isaac's family feel His displeasure strongly.

    a. Esau was bitter, angry, and had murder in his heart. He wanted to kill his brother.

    b. Isaac's disobedience had made his whole family displeased with him, and he was uneasy before God.

    c. Jacob was forced to run away because he was afraid; and he was sad because he did not get the covenant blessing.

    d. Rebekah lost her favorite son.

2. Rebekah was still not cured of her tricks. She did not give Isaac the real reason for Jacob's running away. Read verse 46 and find the reason she gave. We will learn more about it in our next lesson.

DO NOT FORGET that these sinful, cheating, lying people were saints of God and heroes of faith. We, too, with all our sins, are God's saints, because He loves us, and has promised to wash all those terrible sins away in Jesus' blood.

WORD STUDIES
1. motive — a reason or cause for doing something
2. conscience — the voice inside a person, telling him the difference between right and wrong

LESSON 27
Jacob at Bethel
Genesis 28

BEFORE WE BEGIN, we will want to know what happened to Esau. The Lord, through Isaac's mouth, sent Esau away from the fatness and blessings of the earth, and made him and his seed live by using their swords, in war and in robbery, and by making Esau's people subject to his brother Jacob's people. Esau is the father of the people of Edom. We will meet them later in our lessons.

Read verses 1-5

LESSON OUTLINE
A. Jacob Gets the Blessing

1. In this unhappy family, where God seemed to make everything go wrong because of their sins, no one was cured as yet of going his own way.

    a. Rebekah still had her secrets. Someone had told her the words of Esau: that he had murder in his heart; and she had to make more sneaky plans.

    b. She told Jacob to run away to her brother Laban in Haran until Esau was no longer angry. But Rebekah told her husband Isaac a different story: that it was time for Jacob to get a wife from their God-fearing relatives there.

    c. Rebekah thought their separation would be a few days. It turned out to be twenty years. Rebekah and Jacob never saw one another again.

    d. By his trick, Jacob was forced to go into exile* alone, away from his family, church, and country. He was supposed to have everything: the riches of the land and God's promised blessings. He did not have God's blessing yet, nor any riches. He ran away with his staff in his hand.

2. Before he left, Isaac called him and told him to go to Padan-Aram (the same as Haran) and marry a God-fearing girl there.

3. Then Isaac, sorry for his sin of wanting to bless the wrong son, gave Jacob the full blessing which God had promised. God, through Isaac, gave Jacob the blessing He had given to Abraham: that God would be with him and his children after him, and give him the land of Canaan. At last Jacob had God's promise of friendship and salvation.

4. But as soon as he had that special blessing from the Lord, he was forced to turn around and leave home and go to a strange place all alone.

B. Esau's Reaction

1. Esau saw that Jacob had left to get a wife from Padan-Aram, and he knew his parents did not want him to have any more wives from the Canaanites. He knew they were displeased with the two wives he already had, so he went to Ishmael and took one of his daughters to be his wife, along with the other two wives he had.

2. Why? He knew that having three wives was wrong. But by marrying Ishmael's daughter, he thought he would get favor from his parents. After all, Ishmael was Abraham's son. Isaac and Rebekah should be pleased.

3. Were they? No, for Ishmael was not the son of promise and he was not one of God's children. The Bible does not tell us whether Ishmael's daughter feared the Lord. We do know that Esau was not interested in doing things God's way.

Read verses 10-15

C. Jacob's Loneliness

1. Alone, Jacob left. It seemed as if Esau, staying at home, would take his place after all. He would enjoy all the riches and comforts in the home of Isaac and Rebekah. If we could look inside this lonely man, we would see that he was troubled, upset, and unsure of the future.

2. Twice he had tried to get the blessing: once when he thought he bought it with his red pottage, and once when he tried to sneak it in disguise. Now just when he had at last gotten the blessing, he had to run away.

3. Does it surprise you that he felt as if God had left him? He was in misery. That always happens when God's children try to do God's work their own way — without God.

Discuss in class whether you have ever felt lonely
and without God after some special sin or stubbornness.

D. Jacob's Dream

1. It was night time. Jacob had walked all day. Now he had no comforts, no place to stay. Stones had to serve for his pillows. Tired, he went to sleep and had a dream. In his dream he saw a ladder and angels going up and down on it.

    a. Everyone has dreams, but this dream was special. God put it in Jacob's soul that this dream was a revelation, that God had a special message for him. He heard God's Words in his dream.

94

b. We know that God did this more often in Old Testament times. Think of the dreams of Pharaoh and Nebuchadnezzar.

2. What was the meaning of this dream? The ladder stretched from heaven to earth and from earth to heaven. The ladder was the way Jacob could look to God in heaven and God could speak to Jacob on earth: it was a type of Jesus. It brought God near to Jacob. The only way Jacob or any of God's children can come to Him is through Jesus, for John 14:6 says, "I am the way, the truth, and the life: no man cometh unto the Father, but by me."

3. The angels on the ladder are the servants of God's people. They bring our needs to God, and take God's comfort back to us.

4. At the top of the ladder, the Lord Jehovah spoke words of comfort and promise. Now Jacob knew from the mouth of God that:

    a. He promised to give him and his seed this land;

    b. all families of the earth would be blessed in him;

    c. God would be with him and bring him back to this land again.

5. All Jacob had to do was to stop trusting himself and lean on his God. He must have felt happy and blessed. Now he had the greatest promise in heaven or on earth from his covenant Friend. All was well. The angels were caring for him. The ladder was a picture of Jesus Who would surely come some day. Jehovah would keep all His promises. Was this the way Jacob felt?

6. The answer is no.

Read verses 16-22

E. Jacob is Not Cured

1. Jacob was afraid. In verse 17, he was really saying, "God is in this place. How awful!" For a long time, he had acted as if God were far away. He had done things his own way. Now he saw God in His mercy and love, very close. He knew he was standing at the gate of heaven. He was standing before God's holiness. And it was all too much for him, a dreadful sinner. He said it was awful, dreadful, to stand before God's holiness.

2. But Jacob was God's child. He set up a stone and poured oil over it, a picture of holiness, and set it up for a memorial.

3. He also made a promise (verse 20): if God will be with me, keep me safe, give me food and clothes, and bring me back, then I will give one-tenth of my possessions to Him. Notice that Jacob was trying to make a deal with the Lord, a bargain: if God does this, I will do that!

4. Jacob was not humble. He was not sorry with tears of repentance for his

sins. He was not yet cured of trusting himself. But he was strengthened. God gave him strength to go on. In a later lesson we will learn how God cured him.

DO NOT FORGET that it is a very serious thing to stand at the gate of heaven. We stand at the gate of heaven when we pray. Who opens the gate? Jesus does. In John 10:7 He says, "I am the door." That is the reason we pray in the name of Jesus.

WORD STUDIES
exile — separation from one's home and country

LESSON 28
Jacob at Haran
Genesis 29

BEFORE WE BEGIN, would you like to know how far Jacob walked alone until he came to Haran (or Syria as it is called today)? About seven hundred fifty miles, the same distance Abraham's servant had traveled to get a wife for Isaac. He had much time to think on his lonely trip, to be sorry for his sins, and to wonder what plans God had for him as He guided him to Haran.

Read verses 1-8

LESSON OUTLINE

A. Jacob at the Well

1. Wells in those days were the most important places of villages and towns. They were not only necessary to water the huge flocks of animals, but they were the meeting places for everyone, the places to get information.

2. When Jacob came to the well, three shepherds and their flocks were there. It was not evening, the time they usually gave their animals water, but only about two o'clock in the afternoon. Jacob asked why they did not roll the huge stone from the mouth of the well and give their flocks water.

3. The shepherds explained that the rule was to wait until every shepherd came. Then together they would roll away the heavy stone.

4. While he talked with them, Jacob asked the all-important question on his mind. "Do you know Laban?" Yes, they knew him, and they pointed out Laban's daughter Rachel coming with her sheep to the well.

Read verses 9-14

B. Jacob and Rachel

1. Can you imagine how happy Jacob was to see a close relative — his cousin? He had been looking forward to this moment through all those weary miles he had walked. When he saw this beautiful girl, he kissed her and wept. In the countries of the east, the usual greeting was often a kiss, while we westerners more often use a hand-shake. At the same time, Jacob must have wished the shepherds were not there, so that he could be alone with Rachel. Probably he had already begun to love her.

2. Jacob was so glad and so eager to help Rachel that he rolled away the stone all by himself. Remember: he was a seventy-seven-year-old man

already. Usually several shepherds rolled the stone away together; but in his eagerness to help Rachel, the daughter of his mother's brother, he easily moved the huge stone. In fact, in verse 10 he mentioned his mother's brother three times.

3. Rachel ran to tell her father about Jacob, and Laban came to meet him and take him home. At last Jacob was with relatives again, and he lived with them for a month. Jacob must have learned many things about Laban's family, and Laban learned at least two things about Jacob:

    a. that he was a good worker and a good shepherd,

    b. that he loved Rachel.

Read verses 15-30

C. Jacob's First Seven Years with Laban

1. After Jacob lived with his Uncle Laban for a month, his uncle asked what seems to be a kind, considerate question: "You should not work for nothing: what shall I pay you?" But it was a selfish question:

    a. Because Laban was treating Jacob as a hired servant instead of a member of his family, his sister's son.

    b. Because Laban was not blind. He saw how much Jacob loved Rachel, and he knew Jacob had no money to give her or to support her.

    c. Because he was a very greedy man.

2. Jacob fell right into Laban's selfish scheme. He offered to work seven years for Rachel, and Laban agreed. It seemed as if all was well: Laban had a free hired man for seven years, and Jacob was getting the best pay he could imagine: the beautiful Rachel.

3. But all was not well, and all was not right, for Laban had another daughter, older than Rachel, whose name was Leah.

    a. Leah was tender-eyed. She had soft eyes, which showed her gentleness and her meekness and her love of the Lord. Leah was a spiritual girl, the girl God chose to be Jacob's wife.

    b. Rachel had flaming eyes. Her blazing dark eyes showed how proud of her beauty she was. Rachel was a worldly girl who loved herself, and the girl Jacob chose as his wife.

4. For Jacob, the seven years seemed but a few days, because of his love for Rachel. During those seven years, he did not stop to ask God whether he was doing the right thing. He did not pray to ask the Lord to guide him to a godly wife, who would be the mother of a son in the covenant line, which would

end in the Lord Jesus. No, Jacob was still doing things his own way.

5. Then it was time for the wedding feast. It was the custom for the bride to wear a heavy veil, so that no one was able to see her face. We do not know whether there was some kind of wedding ceremony or not.

6. The veil was the perfect cover to hide Laban's nasty prank, for Leah, not Rachel, was wearing the bride's veil.

   a. Often the blame goes only to Laban for this trick. He was the one who thought of it and who planned it all.

   b. But Leah took a part in this trick. She could have run to Jacob and told him the truth. But, as we will soon find out, Leah loved Jacob, and this was probably her only chance to be married. So she went along with the lie.

   c. Rachel, who loved herself, agreed to the plan, too, although the Bible does not tell us how she felt about it.

7. How amazed Jacob must have been, and how angry, when he discovered that he was married to the wrong girl. Was he? Not really. Leah was God's choice; and God showed Jacob that He could use even the wicked trick of Laban to work out His perfect plan.

> Discuss in class other examples of God
> using evil men to work out His plans.
> Here is a start: the men at the tower of Babel.

8. Jacob must have seen God's hand working in his life; and he must have been reminded of the sneaky tricks he had used in his life. He must have known he was getting a dose of his own medicine, because he did not have much to say to his Uncle Laban, verse 25. And Laban, not at all ashamed of his deceit, told Jacob that the custom in his country would not allow him to give the younger daughter before the older one. It was a fine time to tell Jacob! Laban knew it seven years earlier!

9. Now that he was married to Leah, what should Jacob have done? With thanks to God for the wife He had chosen, Jacob should have accepted her and learned to love her. But Jacob was head-strong and he wanted Rachel, whom he loved only for her beauty and her flashing eyes.

10. Greedy Laban was ready with another evil plan. Weddings in those days lasted a week. He suggested (in verse 27) that he marry Rachel after the seven days of Jacob and Leah's wedding were over. Laban knew he would get seven more years of free work from Jacob, because now he had to work seven years

for the real Rachel. Jacob gladly agreed: and he married two wives in eight days.

11. Was it right for Jacob to marry two wives? Read Genesis 2:24. God created man to have one wife. Jacob disobeyed. His was the sin of bigamy*. Why did he do it? Jacob felt that he was in the power of Laban. He was afraid to go back to Canaan. And he still had no possessions of his own. But he knew, and God knew, that it was wrong. In later lessons we will learn how God taught Jacob some bitter lessons as a result of his sin.

Read verses 31-35

D. Leah's Children

1. When the Lord saw that Jacob hated Leah, He gave her children; but to Rachel He gave none.

2. The names of Leah's first four children show us her feelings.

a. When Reuben, Simeon, and Levi were born, she gave them names reminding Jacob and herself that, because she had children, Jacob would love her.

b. When Judah was born, she was ready to "praise the Lord."

DO NOT FORGET that we can learn to love one another, as Jacob had to learn to love Leah. If we look only at the faults and nasty characters of our family or friends, we will have a hard time loving them. But when two of God's children try to love one another with the love that comes from our Lord Jesus, Who loved us so much that He died for us, we will find that we can learn to overlook the faults of others and live in peace and happiness.

WORD STUDIES

bigamy — one man having two wives at the same time

LESSON 29
Jacob Leaves Laban
Genesis 30:25-31:24

BEFORE WE BEGIN, in our last lesson we tried not to forget that true love and peace comes from God, through the love of Jesus in our hearts. When God's children try to run their own lives, they have only trouble and misery, as we will learn in this lesson.

LESSON OUTLINE

A. Jacob's Wives and Children

1. We will not study all the details of Jacob's family from chapter 30, but will look at a few words at the beginning of the chapter. Open your Bibles and find the words envied* and give me in verse 1; the words anger and am I in God's stead? in verse 2; God hath judged me in verse 6; and wrestled in verse 8. Do these words lead you to think that Jacob's family was a happy family?

2. After Rachel saw that God gave Leah four sons, she was jealous because God did not give her any children. To get her own way, she gave Jacob her maid Bilhah as his wife, and when Bilhah had two sons, she said these boys were her sons. Then Leah, to get even with Rachel, gave her maid Zilpah to Jacob as his wife, and she called the two sons God gave Zilpah her sons.

3. After that, Leah had two more sons; and then God remembered Rachel and gave her a son, Joseph. On our worksheets we will study Jacob's family in more detail.

4. Jacob now had four wives and eleven children and an unhappy, bickering, quarreling family. He was still running ahead of the Lord and trying to live his life his own way. The Lord let him go, teaching him at the same time that his own way brought him nothing but grief.

Read chapter 30:25-36

B. Laban and Jacob Make a Deal

1. For fourteen years Jacob had worked for Laban to gain his two wives. Laban should have given him his daughters and paid him a handsome wage besides. But by selling his two daughters, he had kept them poor; and Jacob and his family had no earthly goods at the end of the fourteen years. Laban's greed had taken it all. Jacob was still a hired man. Is it any wonder that he wanted to take his family and leave (verse 26)?

2. Laban did not want that at all. He had become rich while Jacob worked for him. And he thought he knew why: that Jehovah had blessed him for Jacob's sake. We know that the Lord gave Laban many animals, but not with His blessing, for God never blesses the wicked.

3. Jacob agreed with his uncle that Jehovah had given him a multitude of animals and even reminded Laban how poor he had been when Jacob had first arrived. During those fourteen years when Jacob worked in the rain and cold, the heat and the storms, Laban had become a rich man for Jacob's sake.

4. Something was bothering Jacob. He was still a poor man. If Laban continued to pay him the wages of a slave, he asked, in verse 30, "How shall I provide for mine own house also?"

5. This is what Jacob proposed: he would not take anything from Laban; but for the next seven years he would take all the speckled and spotted cattle and goats, and the brown sheep which were born in those years. Everything else would be Laban's possessions. Laban agreed.

6. Why did Jacob choose these wages? Because neither Jacob nor Laban could do anything to make the animals have spots or speckles. Only God can govern what kinds of animals will be born. And Jacob put himself in the hands of Jehovah by faith, knowing that the Lord had promised to bless him.

7. Did Laban realize what would happen? Did he know that the Lord would bless only Jacob? No, for he agreed when he said, "I would it might be according to thy word." Laban thought that God would certainly keep giving him large flocks and herds of animals. He knew, too, that in this country of the East the cattle were usually unspotted and unspeckled. We might think that Jacob chose the wrong kinds of animals. But he didn't. God had come to him in a dream (ch. 31:10-12) and promised him that the spotted, ringstraked, speckled, and grisled animals would be his; and Jacob trusted God.

8. Before the deal between Jacob and Laban went into action, Laban told his sons to take all the spotted, speckled, and brown animals away, and walk for three days, so they would be far away from Jacob. Laban would not leave them near Jacob's animals. He did not want Jacob's animals to have speckled babies (verses 35, 36).

9. What did Jacob do? He had begun by trusting God, but now he wanted to help God along again, to make sure that his animals would be speckled.

    a. Near the watering places where the animals mated, Jacob peeled branches of trees, so they were spotted and speckled, and he placed these branches before the watering troughs, where the cattle would see them. When they looked at the spots and speckles, Jacob thought they would have spotted and speckled baby animals. But he put only the stronger cattle in front of the branches (or rods) so that his baby animals would be born not only spotted and speckled, but strong, too.

b. Did his trick work? Yes, it did. Why? Because God made it work. He wanted Jacob to have the best cattle, and He gave him success. However, it was sin on Jacob's part to try to help God along; and he could not feel in his heart that he had put himself completely in the arms of the Lord. As a result, he continued to have trouble with Laban.

Discuss in class how often we are just like Jacob.

Read chapter 31:1-9

C. Jacob Leaves Laban

1. Laban was not happy. He was jealous and angry, and Jacob could see his feelings in his face. Besides, he heard the words of Laban's sons, that "Jacob hath taken away all that was our father's" (chapter 31:1). That was not true, of course. In verse 16, Rachel and Leah tell the truth: "God hath taken the riches from our father."

2. Now God told Jacob to go back to Canaan. Jacob called his wives and told them:

    a. how he had faithfully served his father

    b. how their rascal of a father changed his wages ten times

    c. that the Lord had come to him with His promise. Read it in verse 13.

3. His wives were more than ready to leave. They felt as if they were strangers in their father's house, sold to make Laban rich.

4. Laban went away to shear his sheep, and Jacob saw his chance to sneak away. Once again, Jacob did not put all his trust in the Lord.

5. Meanwhile, Rachel stole her father's images. Not only was the stealing wrong, but it shows that Rachel was not a truly godly wife. She was an idol-worshipper.

6. Three days later Laban heard the news of Jacob's escape, and he chased after him. He wanted to take Jacob back to Haran. All the troubles in the family were still there.

DO NOT FORGET that the difference between Jacob and Laban was that, though both sinned, Laban sinned as an ungodly man. God did not make him sorry, and He had no forgiveness for Laban. Jacob sinned grievously, but he sinned as God's child, and God loved him and forgave him and washed away his sins for Jesus' sake.

WORD STUDIES

envy — wanting to have what someone else has

LESSON 30
Jacob at Peniel
Genesis 31:24-32:32

BEFORE WE BEGIN, and before Laban could catch up with Jacob, the Lord came to him and warned him not to do anything to harm Jacob and his family. This is another example of the special care God takes for His children.

Read Genesis 31:25-32

LESSON OUTLINE
A. Laban Scolds Jacob

    1. After seven days Laban caught up with Jacob and his family. God could have stopped Laban and made him turn around and go home. But he let Laban go right on. Why? Because Jacob needed a scolding, and He used Laban to give it.

    2. Before we listen to Laban's scolding, we should remember that both men had done wrong, and both needed a scolding.

        a. Laban's scolding seemed reasonable: he was unhappy because Jacob had sneaked away; because he had taken Laban's daughters away as if they were captives; because he could not kiss them good-bye, nor make a farewell party for them.

        b. Underneath, Laban was very angry. His pride was hurt because they did not let him say good-bye. But his real problem was his greed. Jacob had all the wealth now.

    3. To prove that Jacob was a sneak and a thief and that he did not truly trust in Jehovah, Laban asked him why he had stolen his gods.

    4. Jacob admitted that he had sneaked away because he was afraid, but he seemed shocked that Laban accused him of stealing his images. When he said that the thief should die, Jacob, without knowing it, was giving the death sentence to his favorite wife, who had stolen them.

B. Jacob and Laban Make a Covenant

    1. Although Laban would not believe Jacob's words, but searched everywhere, he did not discover that his clever daughter was sitting on them.

    2. Then it was Jacob's turn to make an angry speech. In it he let Laban know that:

        a. he was not a thief, verse 37;

b. he had worked faithfully in all kinds of weather for Laban, and had always taken the losses himself, verse 39;

c. he had his wages changed ten times by Laban, verse 41.

3. But in his speech he made himself to be a godly man who trusted Jehovah with all his heart, and with no faults at all. Jacob and Laban were both wrong.

4. Laban suggested that they make a covenant — that they be friends. Jacob quickly took a stone and set it up as a pillar, a sign of their friendship. Then they gathered stones, sat on them, ate and drank, and made an agreement not to pass over the pillar or the heap of stones to do one another harm. Jacob and Laban gave names to this place, verses 48, 49. In the morning Laban kissed his children and left.

Discuss in class the meaning of the words
"Galeed*" and "Mizpah*."

Read Genesis 32:1, 2

C. Jacob Gets Ready to Meet Esau

1. In these two verses we find Jacob back at the border of Canaan, his homeland. He must have been thrilled and happy, but afraid, too, for he would soon have to meet Esau. Would Esau still want to kill him?

2. On his way, something wonderful happened. The angels of God met him. Did you notice that they were there, but they did not speak to him? Why not?

a. They came as a silent reminder of the time they had come to him at Bethel. That was the day Jacob left Canaan. Now their presence when Jacob came back reminded him of the ladder with the angels. It reminded him, too, of God's promise that He would bless Jacob and bring him back. The angels did not have to speak.

b. Jacob called the place "Mahanaim" which means "double host:" the host of angels and the host of Jacob.

Read verses 3-8

3. Now it was time to meet Esau. Jacob sent his servants to Edom, south of the land of Canaan, where Esau lived. His message to Esau was simple: "I have come back." He also made sure his servants called Esau "lord" and called Jacob "thy servant." Jacob wanted to come to Esau in a peaceable and humble way. He knew that Esau and his men were proud, wild, lawless men, and he did not want to make Esau angry before they even met. He also made

sure that Esau knew that he was now a rich man with flocks and herds. He was not interested in Esau's possessions.

4. The servants came back from Esau with the news that four hundred men were coming with Esau to meet him; and Jacob was greatly afraid.

Read verses 9-12

D. Jacob's Fear

1. Can you tell that Jacob is changing? He is learning to lean on his Father in heaven. As soon as he heard the news, he talked with God, the God of his grandfather Abraham and his father Isaac. He asked Him to remember His promise that He would be Jacob's God, too, and give him children without number in the promised land; and he begged God to save him from any harm that Esau would do.

2. Jacob knew that God would hear him and answer him and help him. At the same time he thought of a plan to make peace with Esau: he prepared a gift of five hundred eighty animals. He divided them into droves*, each drove in charge of a servant; and each servant was told to say the same words to Esau (verse 18).

Read verses 22-32

E. Jacob Wrestles with the Angel

1. Jacob was restless and ill at ease. He had prayed to the Lord, but as yet the Lord had not answered him. He could not sleep.

2. In the middle of the night he sent his wives and their maids over the brook Jabbok (we will find it on the map on next week's worksheets). He stayed alone on the other side.

3. There the Angel of Jehovah, in the appearance of a man, wrestled with Jacob. All night they wrestled. Jacob was wrestling not only with his body, but with his heart and soul and spirit. What was he wrestling for? The blessing of the covenant promise. Jacob began to realize that he was wrestling with the Angel of the Lord. Who was this Angel? It was the Lord Jesus as He appeared in Old Testament times, before He was born as our Savior.

4. All his life — but very imperfectly — Jacob had fought for God's blessing. Now he took the offensive in this wrestling match, and even though the Angel touched him with a heavenly touch and made him limp, he hung on and said, "I will not let thee go, except thou bless me."

5. Jacob did not want just any blessing. He wanted the blessing that his seed would end in the seed, the Lord Jesus Christ, his Savior, Who would take

107

away all his sins and the sins of all His children, and take His people to heaven to live forever.

6.   Jacob called the place "Peniel," for he saw God face to face. There God gave him a new name: Israel, a prince who has power with God and man.

DO NOT FORGET that Jacob was fighting the battle against sin. Hosea 12:4 tells us that he fought with begging and with tears. For what? For forgiveness — for forgiveness of his sins of running ahead of the Lord and trusting in his own strength and not leaning on Jehovah. In this story, God tells us to fight with tears and sorrow for our forgiveness, too.

WORD STUDIES
1.   Galeed — the heap of witness
2.   Mizpah — the Lord watch between me and thee, when we are absent one from another
3.   drove — a collection of animals

LESSON 31
Jacob Meets Esau and Goes to Bethel
Genesis 33 and 35

BEFORE WE BEGIN, we will picture a limping, wounded man leaving Peniel early in the morning to join his family on the other side of the brook Jabbok. He was a humble man, too. His name was Jacob-Israel.

Read Genesis 33:1-7

LESSON OUTLINE
A. Jacob and Esau Meet

1. At last, at the brook Jabbok, Jacob was converted* from his sin of running ahead of God, and from now on he would trust in Jehovah. He could never do that perfectly, of course, for he was still an imperfect sinner.

2. Before Jacob wrestled with the Angel of Jehovah, he had heard that Esau was coming with four hundred men, and Jacob was terrified. He had plans: to make peace by giving Esau a present of flocks of animals. His plans were to let the two maids with their sons meet Esau first; then Leah and her children, and at the end his favorite wife, Rachel, with Joseph.

3. He kept his plans, but now that he learned his lesson at Peniel, Jacob went to meet his brother in faith, trusting in the Lord instead of trusting in himself. The Lord had fully cured Jacob of his lifelong sin.

4. Jacob went first to meet Esau, and as he came close to his brother, he bowed himself, with his head down to the ground, seven times. Bowing was more common in these Eastern countries in Bible times than in our land today. But Jacob had a special reason for bowing: he humbled himself before Esau his older brother.

5. When Esau had come to meet Jacob with his four hundred warriors, he had evil plans in his heart. Suddenly, in verse 4, we read that Esau ran to meet his brother, hugged and kissed him, and wept. What made Esau change? He may have realized that Jacob was not coming back to try to take Esau's wealth away from him, for now he knew that Jacob was a rich man; and he may still have had a sort of brotherly love for his long-lost brother. But the main reason is that the Lord turned Esau's heart toward Jacob, so that he welcomed him. How do we know?

  a. We know that God always works His plans in men's hearts. Proverbs

21:1 tells us that God turns men's hearts the way He wants to turn them. Read that verse in class.

b. God always uses wicked men to serve for the good of His people. Jacob was God's dear child, and God turned Esau's heart in kindness toward his brother. Esau even ended their meeting by offering to be Jacob's guard as he traveled into Canaan, verse 12.

Read verses 8-15

B. Jacob and Esau Part

1. Esau, who had wanted his father's earthly possessions more than anything in the world, refused to take Jacob's present. Jacob urged him, and in the end he took the animals.

2. Why did Jacob insist that Esau take his present of animals? He said, "For therefore I have seen thy face, as though I had seen the face of God," verse 10. It means: "in your face I saw God's friendliness." Jacob saw that God had changed Esau's hatred into friendliness.

3. When Esau wanted his men to act as a guard for Jacob's huge company, Jacob would not hear of it. In their inner beings, their hearts, Jacob and Esau were totally different, and Jacob did not want to put his trust in a brother he knew to be wicked.

Read verses 16-20
Have your worksheets for Lessons 31-33 on your desks.

C. Jacob Goes to Succoth

1. Esau went home with his four hundred men to the south country of Seir. Later this land would be called Edom. Find it on the map on the worksheets for Lessons 31-33.

2. Remember: Jacob was still at Peniel, near the brook Jabbok. He and his family traveled to Succoth. Now find Succoth on the map. Did you notice that it is on the east side of the Jordan River, outside the land of Canaan? There he settled and built a house for himself. Notice that he did not live in a tent. He also made pens for his cattle.

3. Jacob had wanted so much to go to Canaan, and had promised God many years earlier that he would go back to Bethel and worship the Lord there, and give one-tenth of his wealth to Jehovah.

4. But Jacob was not in a hurry. He did not rush to see his old father Isaac, either. He must have stayed in Succoth for some years, for when he finally crossed the Jordan, moved into Canaan, and settled at Shechem, a city of

idol-worshippers, his children were grown. His oldest sons were grown-up men. Find Shechem on the map.

5. There at Shechem Jacob built an altar to God and called it El-elohe-Israel, which means, "God the God of Israel." Later in our lesson we will find out why he did that.

Read Genesis 35:1-5

D. God Comes to Jacob

1. During all his life, since God had come to him at Bethel on his way to Haran, God had taken care of him, and Jacob knew it. Jehovah kept him from danger on his way to his Uncle Laban, blessed him at Laban's house, saved him from Laban's anger when he left Haran, sent angels to meet him at the border of Canaan, and had blessed him at Peniel. But he stayed at Shechem instead of keeping his promise and going to Bethel.

    a. Now God told him to go to Bethel. Had Jacob forgotten his promise to go to Bethel? How could he? The Lord's appearance to him at Bethel was the greatest event of his life, outside of Peniel. He could not forget how God had helped him. But Jacob did not go to Bethel.

    b. Connected with this is another question: did Jacob forget to go to see his father? How could he? Yet he was in Canaan for years without going to see his father. Why? Because his father lived south, in the Plains of Mamre, near Hebron; and Jacob would have to pass through Bethel to get to Hebron. He did not want to go near Bethel. Find the way from Shechem through Bethel to Hebron on your map.

    c. At Peniel, Jacob's faith was very strong, but Jacob did not stay on those high peaks of faith. Part of the reason was that Jacob did not rule his house very well, but allowed his family to worship idols. Some of his children were very evil, and did not live as godly examples to the Canaanites; and Jacob was afraid to travel through the land because of his evil sons. Besides, there were many more people in the land now than there were in Abraham's time. It was more dangerous to travel.

    d. At Shechem he had tried to satisfy the Lord by building that altar. He had tried to make God do things Jacob's way. But it was the wrong place to build an altar.

2. Because Jacob would not go, God came to him at last, and told him to go to Bethel, verse 1. He said, "and dwell there," not here in Shechem. Jacob obeyed, and made his family bury their idols under an oak tree. As they

traveled, Jacob did not have to fear, for God had put His terror into the hearts of the heathen Canaanites, and they did not harm him.

Discuss in class whether God calls us to bury our idols,
and what kinds of idols we must bury.

Read verses 6-8

E. Three Deaths in Jacob's Family

1. Jacob obeyed God and went to Bethel, built an altar, and God blessed him with all the blessings of his grandfather Abraham. Once more God gave him the name of Israel (Prince).

2. There Deborah, his mother's nurse, died, the nurse who had taken care of him since he was a baby. She was probably about one hundred seventy years old. They buried her in a place called the "Oak of Weeping."

3. As they traveled south, at Ramah, on the way to Ephrath (or Bethlehem), Rachel died when her second son was born. See Matthew 2:18. She called him Benoni, son of my pain (or sorrow), but Jacob named him Benjamin, son of my right hand.

4. Then Jacob traveled to Mamre to see his father. His mother had already died. Although Isaac lived twelve years after Jacob came back to him, in fact almost until the time that Jacob went to Egypt to see Joseph, the Bible tells us here about his death, when he was one hundred eighty years old.

DO NOT FORGET that we should not be too hard on Jacob for not keeping his promise to God to go to Bethel. Are we any better? Do we always keep our promises to God — our promises to obey, to love our neighbor and help him, and to pray to our Father with all our hearts?

WORD STUDIES

converted — to be turned from a sinful way of life to a righteous way of
life

LESSON 32
Joseph and His Brothers
Genesis 37

BEFORE WE BEGIN, if you watch closely as you read this chapter, you will not see any name of God in it. You will read about the wicked plans and wicked deeds of Joseph's very evil brothers, and it may seem to you, as you study this chapter, that God is far away. But He isn't!

Read Genesis 37:1-4

LESSON OUTLINE

A. Joseph's Evil Brothers

　1. Jacob and his sons now lived in the region of Mamre, and the brothers took care of the flocks and herds of animals. Joseph, at the age of seventeen, was the youngest brother to work in the fields (Benjamin was too young yet).

　2. Already when they had lived in Shechem, Joseph's brothers had very bad reputations*. Some of their evil deeds were worse than those of the heathen around them. Yet father Jacob sent young Joseph out to the fields with his brothers, who at this time were very evil men. Later in life some of them repented.

　3. His brothers hated Joseph. Why?

　　a. Joseph was a godly, righteous, young man. He was bothered by the evil deeds of his brothers, especially when they were out in the field where father Jacob could not see them.

　　b. Joseph brought their evil report. That does not mean that he was a tattle-tale. He brought a report. It means he told what the people of the land thought of his brothers. They thought evil of them. The Bible mentions in verse 2 that the sons of Bilhah and Zilpah, Dan and Naphtali, Gad and Asher, were very evil.

　　c. The brothers hated Joseph because father Jacob showed that he loved Joseph more than his other sons. He showed it by making him a coat, probably not a coat of many colors, but more correctly a long coat worn by noblemen and king's children. It was not wise of Jacob to show his special favor toward only one son, and it would lead to more trouble and jealousy in his family. The seeds of hatred were taking root.

Read verses 5-11

113

B. Joseph's Dreams

1. What was it that made their hatred burn white hot? Joseph's dreams. Dreams in Old Testament times were often used by God to speak to His people. When God sent him his dreams, Joseph knew that God was showing him what would happen, and father Jacob knew it. So did his brothers, and they were angry and jealous that the Lord favored Joseph, too. Joseph's two dreams had the same meaning.

a. In the first dream, the Lord used the figure of the bundles (or sheaves) of grain that Joseph worked with in the fields. In his dream, his brothers' sheaves bowed down to him.

b. In the second dream, with the sun, moon, and eleven stars, Joseph's parents were also pictured as bowing down to him, along with his eleven brothers. His father scolded him because he could not understand how he and Joseph's mother would bow down to him, their child.

2. But Joseph knew that God was telling him that some day he would be a ruler over his family.

3. Why did God tell this now, so many years before it really happened? So that, when Joseph would soon be in deep trouble and loneliness, he could remember God's promise which He showed him in his dreams, and it would comfort him.

4. If you follow the words in this chapter, you will see how the hatred of the brothers grew. In verse 4 we read that they could not speak peaceably to him. They could not give him a cheery, "Good morning, Joseph!" After Joseph told the dreams, they envied him (verse 11). Then that hatred turned to murder. Verse 20 says, "Let us slay him."

Discuss in class the way we use the playground words,
"My mother will kill me if she finds out."

Read verses 12-28

C. Joseph is Sold

1. In this section of the chapter, we find Joseph's brothers a long way from home with their animals. They were finding pasture far north at Shechem. Joseph was at home with his father at this time.

2. Jacob was concerned about his sons. He knew their wicked ways, and he wanted to know whether all was going well. He sent his seventeen-year-old son, whom he knew his brothers hated and envied. He sent him all alone on this long trip to the north to find out how his brothers were faring. Was Jacob wise to do this?

114

3. Joseph came to Shechem and could not find his brothers. A man who saw him wandering in a field told him he would find them at Dothan. Find it on your map.

4. The hatred of his brothers was so strong that when they saw him far off, they could think only one thought: murder. Notice that they called him "this dreamer." They did not want his dreams to come true so that he would rule over them. If they got rid of Joseph, they thought they would make it impossible for his dreams to come true. The brothers' purpose was to stop God's plans. But God in heaven was ruling over all their plans, for exactly when they got rid of Joseph, God put him on the road to Pharaoh's palace, where some day he would rule over them.

5. God had also put Joseph on the main road for travelers from the east going down to Egypt. If Joseph had found his brothers in Shechem, he would not have been near a busy highway, traveled by buyers and sellers going from Gilead to Egypt.

6. Now we will go back to Joseph's brothers.

a. In their evil hatred, their first plans were to kill him, and tell the lie that a wild animal had eaten him. They did this to "see what would become of his dreams," verse 20.

b. Reuben was not ready to kill his brother. But he was not strong enough to scold his brothers and make them stop their evil plans. Reuben went along half-way with his brothers, and suggested that they throw Joseph into a deep pit. He planned to rescue him later. Reuben was guilty with his brothers, for he would not stop them from their evil plan.

c. The brothers took off Joseph's robe, threw him into the pit, and sat down to eat. God tells us in chapter 42:21 that Joseph begged them to take him out, but they paid no attention. Their hearts were hard.

d. Judah was the one who felt horror about killing his own brother. He was afraid to kill him, but not to sell him, verse 26.

7. For at that instant God sent merchantmen* past Dothan. They were Ishmaelites, descendants of Ishmael, and verse 28 really says they were "Midianitish men." It means that the Midianites were merchants, too, and all these merchants looked alike. Without any pity, the brothers pulled Joseph from the pit and sold Joseph to the Ishmaelites for twenty pieces of silver.

Read verses 29-36

D. Joseph Goes to Egypt

1. Verses 29 and 30 tell that Reuben came back too late to rescue him. What could he do now but go along with their lie? Joseph was sold and the brothers went home and faced their father with the coat they had bloodied, and lived a lie in their father's house for many years. Father Jacob would not be comforted.

2. In all this sinful history, God was not far away. He was using the evil hands and hearts of Joseph's brothers who made the plan to get rid of him. He sent the Ishmaelites to Dothan at just the right time to take Joseph to Egypt.

DO NOT FORGET that this story is the first step in taking Jacob's whole family to Egypt, where they would grow to be the mighty nation of Israel. God did not want His people to become great in Canaan, but he led them to the land of Egypt, where they could live separately and become God's chosen nation.

WORD STUDIES
1. reputation — what others think and say of a person
2. merchantmen — travelling store keepers

LESSON 33
Joseph in Potiphar's House
Genesis 39

BEFORE WE BEGIN, do you wonder why God would take his father's favorite son away from him? God loved both Jacob and Joseph. Why did He make all that sadness in their lives? Because Jacob had to learn to love Joseph for God's sake, not because Joseph was so nice; and both Jacob and Joseph had to learn, through their troubles, to trust in the Lord's goodness. As we study this lesson, God will teach us to trust in His goodness, too.

Read Genesis 39:1-6

LESSON OUTLINE

A. Joseph Alone

1. All along the sad and miserable trip to Egypt, the Ishmaelites kept Joseph with them. They did not sell him until they came to Egypt. There they sold this handsome young man, probably at a profit, to Potiphar, captain of the king's bodyguard, who was also the man in charge of killing criminals.

2. Have you ever wondered how Joseph felt? In his dreams, God had promised that he would be a ruler, but he was a slave, sold for money. Did Joseph wonder why, although he was righteous and his brothers wicked, he was the one being punished? Would you have felt that way?

3. But Jehovah had not left Joseph. Read the first six words of verse 2. Verse 2 tells us that God's Spirit in his heart made him work hard, made him wise, made him able to do Potiphar's work better than anyone else ever had. Joseph prospered*! The Lord made Potiphar's house great and rich because He was blessing Joseph, one of the slaves.

4. Potiphar favored Joseph, not because he loved Joseph's God, but because, as verse 6 says, he was a goodly person and well favored (handsome). Besides, Potiphar could see that God blessed his house because of Joseph. Soon Joseph was manager of his house. Potiphar did not bother himself with the details of running his house anymore.

Read verses 7-20

B. Joseph in Trouble

1. It is possible that Joseph thought that the Lord was starting him on the road that led to his being some kind of great ruler, as his dreams had told him. That is what Joseph probably hoped, and what we would hope. But God, in

117

His perfect plan, said that Joseph was not yet ready to be a ruler. He had more to learn. God must teach him through more troubles and disappointments.

2. His trouble came in the person of Potiphar's wife:

    a. Joseph was a son of the beautiful Rachel, and had inherited her beauty. Potiphar's wife saw how handsome this new slave was. He was also an intelligent young man, quick to understand. He succeeded in all that he did. Potiphar's wife liked Joseph.

    b. The first part of this chapter tells us something about Potiphar's character: he was interested in his job, but not in the running of his house. He cared little about how things went in his household, and they probably did not go well before Joseph came and ruled his household.

    c. The first part of this chapter makes us think that Potiphar cared for his position in the king's army, but not about his home and his wife. He was a weak man, as we shall see later.

    d. Potiphar's wife was a godless, heathen woman, with too much time on her hands, and she noticed this handsome slave. She wanted to have a love affair with him behind her husband's back. She was not satisfied with the husband she had married. She pestered Joseph to pay attention to her.

3. Was Joseph tempted to listen to her? To be friendly with the wife of one of the greatest men in Egypt, close to Pharaoh? Maybe they could get rid of Potiphar and then Joseph would take his place. Those were words of temptation straight from the devil. The devil was there in Egypt, in Potiphar's house, and tempted Joseph to do wrong.

4. We have just read that God was with Joseph. Yet He let the devil tempt Joseph. Why? So that he would come through the temptation clean and purified; for God would not let him fall.

> Discuss in class how, after you have been greatly tempted to sin,
> and probably even fallen into a bad sin,
> God made you hate and shudder at that sin more than you ever did before.
> Has this happened to you?

5. Potiphar's wife bothered Joseph for a long time, trying in every way, day by day, to make him be her lover, verse 10. Joseph, with the fear of God in his heart, was strong enough to say no day after day. He had three good reasons for saying no to that wicked woman:

    a. His master Potiphar trusted him to take care of all his possessions, and Joseph could not betray that trust. He could not become a "double-crosser."

b. The only possession of Potiphar which belonged to him alone was his wife; and Joseph could never take what belonged only to Potiphar. It would be sinning against their marriage.

c. It would be a sin against God. This was Joseph's deepest reason for saying no. God's law says, "Thou shalt not commit adultery;" and Joseph, with God's love in his heart, wanted to obey that command. See verses 8 and 9.

6. One day, when no one was around, Potiphar's wife grabbed him, and Joseph ran, leaving his garment — his outer coat — in her hands. Immediately after Joseph ran away, this hateful woman thought of an evil plan:

a. She screamed and brought the servants running.

b. She lied about Joseph and said he wanted to mock her.

c. She had been hurt because Joseph would not listen to her, and now she was afraid her husband would discover her adulterous plans. She would blame Joseph.

C. Joseph in Prison

1. We do not know whether Potiphar believed his wife or not. He simply threw Joseph into the prison where the king's prisoners were kept.

2. We would ask: Was it fair? Joseph did only good to Potiphar and his household. He served with the fear of the Lord, and he did not meddle in his master's marriage.

3. He suffered for doing well. Psalm 105:18 tells us: "Whose feet they hurt with fetters: he was laid in iron." He was in prison! He hurt! He was humiliated!

4. In all this, the Lord was with him. Joseph learned to trust his life in prison to the Lord, and the Lord made him advance to be the servant to the care-taker. It was in this prison that the Lord had planned to have Joseph meet the butler and the baker, and then go on to Pharaoh's palace.

DO NOT FORGET that Joseph suffered because he was obeying Christ. And our Lord Jesus Christ, Who was born long after Joseph died, suffered because His people sinned, so that He could save them. He puts His love into our hearts, too, so that we want to obey Him.

WORD STUDIES

prosper — to have things go well, to succeed

LESSON 34
Joseph Interprets Dreams
Genesis 40-41:45

BEFORE WE BEGIN, it will help us to know how much time went by from the time of Joseph's coming to Egypt and the time of his ruling over Egypt. It was thirteen years. We do not know how these years were divided. Perhaps most of them were spent in prison.

Read Genesis 40:1-5

LESSON OUTLINE

A. Joseph and the Butler* and the Baker

1. These two men had made the king angry. They may have planned to kill the king, but we do not know whether they were guilty or not.

2. The captain of the guard put Joseph in charge of the two new prisoners, and he served them for some time. One night each man had a dream, a special dream. They knew their dreams were special, but they did not know the meanings. They were unhappy.

3. Joseph, a godly man, noticed their sadness and asked them in kindness, "Wherefore look ye so sadly today?" They were sad because they did not know the meanings of their dreams.

4. Joseph said just the opposite of what the magicians and wise men of Egypt would say. They boasted that they could tell meanings of dreams. Joseph said, "Do not interpretations belong to God?" (verse 8) Joseph knew that his God, Who was with him in prison, would tell him the meanings. Then the two men told Joseph their dreams.

Read Genesis 40:9-19

5. In his dream, the butler saw himself at his old duty of making wine and serving it to the king. In his dream he also saw a number: three branches of grapes. Joseph told the meaning. In three days the butler would be back at the palace, serving the king wine.

6. Very humbly, Joseph asked the butler to remember him when he stood before Pharaoh again, and tell Pharaoh that he was stolen from his land, that he had done no wrong, and that he would like to get out of prison. Joseph probably thought that this might be the time for his dreams of long ago to come true. But it was not God's time yet.

7. Then the baker, hopeful that he, too, would go back to the palace, told his dream. But Joseph had to tell the baker that in three days he would be beheaded, and the birds would eat his flesh. The Bible does not tell us whether the baker was guilty or not.

8. Joseph's interpretations came true. In three days, on Pharaoh's birthday, the butler went back to the palace, and the baker was hanged.

9. Read the last verse of chapter 40. Are you asking, "How could the butler forget? Didn't he have to think of Joseph every time he served the king wine?" The answer is yes. The butler's forgetfulness was willful. After he was back in the palace, he did not think it important to bother the king with the matter of a lowly Hebrew slave. The king might be annoyed or angry with him. Besides, what did Joseph mean to him? The butler was interested only in himself. He willfully forgot.

10. At the same time, Joseph knew and we know that the Lord directed the butler to keep silence. It was not yet God's time to take Joseph out of prison.

Read Genesis 41:1-7

B. Joseph and Pharaoh

1. Two years later God sent Pharaoh two dreams. The river in his dreams was the River Nile. Find it on your map on the worksheets for Lessons 34-36. You have just read his dreams. After he dreamed about the seven fat and healthy cows and the seven thin and scrawny cows, he awoke, but fell asleep again. After his second dream of the seven full and juicy ears of corn and the seven thin and withered ears, his dreams had seemed so real that he was surprised when he awoke that they were dreams. What did his two dreams mean?

2. Notice in verse 8 that Pharaoh called all the magicians and wise men of Egypt to tell him what his dreams meant. These men were priests in Egypt, who told people what charms to wear to keep them from harm, which days were lucky and which were unlucky, and what people's dreams meant.

3. But they could not tell Pharaoh the meaning of his two dreams. Why not? Because they were wicked men, the servants of Satan, and God will not tell His secrets to Satan's servants. But to a humble servant in prison, to His child and His friend, God would tell His secrets.

4. Suddenly the king's chief butler remembered his faults, verse 9. This shows that he never really forgot Joseph, but now was the time to tell Pharaoh the story of this young Hebrew slave. He told Pharaoh how he and

the baker both had dreams, that this young man had told the meanings, and that Joseph's interpretation* of the dreams had come true.

    a. The butler called him "servant to the captain of the guard" in verse 12.

    b. He did not tell Pharaoh that the young man was an innocent Hebrew slave.

5. Joseph was sent for, and he came after he shaved and changed his clothes. Once more Pharaoh told his two dreams, verses 18-24. Jehovah his God put the meaning of those dreams into Joseph's mind, so that he could tell the meaning immediately. He told the king that:

    a. Both dreams had the same meaning. God sent the same dream, one with cows and one with ears of corn. God sent the same dream twice, to impress on Pharaoh that it was an urgent dream. The meaning of these dreams would happen soon.

    b. The seven good cows and the seven good ears meant seven years of great, abundant yields of crops, such as Egypt had never seen. The seven poor cows and seven withered ears meant seven years of famine such as Egypt had never known. This famine would be so bad that they would scarcely be able to remember the years of abundance.

6. How did Pharaoh know that Joseph's words were the correct interpretation of his dreams? God's Spirit made it ring true in his heart. He knew this came from God. God put it into Pharaoh's heart, for, remember, Proverbs 22 says that the hearts of kings are in the hand of the Lord as rivers of water.

    a. Joseph made an impression on Pharaoh. He was humble and polite, but bodly spoke the words of the Lord.

    b. Pharaoh had to confess that the Spirit of God was in Joseph, verses 38, 39, and there was no one so discreet* and wise as Joseph. Joseph showed that he was godly.

Discuss in class how our godliness makes a good impression on others.
Give examples.

7. Joseph suggested to Pharaoh a wise and orderly plan to collect food during the seven years of plenty: to collect the fifth part of all the crops from everyone, and store them in an orderly way in storage cities.

Read verses 41-44

8. Suddenly Joseph became the "man of the hour." Pharaoh dressed him in

122

royal clothes, and only Pharaoh was higher than Joseph in the land of Egypt.

9. Pharaoh gave him a new name: Zaphnath-paaneah, which most likely means "preserver of life."

DO NOT FORGET that although God made Joseph's dreams come true and led him at last to be ruler of Egypt, that Joseph was still a lonely child of God in a heathen land. But Jehovah kept His arms of grace and love around Joseph. Even though he had to work with the heathen government, the idol-worshipping Pharaoh and his men, God kept his faith strong.

WORD STUDIES
1. butler — a servant in charge of the serving of wine; the head servant in the house
2. interpretation — to give the meaning, to explain
3. discreet — wise, careful

LESSON 35
Joseph's Brothers Come to Egypt
Genesis 41:46-end of 42

BEFORE WE BEGIN, we will understand that Joseph was the second highest ruler in Egypt. When he rode in his chariot, servants called to everyone, "Bow the knee!" Joseph was now thirty years old, and Pharaoh gave him Asenath, the daughter of a heathen priest, as his wife.

Read Genesis 41:46-49

LESSON OUTLINE
A. The Seven Years of Plenty

1. We do not know whether Asenath turned to Jehovah and worshipped Him. Probably, in God's plan, through her husband's godly example, she was brought to the fear of Jehovah, too.

2. They had two sons, and the names which Joseph gave them tell us much about Joseph.

    a. Read Genesis 41:51. When he named Manasseh, he said, "God made me forget." No, he could never put all his troubles out of his mind. But God made him forget all the torture the wickedness of his brothers caused him.

    b. When he named Ephraim, verse 52, Joseph thanked God for making him fruitful, for making everything well. But he could not forget that he was living in the "land of my affliction." He was not in the promised land anymore.

3. Have you wondered why Joseph, when he became ruler, did not send someone to find his family in Canaan, and tell the good news? He must have understood, from his dreams, that his whole family was to come to him and bow down to him. And he must have looked ahead, and seen that when the seven years of famine came upon the world — for famine would come not only on Egypt, but on all lands — his family would have to come to Egypt for food, verse 57.

Read Genesis 42:1-4

B. The Brothers Start Out

1. Two years of famine had passed. We must not imagine that the famine in Canaan was so severe that nothing would grow. They grew some foods such as fruits and nuts and root food-plants, but the grain for their cattle was gone.

2. Back in Canaan, Jacob had seen his neighbors going to Egypt, and had heard from them that there was grain for sale.

a. But his sons acted strangely. They were silent, and did not seem to want to go to Egypt.

b. We know what the brothers were thinking when that country was mentioned. It was twenty-two years ago that they had done that awful deed to their brother. Was he a slave in Egypt now? Their consciences were bothering them and their hearts were troubled because of their plot against Joseph.

c. Jacob noticed their behavior, and said, "Why do ye look one upon another?"

3. He told them to go to Egypt, and ten brothers left. Jacob would not let his youngest son, Benjamin, the son of his Rachel who had died, go along, for he said, "Lest mischief befall* him." It seems as if Jacob suspected that his ten sons had something to do with the mischief which befell Joseph twenty-two years ago.

Read verses 5-24

C. The Brothers in Egypt

1. When the brothers arrived in the land that they dreaded more than any other land, they met the Egyptian ruler, who was Joseph, the brother who was looking for them.

2. Verse 6 tells us that Joseph did the selling to all the people who came to buy food. No one could escape his notice. In that way, he immediately saw his brothers. They must have changed in twenty-two years, but he knew they were his brothers.

Discuss in class what must have gone on
in Joseph's mind when he first saw his brothers.

3. From the rest of the story, we learn that Joseph had prepared himself for this moment. He was a clever and a godly man; and he made plans because he knew it was necessary to remain unknown to them at first. Before he told them who he was:

a. He must know whether they were his brothers with the same wicked hearts which they had in Dothan, or whether they were his brothers who had repented and changed.

b. If they were sorry, he could forgive them and take his family into Egypt to live with him.

c. In order to find out whether they had changed, he planned to separate them from the crowds of people buying grain. To separate them, he had to have a reason for taking them and shutting them up. His reason would be to accuse them of being spies. Does this sound like a mean or unreasonable plan? No, it was not. Joseph had to know his brothers' hearts, and his brothers had to learn a hard lesson.

d. When he accused them of being spies, he knew he would get his brothers to talk. They would tell about his family. Joseph couldn't wait to hear!

e. Then he would put them in ward, a private place of safety. They would be filled with terror, and would tell one another their thoughts. They would not know that the ruler could understand their language and would know what was in their hearts. These were Joseph's plans.

4. That is why Joseph made himself strange to his brothers when they came. He looked and acted and dressed as an Egyptian, and though he understood them, he talked with them through an interpreter.

a. He was stern and spoke roughly with them, and accused them of being spies. He argued with his brothers, verse 12, and as Joseph had planned, his brothers talked and told him that their father still lived, that their youngest brother was at home, and one brother was not. They did not say what happened to him.

b. The brothers played right into Joseph's hands. Now Joseph knew about his father and Benjamin. At first he decreed that he would send one man home to get Benjamin and keep the other nine in Egypt, to make sure they were not spies. Then he put them in ward for three days. It was like being in prison. Can you imagine the fear in the brothers' hearts?

c. Joseph changed his mind. He would let nine brothers go home and keep one brother, Simeon. The brothers did just as Joseph had planned. They talked together about how guilty they were of their heartless crime against their brother Joseph, and Reuben reminded them that he had told them not to sin against Joseph, verse 22.

d. And Joseph heard and understood it all. He had to leave and weep.

5. Joseph knew their consciences were bothering his brothers. But was it because they were afraid or because they had changed and were sorry? He must wait for that answer.

Read verses 25-28

126

D. The Brothers Go Home

1. After Joseph bound Simeon in front of their eyes, he commanded his servant that their sacks were to be filled and their money put back in the top of the sacks.

2. What a scare the brothers had when they found their money in their sacks at an inn on the way home. In fear because of their sins, they asked, "What is this that God hath done unto us?"

3. How they must have dreaded to face their father!

4. They told him (verses 30-35) all the unhappy things that happened to them in Egypt, and ended by telling their father that Benjamin must go along next time: beloved Benjamin, who was Rachel's son.

5. Read verse 36. Jacob blamed his sons for taking away three of his children: Joseph, Simeon, and Benjamin. He said that all these things were against him. He did not say it with a heart of faith, for all his sons were safe. Two were in Egypt and ten safely at home; and God was for him, so that nothing could be against him.

DO NOT FORGET that we are Jacobs, too. When God sends trouble into our lives, or when we are punished for a serious sin, we may want to say that all things are against us, but we will learn to say, "If God be for us, who can be against us?" (Romans 8:31)

WORD STUDIES

befall — something which happens to someone

Joseph Tests His Brothers
Genesis 43:1-44:17

BEFORE WE BEGIN, can we understand the hard choice father Jacob had to make? He could send his son Benjamin with his brothers to Egypt and lose another son, or he could keep all his sons at home and watch them and their cattle starve.

LESSON OUTLINE

A. Jacob's Hard Choice

1. "The famine was sore in the land," says verse 1. God did not give sunshine and rain for the crops to grow, and Jacob's family had no more grain. They had to have grain to survive, and Jacob said, "Go again, buy us a little food." He was acting as if he had no problem: "Just go!"

2. Judah was the son who reminded his father that they could not go without Benjamin. The stern ruler in Egypt would not even look at them. But Judah also felt sorry for his old father. He had a plan: he would be a "safety" for Benjamin. If anything were to happen to Benjamin, Judah would take the blame and the punishment.

3. Sadly, father Jacob gave in. He understood that there was no other way. To make peace with the ruler in Egypt, Jacob suggested that they take a present of a few of the fruits, nuts, and spices which still grew in the land, and double money in their sacks.

Read Genesis 43:15-25

B. Dinner at Joseph's House

1. The Bible does not tell us whether they had heavy hearts all the way, but they must have dreaded to go to Egypt again. Joseph, on the other hand, must have been eagerly waiting for them. He knew that the famine would drive them to Egypt, and he wanted to see Benjamin! He had his plans made.

2. When he saw his ten brothers, he quickly made arrangements to get them away from the crowds of people again. How did he do it this time? He ordered them brought to his house, the house of the great ruler of Egypt.

    a. Were they thrilled? No, they were frightened. They were sure they knew why they were going to the ruler's house. He would arrest them for being thieves, for keeping back their money, and he would put them all in prison.

b. To prove that they were innocent, they explained to the steward* of Joseph's house that they were honest men and that they had found the money in the tops of their sacks and had brought double money this time.

c. The steward's answer showed that he knew who they were: Joseph had told his steward his secret. He put the brothers' fears at rest by saying, "Peace be to you. I had your money." That was true. He left out the rest of the truth, which was that he had put the money back: that it was really God Who gave it back, verse 23. Although this little plot of the steward makes us smile because we know the truth, can you imagine how confused the brothers were?

d. The steward brought Simeon to them, washed their dusty feet, and gave their animals food. By this time the brothers had heard that they were to have dinner with the great ruler.

Discuss how the brothers felt
when they sat down to eat with the Egyptian ruler.

3. Once again all the brothers made a low bow to the ruler, and Joseph remembered his dreams. If the brothers had not been so nervous and frightened, they might have noticed the ruler's great interest in their old father and their younger brother, when he asked, "Is your father well?" and "Is this your younger brother?" And when he blessed Benjamin by saying, "God be gracious unto thee, my son," he could hardly control himself. He wanted to tell them "I am Joseph!" But it was not yet time. So he rushed from the room to weep. His tears helped to relieve the strain inside him.

4. When he came back, the dinner was served. The ruler sat by himself because of his high position. The Egyptians ate by themselves because they might not eat with Hebrews. And the brothers sat by themselves in the order of their ages. They were amazed! How could the Egyptian ruler know the ages of eleven grown men? Did they have any idea that this ruler was not the Egyptian he seemed to be? No. They were totally puzzled.

5. Joseph tested them by giving Benjamin five times as much food as the brothers had. Would they be jealous? No, the brothers passed this test well. They were not jealous of Benjamin, and they even had a good time with the ruler.

Read Genesis 44:1-13

C. The Silver Cup

1. As soon as it was light the next morning, the brothers were ready to go back home. And Joseph was ready for his last and greatest test. It was a test Joseph had to give to be sure his brothers had changed. He had given orders

129

to load grain into the sacks, put their money on top, and put his silver cup in Benjamin's sack.

2. The eleven puzzled brothers started out. The Bible does not give us the details of what they talked about on their way home, but they must have been happy. Simeon was back with them, Benjamin had been the guest of honor: but how had the ruler known their ages?

3. Their happiness came to a sudden end. Verse 4 tells us that they had not gone far before they heard the stern voice of the steward, and he wanted to know who stole his master's silver cup, his special silver cup by which he divined*. Joseph did not really use his silver cup to divine, but he wanted his brothers to think so.

    a. Horror filled the hearts of the brothers, for they were in trouble again, and this time they were innocent.

    b. They tried to tell the steward how impossible it was for them to steal it. Did they not bring back their money from their first trip? Were they not honest men? Why would they steal from the master's house? They were so sure they were innocent that they said the brother with the silver cup deserved to die.

4. The steward, who knew where the cup was, started looking in the sack of the oldest brother, building up suspense until he came to Benjamin's sack, in which he had put the silver cup.

5. When the brothers saw the silver cup in Benjamin's sack, they could have let him go back to Egypt alone and taken his punishment, and they could have gone home free. Instead, they tore their clothes, as a sign of their misery.

6. With long faces and heavy hearts they went back and bowed to the stern ruler who must have felt as sad as they did, but who scolded them anyway, verse 15.

DO NOT FORGET that they were innocent of this sin. Neither Benjamin nor any of his brothers took the cup. Did they suspect that the ruler had laid a trap for them and put it in Benjamin's sack? They did not dare think that! But they felt guilty for their sin of twenty-two years ago, and they could not forget that God saw that sin in their hearts.

WORD STUDIES
1. steward — manager
2. divine — to find out hidden things, or foretell the future

LESSON 37

"I Am Joseph"

Genesis 44:18-45:28

BEFORE WE BEGIN, we might ask: Was Joseph too hard on his brothers? Was he trying to get revenge? No, Joseph was a man to whom God told His secrets, and Joseph understood that his father and brothers must come to Egypt for a time, to keep alive the covenant line of believers. Before they came to live there, Joseph must know what was in his brothers' hearts.

Read Genesis 44:18-34

LESSON OUTLINE

A. Judah's Speech

1. In his sad and beautiful speech, Judah told the ruler of Egypt:

a. We did not want to take Benjamin, but you insisted that he come with us.

b. We obeyed you and refused to go to Egypt without our younger brother.

c. Our father loves him so much, he would die if something happened to him.

d. I promised to be surety* for him. Now let me be your servant and let my brother go back home.

2. Judah ended his speech with a question: "For how shall I go up to my father, and the lad be not with me?" Twenty-two years ago he had said about his brother Joseph, "Let us sell him." He had not loved Joseph because the love of God was not strong in his heart. But God made him sorry for his sin and forgave him and put His love in his heart. Now Judah could say about Benjamin, "I shall bear the blame forever," verse 32.

Read Genesis 45:1-4

B. "I Am Joseph"

1. Judah's very touching speech brought tears to Joseph's eyes. He knew he had tested them long enough, and he could keep his secret no longer.

2. He ordered all his Egyptian servants and attendants to leave. No one else may be in the room when he tells them who he is. Then Joseph wept loudly.

3. Can you put yourself in the brothers' place and imagine how they felt when he cried out, "I am Joseph!" They must have been startled, stunned, unable to believe their ears.

a. His next question, in the same sentence, was: "Doth my father yet live?" He knew old Jacob was still living. But now it was so nice to ask the question with the words my father in it.

b. Joseph had not prepared his brothers for this shocking revelation. He was too eager to tell them the news. He was almost bursting to tell it! The moment he had been looking forward to had come at last.

c. The brothers could not answer him. They were troubled and afraid. This Egyptian — their brother? Joseph's dreams — coming true this way?

4. So Joseph said, "Come near to me." Reuben, the oldest brother, was not guilty of selling Joseph, but he had known the secret for twenty-two years. Benjamin, the youngest brother, probably never was told what had happened. Now he knew that they had gotten rid of their brother. He had not lived with the secret for twenty-two years. The rest of his brothers had.

Read verses 5-15

C. Joseph Talks with His Brothers

1. He had so much to say, and while he talked with them, he probably began to calm his brothers, too. He told them: You did the evil deed, but God worked through your evil deed to preserve* life (verse 5). In verse 7 he told them that God sent him to Egypt to save their lives and to save them a posterity*. God was ruling, even in the way of their evil deeds.

a. They sold Joseph to be sure his dreams did not come true.

b. God, through their wickedness, made sure Joseph's dreams came true.

c. God's purpose was that He had chosen Joseph to save his brothers from starving so that they would come to live in Egypt and grow into a nation of God's people, the nation which would look ahead to the birth of the Savior.

Discuss in class other examples of God working
His will through evil deeds of men.

2. Joseph could hardly wait to see his old father. Twice (in verses 9 and 13) he told them, "Haste ye." There were five more years of famine left, and Joseph had already made preparations for his father and brothers. He must have talked with Pharaoh about a place for his family, for in verse 10 he told them that the land of Goshen was ready for them. After he kissed his brothers and wept, the brothers at last were able to talk with Joseph, their ruler-brother.

Read verses 16-24

D. The Brothers Go Home

1. The news spread through Pharaoh's house: Joseph's brothers are here! Pharaoh was pleased and told them to go back to Canaan and get their families and possessions and come to live in Egypt. He and Joseph gave them clothes and money, and wagons of food for the people and their animals.

2. Pharaoh promised the good of the land and the fat of the land of Egypt to them and their families. This proud Egyptian Pharaoh, whose heart was in God's hands, would give Jacob and his family the best part of the land. God always takes care of His people.

Read verses 25-28

E. Jacob Hears the News

1. Joseph warned his brothers not to get into trouble on the way. They could easily quarrel about who of the brothers had the greatest sins against Joseph. Joseph wanted them to go home without anger.

2. Father Jacob was waiting for them. He could not believe their words. They told him the news too soon. They forgot to prepare him for such shocking news, and he felt numb. When Jacob saw the wagons, he began to revive. And, although the Bible does not tell us, the brothers had to confess, at last, their terrible sin. The old Jacob's heart was faint because of it. But when he knew it was the truth, he was ready to go to see his son Joseph.

DO NOT FORGET that it was not easy for Jacob's sons to confess a sin they had hidden for twenty-two years. God teaches us about hidden sins, too. In Psalm 19:12 He teaches us to pray, "Cleanse thou me from secret faults." Sing Psalter number 40:5, which is taken from Psalm 19.

WORD STUDIES

1. surety — one who promises to be responsible for another
2. preserve — to keep in safety, to protect from danger
3. posterity — descendants, future generations of children

LESSON 38
In the Land of Goshen
Genesis 46, 47

BEFORE WE BEGIN, we already know that Jacob's sons did not prepare him for the amazing news that Joseph was alive. He almost fainted from the shock. But when he finally knew it was true, he said, "I will go and see him before I die."

Read Genesis 46:1-4

LESSON OUTLINE
A. Jacob Goes to Egypt

1. Many years earlier Jacob's grandfather Abraham went to Egypt. He went sinfully, to escape a famine in Canaan. When Jacob's father Isaac planned to go to Egypt, God prevented him from going. But the Lord led Jacob to Egypt, to save his life and the lives of his family. Even so, after Jacob started out and arrived at Beersheba, he built an altar and offered sacrifices. He did not run ahead of God anymore. He wanted to know whether he was doing right; and God came to him in a vision and told him to go to Egypt. Find Beersheba on the map.

    a. God gave him a promise: to make of Jacob's chosen family a great nation.

    b. God led the way to the land of Goshen, in Egypt. Find it on the map. This part of Egypt had very few people living in it, and the land was good land for grazing animals. Look ahead to chapter 47:6. There Pharaoh calls it "the best of the land."

    c. In Goshen, Jacob's family could live separately. The Egyptians, whose gods were animals, would not go near the Israelites, who sacrificed animals. Here in Goshen, all by themselves, they could grow into a great nation, God's special children.

Read verses 5-7

2. Jacob was old, and most old people want to stay where they are. Jacob had two reasons for wanting to move, and to go to Egypt.

    a. He longed to see his favorite son of his favorite wife once more.

    b. He wanted to go the way that the Lord was leading him.

3. Jacob and his sons took everything with them: household goods, animals, and every member of their families, and loaded them into the wagons of Pharaoh.

4. Jacob's children in Canaan numbered sixty-six people. With Joseph and his wife and two sons in Egypt, his descendants were seventy people. That number is a symbol*. It is made up of three (the number of God) plus four (the number of man) times ten, the number of completeness. It is a number which counts the whole nation of God. See verses 26 and 27.

Read verses 28-34

B. Jacob's Family Meets Joseph

1. When they were near to Goshen, Judah, the brother who had given a beautiful speech to a Joseph he did not know, was chosen to go ahead and let Joseph know they had arrived. The rest of the family went on to Goshen.

2. Joseph hurried with his chariot to see his father, and after twenty-two years, they had a happy reunion, even though Joseph wept a long while. Jacob was satisfied. He was ready to die now that he had seen Joseph once more. But the Lord let him live seventeen years longer.

3. Next, Joseph prepared his brothers to speak to Pharaoh. He told them to tell Pharaoh that they were shepherds and had many flocks and herds. And he urged them to ask Pharaoh for the land of Goshen.

Read Genesis 47:1-6

4. Joseph had more planning to do. He told Pharaoh that his brothers had flocks and herds of animals, so that Pharaoh would know they had to live separate from the Egyptians. The Egyptians thought they were far more civilized and refined, far above these shepherds with their dirty work. The Egyptians would not go near them.

5. Joseph was not finished planning. He took five of his brothers to Pharaoh to ask for the land of Goshen to live in, verses 3 and 4. Notice that God's chosen people asked a heathen king for a little bit of land where they might live.

6. Why was it so important to Joseph that his family live in Goshen? Because he knew the promise of God: that some day God would return them to Canaan, the promised land. Meanwhile, they must be kept separate and not become friends with the wicked Egyptians and begin to marry them. God's people might not be swallowed up in Egypt. Joseph knew God's promise to save a special people who would be saved through His Son.

Discuss in class how we live separate from the evil world.

Read verses 7-10

7. Joseph brought his father Jacob to meet Pharaoh. Pharaoh asked him

how old he was. Jacob looked older than the Egyptians, for the Egyptians probably did not live to be so old. Jacob answered Pharaoh that his days were few and evil. He was most likely thinking of his many troubles all through his life, troubles which he brought on himself by trying to run ahead of the Lord. He called his life a pilgrimage. A pilgrim* has no home where he is. He is going somewhere else. Jacob was going to heaven. Jacob "blessed" Pharaoh when he met him and when he left. He did not bless Pharaoh with God's blessing, for Pharaoh was an evil man. The kind of blessing he gave was saying, "Hello, good-bye," or "Long live the king!"

C. The End of the Famine

1. There were five more years of famine left. The rest of the chapter tells how Joseph kept the people alive.

    a. When they ran out of money to pay for food, Joseph said he would take animals in payment.

    b. When their animals were gone, the people offered to sell themselves and their land to Pharaoh for food.

    c. Near the end of the famine, Joseph put the people in cities so it would be easier to distribute food to them.

2. At the end of the seven years of famine he gave them seed for planting their crops.

DO NOT FORGET that we, too, are a separate people, not living in a separate country from evil people, but living our lives separately and serving God in our homes, schools, churches, and in our hearts.

WORD STUDIES

1. symbol — something used as a picture of something else
2. pilgrim — one who journeys to another land (to heaven)

LESSON 39
The Last Days of Jacob
Genesis 48-50

BEFORE WE BEGIN, we know that Jacob lived with his family seventeen more years in Egypt. The Bible does not tell us about those years, except that the people grew to be a great nation. The Lord did not call His people back to Canaan either, and they understood that it was God's will that they stay in Egypt.

Read Genesis 48:1-5

LESSON OUTLINE
A. Jacob Blesses Joseph's Sons

1. Joseph heard that his father was sick, and he came to him with his two sons, Manasseh and Ephraim. Jacob knew that he would soon die, and he wanted to bless the two sons of Joseph as his own children. He said, "They shall be mine," verse 5. Jacob was still amazed that the Lord let him see Joseph's children, verse 11, and now he wanted to treat them as his own.

2. This blessing was not just some good wishes, but Jacob, as God's prophet, spoke God's words. The words which Jacob spoke would come true, because God put His Words into Jacob's mouth. You will remember that in Israel the oldest son usually had the special blessing of the birthright.

Read verses 10-20

3. Jacob's eyes were not very good in his old age, and Joseph helped him by leading Manasseh, the oldest, to Jacob's right hand. He led Ephraim to Jacob's left hand. Joseph thought this was the way it was supposed to be. As soon as he did this, father Jacob crossed his arms.

4. Joseph thought his father had it all wrong. "Not so, my father," he said, "for this is the firstborn; put thy right hand on his head."

5. What did Jacob say? "I know it, my son, I know it." Joseph could not help his father along, for Ephraim, the younger, would get the birthright blessing and grow to be a stronger nation than his older brother Manasseh.

6. Jacob blessed them in the name of the Angel, verse 16. Remember, the Angel of Jehovah is the Christ of the Old Testament. Grandfather Jacob blessed the two lads in the name of the Angel Who redeemed* him from all evil. Now God would bless Ephraim and Manasseh and their seed. Not everyone of their descendants would be God's child, but Ephraim's and

Manasseh's seed would be God's children, the church. We are God's children, too, His church, and that promise is for us, too.

B. Jacob Blesses Judah

1. We will not study the blessings on all of Jacob's sons in chapter 49. We will work with some of them on our worksheets.

2. Before he died, Jacob called all his sons to his deathbed and prophesied what would happen to them, verse 1.

3. Read verse 3. Would you expect Reuben, the firstborn, to get the special birthright blessing and to be ruler over his brothers? He did not. Verse 4 tells us that he was unstable as water. Jacob passed by the cruel Simeon and Levi, too, verse 5.

Read Genesis 49:8-10

4. When father Jacob came to the next son, he said, "Judah, thou!" You are the one! Your brothers will praise you! Judah would rule over his brothers!

a. Jacob made a picture with his words of lion's whelp*, a type of royal power and strength. From Judah would be born the Lion of God. Who is He?

b. God, through Jacob's mouth, gave Judah the scepter*, the staff of power to rule. Only kings use sceptres of power. From Judah would be born the line of the kings, until Shiloh, the Prince of Peace, came. Shiloh, means to rest and to have peace. Judah's kings would rule until they rested in Christ.

5. On our worksheets we will study more of the blessings in chapter 49. After Jacob blessed all his sons, verse 28 tells us that these are the twelve tribes of Israel. That is what we will call them from now on.

Read Genesis 50:1-6

C. Jacob Dies

1. Jacob had one last thing to take care of: he must be buried with Abraham, Sarah, Isaac, Rebekah, and Leah in Canaan, the picture of resting forever in peace in heaven. Then Jacob died.

2. The Egyptians embalmed Jacob's body by wrapping it and treating it with spices and sweet-smelling perfumes to preserve his body. The Egyptians, who did not look forward, as we do, to a new body in heaven, wanted to keep their dead bodies. It took forty days to finish embalming Jacob.

Discuss in class why we want to be buried after we die.

3. Joseph asked permission from Pharaoh to travel to Canaan to bury his father, as his father had made him promise (swear).

4. The custom of the Egyptians was to have an elaborate celebration at a funeral. Jacob's family, with the horses, chariots, and important noblemen from Egypt, went to Canaan in the funeral procession. They mourned for him for seven days near the entrance to the land of Canaan, and buried him in the cave of Machpelah.

D. The Last Years of Joseph

1. His brothers were afraid that, since their father had died, Joseph would show hatred to them and try to get even. Would Joseph punish them now for their sins?

2. Joseph spoke kindly to them, and told them, "Fear not." Then he spoke the beautiful words of verse 20: "Ye thought evil against me, but God meant it unto good." Joseph knew that when they sold him, it was his first step on the stairway to the throne of Egypt.

3. Joseph lived fifty-three years after his father's death, but the Bible does not tell us about these years. Before he died, he told the children of Israel that God would lead them out of Egypt, and made them promise to take his bones along with them to Canaan.

DO NOT FORGET that although the line of the kings of Israel from Judah's family are long gone, and Shiloh has come, it is not the end. We are in the line of believers, of Judah's children, and are looking for Shiloh to come again.

WORD STUDIES

1. redeem — to free, or rescue by paying a price
2. whelp — the young of a dog, wolf, lion, or other beast
3. scepter — a rod which is the symbol of authority and power

LESSON 40

The Birth of Moses

Exodus 1:1-2:10

BEFORE WE BEGIN, did you notice that we have finished the book of beginnings (Genesis) and will start the book of Exodus in this lesson? Exodus means to leave, to go away from a country or place.

Read Exodus 1:1-10

LESSON OUTLINE

A. Pharaoh Afflicts* the Israelites

1. A long period of time, about three hundred years, passed since Joseph's death, which we studied in our last lesson. The Bible skips over these years and does not tell us about the descendants of the twelve sons of Jacob. Suddenly we learn that these descendants were exceedingly great and mighty, and they filled the land of Goshen. In verse 7 they are called the children (or people) of Israel.

2. Now a new king, probably not from the same family of kings who ruled when Joseph was living, was on the throne. He was still called Pharaoh, the name for all Egyptian kings. This Pharaoh did not know or care for the Joseph of long ago. He was not friendly toward the people of Israel, but he was afraid, for two reasons:

   a. the people of Israel were strong, and they might join Egypt's enemies in war and fight against the Egyptians.

   b. they might win, and leave the land, and Pharaoh would lose all his slaves.

3. Verse 10 tells us that Pharaoh wanted to "deal wisely" with the Israelites. As you read the rest of this lesson, decide whether he was wise. He made plans to make the people of Israel become weak, so that many would die. We will learn how he tried to do this in the next part of our lesson. First we must learn why he did this to God's people.

   a. Because the devil was busy in Egypt. He worked through the wicked Pharaoh. The devil knew that the Israelites were God's people. He knew that Christ, the One Who would crush his head, would be born from them; and the devil had one purpose: to destroy God's people so that Jesus could not be born. The devil used Pharaoh as the person to make it all happen. It is important to remember as we study Exodus, that the devil used Pharaoh as his tool to try to destroy the Israelites.

b. Because God was busy in Egypt. Before Pharaoh made them slaves, the Israelites loved Egypt. They were comfortable and happy there. Many of the Israelites were starting to worship Egypt's idols. Now God was ready to make the people hate Egypt and want to go back to Canaan. To make them hate Egypt, God made them suffer so much pain and trouble that they could not stand it any longer. They would be eager to leave.

Read verses 11-14

B. Pharaoh's Three Plans to Make Israel Weak

1. Pharaoh needed the people of Israel for slaves, but he wanted to make them weaker slaves so they could not rebel against him. He wanted not too many Israelites and not too strong Israelites. How was he going to "deal wisely" with them? By making their lives bitter with bondage*.

a. They worked in the fields. In Egypt they carried water by hand from the Nile River to water the crops, a back-breaking task.

b. They made bricks of baked clay in hot ovens for building material.

c. They built two storage cities, Pithom and Raamses, for extra food and for extra weapons for war.

2. Pharaoh's plan did not work. By a wonder of the grace of God the people of Israel grew stronger and increased greatly.

3. For his next evil plan, Pharaoh talked to the midwives of the Israelites, those who helped the mothers when babies were born. Pharaoh commanded them to kill all the sons born to Israelite women, but let the daughters live. What would happen if they did this? Without boys to grow up to be men, there would be no more nation of Israel. But the midwives feared and obeyed God and refused to obey the wicked Pharaoh. This plan did not work, either.

4. Read verse 22. This cruel man ordered that every baby boy in Israel be murdered by drowning in the river. It was a very sad and dark time for Israel. For a short time Pharaoh enforced this law strictly, but soon even the godless Egyptians did not want to obey a law of murder for baby boys. Remember, God was working His will through these troubles. He was bothering the Israelites so they would beg Him to let them leave Egypt. And the Lord was teaching His people to put their trust in Him.

Read Exodus 2:1-4

141

C. Moses is Born

1. In these very dark days in Israel, just when the law was strictly enforced, the baby Moses was born. It was the time of spies and soldiers hunting out all the Israelite baby boys. These were days of horror.

2. It was the Israelite's darkest, most hopeless time in Egypt. They couldn't stand the cruelty any longer! They wanted God to deliver them from Egypt right away.

3. This was the time that the Lord let the baby Moses be born, the Moses who would lead them out of Egypt. It would take eighty years to train Moses to be their deliverer. The Israelites thought they needed their deliverer now. Do you think God was eighty years too late?

4. The answer, of course, is no. The Israelites were in a hurry, just as we are. They wanted God to help them their way. But God, Who knows all things and is perfectly wise and calm, knows just when it is the right time for everything to happen.

Discuss in class how we often do not have
faith and patience to wait for God's time.

5. Find the names of Moses' parents in Exodus 6:20. Chapter 2:2 says that Moses was a goodly child. Acts 7:20 calls him exceeding fair, and Hebrews 11:23 says he was a proper child. Amram and Jochebed had faith in God that He would save this special child. They hid him for three months.

6. When it was too hard to hide him any longer, they obeyed the king's order in a special way by putting Moses in the river in an ark (a small boat) in the reeds near the shore. They trusted the Lord to take care of him.

Read verses 5-10

7. When Pharaoh's daughter came to bathe in the river, she saw how beautiful the baby was. She wanted him to be her son.

8. Miriam, his sister, a quick-thinking girl who was watching from a distance, offered, "Shall I get you a nurse?" The nurse was Moses' mother, probably the only mother who was ever paid by a princess for taking care of her own child. God made these things happen so that Moses could learn God's fear from his parents while he was young.

9. Pharaoh's daughter called him Moses: drawn out of the water. When he was old enough, he lived in the king's court, perfectly safe, and went to school there.

DO NOT FORGET that Pharaoh's daughter was an ungodly woman, but God used her to keep Moses safe, and God used Pharaoh's court to teach and to train Moses for his work of leading Israel back to Canaan.

WORD STUDIES
1. afflict — to distress with suffering, to trouble
2. bondage — forced slavery
3. exodus — the going away of a multitude from a country

LESSON 41

Moses in the Desert

Exodus 2:11-3:6

BEFORE WE BEGIN, we will learn that Moses is already forty years old. The Bible does not tell us about these forty years. We would probably like to take a peek at his life in the palace of the Egyptian king, but God says it is not necessary for us to know. We do know that the Israelites were still living in hard bondage.

Read Exodus 2:11-14 and Acts 7:23-25

LESSON OUTLINE

A. Moses is Ready

1. Acts 7:25 tells us that Moses knew that God had called him to deliver the Israelites from Egypt. He believed by faith that God would make him their leader. He was forty years old, well educated, and impatient. He decided it was time to show that he sided with his brethren, not just because they were Israelites, but because they were brothers in the faith of Jehovah. It was time to make a break with Egypt.

2. One day he went to visit them in their slavery. His purpose was to show his brothers that he loved them because they were his people, the people of God. And he supposed they would understand that God would use him to deliver them. Moses went to stir them up!

3. These were Moses' thoughts:

   a. he could no longer be called the son of the godless daughter of Pharaoh

   b. he wanted to leave the rich world of the palace and the honor of being Pharaoh's daughter's son

   c. he chose to suffer affliction with the people of God.

4. Moses saw an Egyptian, perhaps a taskmaster, mistreating a Hebrew, beating him. Moses was not interested in killing just one cruel Egyptian, but in showing to everyone that the time had come to make a break with Pharaoh and the Egyptians. He did not kill the Egyptian in a sudden fit of anger. He wanted this murder to say to the Israelites, "I am here to help you. It is time to follow me out of the land."

5. Moses was not sorry he killed the Egyptian, for he came back the very next day to his brothers. He thought they would understand that he was helping them to rebel against the king and to leave Egypt. Instead, he saw

two Hebrews fighting. When he asked them why, one of them gave an angry answer: "Who made you a judge over us? Will you kill me, too?" Moses did not understand. His own people did not want Moses to fight for them.

6. Moses was ready. God was not. In God's eyes, Moses was too big. He tried his own methods to help the Israelites. Moses forgot that God would be Israel's deliverer in His time. Moses was not ready yet to let God do it all. He needed forty more years of training.

Read verses 15-22

B. Moses Runs Away

1. In verse 14 we read, "And Moses feared, and said, Surely this thing is known." He knew Pharaoh would be angry. He must run away for his life.

2. But Hebrews 11:27 says, "By faith he forsook Egypt not fearing the wrath of the king." How can that be? Was Moses afraid and not afraid? He was afraid that Pharaoh would kill him. Therefore he ran away. But he was not afraid to take a stand with the Israelites, God's chosen people; and he would never go back to live an easy life in Pharaoh's godless courts again.

3. When Moses said no to Pharaoh, he said yes to Christ. Hebrews 11:26 tells us he chose the reproach* of Christ. Now he had to flee and live in exile in the desert.

4. He ran away to the land of Midian. Find it on the map on your worksheet. Remember: Midian was the son of Abraham and Keturah, and a half-brother of Isaac. There was still some fear of God among the descendants of Midian. Jethro, whose name means Excellent, and who was also called Reuel (Friend of God), was a priest of God and a wise man.

5. Moses came to a well, a place to meet people. There he saw the seven daughters of Jethro in trouble because cruel shepherds chased them away from the well. The girls did not show much friendliness to Moses after he helped them and drew water for their flocks, but they came home much earlier than usual. Their wise father questioned them and sent them back to Moses with an invitation to "eat bread" with them. That is the way the Lord led Moses to the godly Jethro's home to live for forty years.

6. For forty years Moses was a shepherd. It was a hard, lonely life. In the desert God taught an impatient Moses patience. Moses learned to wait for God's time. In the desert Moses became a meek man. He married Zipporah and had two sons: Gershom, which means "I have been a stranger in the land," and Eliezer, "God is Help."

Read Exodus 3:1-6

145

C. The Burning Bush

1. Moses was feeding the flocks of Jethro at Horeb. Find it on your map. There he saw a strange sight: a flame of fire in a thorn bush of the desert. Though the fire was burning, the bush was not consumed (burned up).

2. When Moses came toward the bush to see this strange sight, God called to him in a voice: "Moses, Moses." When Moses answered, "Here am I," the Lord warned him not to come near, and told him to take off his shoes. This was holy ground and he might not walk on it as he would on any common kind of ground.

3. God introduced Himself to Moses as Jehovah, the God of his fathers, verse 6, and Moses hid his face. He was afraid to look upon his holy God.

4. Why did God appear in a burning bush?

a. The bush was a picture of the children of Israel. These poor slaves in Egypt seemed no more important than a thorn bush in the desert.

b. The fire was a picture of the Egyptians who were putting the Israelites into the fire of hard slave labor, the fire of trying to destroy them. At the same time this fire has another meaning: the holy presence of God. The Bible often says that our God is a consuming fire. Can the fire have two meanings? Yes, for God's fire was troubling His people. God's fire was using the cruel Egyptians to make them so miserable that they would cry to Him to be delivered from their bondage.

5. When Moses looked at the burning bush, it seemed helpless against the fire, just as the Israelites seemed helpless in Egypt. It seemed as if they would be destroyed in the fire of slavery. But the bush was not burned! Neither were the Israelites! Why not? God's fire burned their sins away, but He would never harm His people, for He promised to save them.

6. That is why the Angel of Jehovah spoke to Moses, verse 2. Remember, He is the Christ of the Old Testament. He was there to say that His people will not be burned because He will take away the fire of God's anger against their sins on the cross. God's people are saved and safe.

DO NOT FORGET that the bush of God's fire did not burn only in Egypt. It still burns today. If we as God's children turn to sin and love it, God sends His fire to trouble us and to judge us and to make us sorry and to purify us. Then we turn to Jesus. It is the only way we can be saved.

WORD STUDIES

reproach — to blame someone for something wrong, to disgrace

LESSON 42
God Calls Moses
Parts of Exodus 3, 4, 5

BEFORE WE BEGIN, we will be ready to discover a different Moses. In our last lesson he was ready to lead Israel in his own strength. But God was not ready. At last it was God's time to take Israel out of Egypt, but a small and humble Moses asked, "Who am I that I should bring the children of Israel out of Egypt?"

Read Exodus 3:10-14

LESSON OUTLINE

A. God's Promise to Moses

1. We can understand all those fears of Moses. God understood, too. That is why He said in verse 12, "Certainly I will be with thee." He even made a promise to encourage Moses: when you travel back to Canaan leading the people of Israel, you will stop at this very mountain to worship Me.

2. Moses had another question: when I go back to the children of Israel and I tell them that the God of their fathers sent me, and they ask me His name, what shall I say? Moses needed an answer for the people, and for himself, too. He could not take up this task alone. He needed the strong Rock of his God to hold on to. That Rock was God's Name.

3. God answered, "I AM THAT I AM." It means that:

   a. nothing caused God, nothing formed Him. He is the independent, all-powerful God Who rules everything.

   b. nothing changes God. He is always perfect. He loves His people, and He always will love them.

4. Now Moses felt better. He knew more about his Rock Who never changes and Who will always love His people.

5. Next God told Moses just what would happen when he went to Egypt.

   a. Moses will tell his people that Jehovah had appeared to him, that the Lord sees what the Egyptians are doing to them, that He is ready to deliver* them.

   b. Moses will tell Pharaoh that he must permit the Israelites to go a three days' journey into the wilderness to sacrifice to Jehovah.

   c. God told Moses that His people would listen, but Pharaoh would not. When he would not listen, God would do great wonders in Egypt until Pharaoh let them go. Now Moses knew just what God had planned.

B. Moses' Objections

1. The Lord had not appeared to His people for hundreds of years. Now He came to Moses, alone in the desert. How could Moses prove that the Lord had called him? It might be his big imagination! The people would listen only if they knew that God really had spoken to him. This was a very important matter, and the Lord took care of it by giving Moses three signs.

2. Moses needed signs from God because the people could not see God. A sign is something God gave them which they could see and understand. These signs were not tricks without meaning, but they told the people what God was saying. These are the meanings of the three signs.

    a. In the first sign, Moses held a rod, a shepherd's staff, a symbol of his work as a shepherd. Moses threw the staff down. It meant he resigned from being a shepherd. The rod became a serpent, the sign of the devil and his power of sin. The devil was at work in Egypt. Therefore Egypt was a picture of the serpent, too, when Egypt tried to kill Israel. When Moses saw the serpent, he was afraid. God told him to pick it up, to conquer it — a sign of conquering Egypt. When Moses picked up the serpent, it became a rod again, this time the rod of God's power.

    b. In the second sign, Moses put his hand into his bosom, a sign of God carrying His people near to His heart. When Moses pulled his hand out, it was full of leprosy. Leprosy is a symbol of sin, a picture of the Israelites as they sinned in Egypt. When Moses pulled his hand from his bosom the second time, it was healed and clean, a sign of God delivering His people by making them holy and pure.

    c. In the third sign, Moses took water from the Nile River. The Egyptians needed water if they were to grow crops and have food and live. Moses took the water from the Nile, their god. When the water turned to blood on the dry land, it was a symbol of death from the plagues on Egypt, and the death of the god of Egypt.

3. Moses was still not ready to obey the Lord and go to Pharaoh. He complained in verse 10: "I am not eloquent*... but slow of speech." The Lord asked him, "Who hath made man's mouth?" And He promised to go with Moses and teach him. Moses did not need anything else. He had a promise from his covenant Friend!

4. God had taken away all Moses' problems, but still he did not want to

go. Read verse 13. That verse really means, "Lord, don't send me."

Discuss in class whether you would have felt as Moses did.

5.   The Lord was angry with Moses, but He knew what a great task it was for this humble, meek man; and the Lord was merciful to him and promised to send Aaron to help him and speak for him.

C.   Moses Goes to Egypt

1.   Moses asked Jethro his father-in-law to let him go to visit his brethren in Egypt. Jethro, a wise man, must have understood that Moses was called by the Lord. He said, "Go in peace."

2.   God led Aaron to meet Moses at the Mount of God (Sinai), verse 27. Together they went to Egypt and visited the Israelites. Aaron spoke and Moses showed them the signs from God. The people received them well and believed. They bowed their heads and worshipped.

Read Exodus 5:1-3

3.   Now Moses and Aaron were ready to appear before Pharaoh. They told him God had an order for Pharaoh: "Let my people go a three days' journey into the wilderness to serve the Lord." Remember:

a.   Pharaoh was not king of the Israelites. They were only staying in his land for a time.

b.   They had never had a holiday, but did the work of slaves every day.

c.   The Israelites could not sacrifice to God in Egypt, because animals were Egypt's gods, and the Egyptians would not allow the killing of animals.

4.   God called Pharaoh to obey Him and to let the people go. And Pharaoh must obey the God of heaven and earth. What was Pharaoh's answer? Read it again in verse 2. His answer does not mean that he had never heard of the Lord, but that he was too proud to stoop down to obey the words of the Lord.

5.   Pharaoh rebelled against God. He gave orders to his servants not to give the Israelites straw, but to let them find their own, and still make the same number of bricks. Here already the Lord was hardening the heart of this cruel ruler.

6.   How did the people of Israel react to the new orders to do the impossible? Read their compaint in verses 15 and 16.

7.   Then they met Moses and Aaron and heaped all their bitterness on them. Moses and Aaron got all the blame. And Moses was very sad and downcast. He told the Lord, "You have not saved the people at all."

DO NOT FORGET that there were two kinds of Israelites, the believers and the unbelievers. All of them shouted in happiness when Moses came to deliver them from slavery, but as soon as trouble came, the unbelievers complained. Only the believers in Israel waited in faith for the Lord to deliver them. We wait for the Lord in faith, too.

WORD STUDIES

1. deliver — to set free from evil and danger
2. eloquent — good use of language, especially in speaking

LESSON 43
The First Three Plagues
Exodus 7:1-8:19

BEFORE WE BEGIN, we remember that we left a very down-hearted Moses in our last lesson. In the first part of chapter 6, the Lord comforted him by saying, "I will take you to me for a people and I will be to you a God." But God reminded Moses that he must obey his God, too. He said, "Go in, speak unto Pharaoh king of Egypt."

Read Exodus 7:1-13

LESSON OUTLINE
A. God's Sign to Pharaoh

1. God promised to make Moses a god to Pharaoh. God gave him His words, but Moses stood apart from Pharaoh and Aaron spoke Moses' words, which were God's Words. From now on Aaron was to be Moses' spokesman.

2. The first time Moses and Aaron appeared before Pharaoh, the Lord did not want them to speak, but to show Pharaoh a sign. When Pharaoh said, "Show a miracle," Aaron was ready with his sign of the rod, the sign that would prove that their wonder came from God.

3. Aaron took his rod (the rod of Moses), threw it down before Pharaoh, and it became a serpent. Pharaoh called his wise men and magicians. When they threw down their magic rods, they became serpents, too. How did the magicians do it? It may have been by the secret magic tricks they had learned, or it may have been that these evil magicians were in the power of the devil, in whose power they performed the trick. All we know is that God allowed the rods to turn into snakes.

Discuss in class how it is possible
for people to put themselves in the power of the devil.

4. But Jehovah had the victory, for He made Aaron's serpent swallow up all the other serpents. When the magicians saw it happen right before their eyes, they knew that all the power belongs to Jehovah. It was a sign that God would destroy Egypt, for the serpents of the magicians were swallowed up. They disappeared, a sign that all the power of Egypt would disappear, too.

5. The sign from God left Pharaoh and his magicians amazed. Pharaoh could no longer say, "Who is Jehovah?" He knew in his mind that Jehovah is God,

151

but in his heart and his will he would not listen to Him. Pharaoh's heart was hardened. The Lord hardened it.

B. The Plagues

1. Before we study each plague separately, we will take a look at all ten plagues to see how and when God planned them, and how He arranged them.

2. Because the Bible tells us the names of certain months and certain crops which were ripe during the plagues, we can figure what time of the year the Lord sent them: most likely from the beginning of October until May, a period of about eight months.

3. God divided the plagues into groups of 3 + 3 + 3 + 1.

    a. In the first group of plagues, God let the magicians imitate Moses in bringing the first two plagues, and then He gave them no more power. They could not imitate Moses in the third plague.

    b. In the second group of plagues, the Lord separated His people Israel. They did not have any more plagues.

    c. In the third group God sent very severe plagues, leaving the land of Egypt bare.

    d. The last plague was a plague of death.

Read Exodus 7:19-25

C. The First Plague — Water Turned to Blood

1. Moses announced the first plague to Pharaoh as he went to the river in the morning. He warned Pharaoh with God's Words: "Let my people go." If Pharaoh did not obey, the Lord would turn the waters into blood.

2. It seems as if Pharaoh paid no attention to his words.

3. Moses told Aaron to stretch out his rod, the same rod which had become a serpent, over the waters of Egypt and all the waters became blood. God allowed the magicians to turn water into blood, too.

    a. Not only the Nile River, but pools and ponds and containers of water all turned into blood.

    b. All the fish died, and the river stank.

    c. The people had to dig to find water.

4. Pharaoh did not pay attention to the plague, but went home. He should have paid attention, for Moses and Aaron stretched out the rod in the sight of Pharaoh and his servants. Why were they at the river early in the morning? To worship their god, the Nile River. The Egyptians had a sort of nature worship, with the sun and the Nile as their most important gods. But they

also worshipped the land that grew crops for them. They worshipped God's creatures.

5. God spoke to Pharaoh in this plague. He was saying, "Your god, the Nile River, which swallowed up the covenant babies, is dead. I am the only God." But Pharaoh did not listen.

Read Exodus 8:1-15

D. The Second Plague — Frogs Over the Whole Land

1. Moses announced the second plague, too. He came to Pharaoh with these words, in verse 1: "Thus saith the Lord, 'Let my people go, that they may serve me.' " Moses even explained the horrors of the plague that was to come. Read about the frogs in verses 3 and 4.

2. When Pharaoh did not listen, Aaron stretched out his rod and frogs came out of all the waters in Egypt and covered the land. The magicians imitated Aaron and brought out frogs, too. The Lord allowed them to imitate these two plagues. Was it a great thing that these magicians did? Hardly. What Egypt did not need was more blood and more frogs.

3. Pharaoh called Moses and told him to ask the Lord to take away the frogs and he would let the people of Israel go. Moses asked him, "When?" and Pharaoh said, "Tomorrow." The next day the plague stopped, and Pharaoh knew that Moses' God was the Almighty, Who sent the plagues and took them away, but he hardened his heart. The frogs, gathered into piles, made the whole land stink.

4. The frog-gods which came from their Nile-god were now stinking heaps which spread sickness and death.

Read verses 16-19

E. The Third Plague — Dust Became Lice

1. Moses did not announce the third plague. Aaron stretched out the rod over the dust and it became a plague of lice. The magicians tried to bring forth lice, but God said, "That's enough." They could not do it. In verse 19, they are really saying, "This is the finger of the gods," the gods of Egypt, not Moses' God.

2. The dust of the fertile land that was one of their gods turned into lice that plagued them. The Lord proved to Pharaoh that his gods were no gods. But Pharaoh's heart was hardened, and he would not bow before the Lord.

DO NOT FORGET that these plagues were great wonders, which only our almighty God can do. In these first three plagues, God showed the Egyptians that their gods were no gods. He showed them that He is God.

LESSON 44
The Second Group of Plagues
Exodus 8:20-9:12

BEFORE WE BEGIN, we must connect the words of our last lesson with today's lesson. Pharaoh and his magicians, with hard hearts, said, "This is the finger of the gods. It is just something that happened. Every now and then there are catastrophies in nature." In the next three plagues God will show them that He is not only God, but He is Israel's God, and they will have to admit that these plagues were not just catastrophies, but that Israel's God, the King, sent them.

Read Exodus 8:20-32

LESSON OUTLINE

A. The Fourth Plague — All Kinds of Flies

1. The Lord told Moses to meet Pharaoh early in the morning at the river. Pharaoh did not go to the river to bathe or to swim, but to worship his god, the Nile. He needed the protection of his gods, for he thought that here in Egypt a battle was going on between Egypt's gods and Jehovah.

2. The first words that Moses said as he met Pharaoh were, "Thus said the Lord, 'Let my people go, that they may serve me.' " He also told Pharaoh what would happen if he would not obey the Lord: swarms of flies would fill the land.

    a. Notice that Moses did not use his staff. Then Pharaoh could have said that the staff was a magic wand which Moses controlled. But God must show Pharaoh that they came from His hand. Moses had nothing to do with bringing the flies. Suddenly they came and filled the land.

    b. The land was thick with them. They were everywhere: in the houses, on the people, on the ground, so that swarms of them flew up at every step. Psalm 78:45 says, "He sent divers sorts of flies among them, which devoured them." Divers means many. And Exodus 8:24 tells us that "the land was corrupted by reason of the swarms of flies."

    Discuss in class how this plague affected the lives of the people.

3. At the beginning of this plague, the Lord put a separation between Egypt and the land of Goshen. There were no flies in Goshen. Why not? God told Pharaoh, "to the end that thou mayest know that I am the Lord in the midst of the earth."

154

a. Usually the Lord does not make a separation between His people and the ungodly when He sends a thunderstorm, a tornado, or a blizzard.

b. But this was a special time of types and pictures. In this plague, God showed Pharaoh that His people are separate because He is saving them. Soon He will take them out of Egypt back to Canaan, which is a picture of their finished salvation in heaven. They are a separate people.

4. Pharaoh called for Moses. He could not stand this plague. He tried to make a compromise, and told Moses to "sacrifice to your God in the land." Pharaoh would not obey, but would try to meet God half way, and do it his own way after all.

5. Moses reminded him that sacrifices were an abomination* to the Egyptians. The Egyptians would stone them if they sacrificed in the land.

6. At last, because he could not find another way out, Pharaoh promised to let the people go, but not far away. Of course he knew God's demand: a three days' journey into the wilderness.

7. Did Pharaoh humble himself before Jehovah? No. Being truly humble is loving God and His goodness and being sorry for one's sins. Pharaoh seemed humble, but only because he wanted to escape punishment. Besides, fear and suffering made his will weak for a moment, but he had never intended to obey the Lord.

8. God took away the plague of flies, even though Pharaoh did not repent. Why? Because God's plan was to destroy Pharaoh and save His people. When the flies were gone, Pharaoh hardened his heart.

B. The Fifth Plague — Sickness on the Cattle

1. Once again we find Moses coming to Pharaoh. He has the same message from the Lord: "Let my people go, that they may serve me."

2. If Pharaoh will not keep his promise, God will send a grievous murrain* on the cattle. The word cattle in the Bible often includes all the animals of the field: horses, sheep, oxen, asses, and camels. This pestilence brought death to the animals.

3. Moses did not use his rod for this plague, either. The Lord set a time: tomorrow. And on the next day the plague came. It came straight from the hand of the Lord.

4. Verse 4 tells us that God made a separation between the animals in Egypt and those in Goshen. Not one of the cattle of the Israelites died. Pharaoh, with a hard heart, did not believe Jehovah's Word that His people's animals

were not harmed. He sent a messenger to Goshen and found out that not one animal of the Israelites was dead.

5. All the cattle — not every single animal, for we read of some live animals in the next two plagues — but a huge number of animals of every kind died.

6. Pharaoh paid little attention to this plague, for his heart was hardened.

Read verses 8-12

C. The Sixth Plague — Boils on Man and Beast

1. Do you remember that God did not announce the third plague, the last one in the first group? He did not announce the sixth plague, the last plague in the second group, either. When this plague came unexpectedly, it was more frightening. It happened without warning, and by it God was telling Pharaoh that his death was soon coming without any warning, too.

2. Moses was in the presence of Pharaoh, verse 8. He took handfuls of ashes and tossed them up toward heaven. Where did the ashes come from? From the furnaces out in the open fields where the Israelites made bricks. Those ashes thrown up to heaven were pictures of the cry of Jehovah's slaves, for their beatings, for the cruelty they suffered, for the wages they did not get. They were a cry to God for justice.

3. Pharaoh was not stupid. He knew that those ashes were pictures of the sufferings of God's people. Now those ashes would become boils with blains* on man and beast. They were so painful and made the people look so disfigured that even the magicians could not stay before Moses.

4. Pharaoh understood that Jehovah sent these six plagues, but he would not pay attention to Him, for the Lord hardened his heart. He was sinking deeper into sin. Soon God would destroy him.

DO NOT FORGET that we started this lesson by saying that Jehovah is King. But to us, His children, He is much more. He is our Rock Who protects us, our Father Who loves us, and our covenant God Who keeps His promises to us.

WORD STUDIES
1. abomination — anything that is disgusting or hateful
2. murrain — contagious disease of cattle; a pestilence
3. blain — a blister

LESSON 45
The Third Group of Plagues
Exodus 9:13-10:29

BEFORE WE BEGIN, we must understand that Pharaoh's heart became more and more hard as Jehovah sent each plague. We might say that the more often he said no, the harder he became. With his mind and understanding he saw that Egypt was being ruined; but with his evil, stubborn heart he said no to God's Word. He would rather be destroyed than obey God. Sometimes he seemed almost ready to give in, but he hardened his heart again.

Read Exodus 9:18-26

LESSON OUTLINE

A. The Third Group of Plagues

   1. In these last three plagues, God showed Pharaoh that He is Jehovah, the only God, and that there is no other god beside Him.

   2. These three plagues began during our month of February, when the flax and barley in Egypt were ripe.

B. The Seventh Plague — Hail, Thunder, and Fire

   1. Early in the morning Moses met Pharaoh again. Most likely Pharaoh went to the Nile River to worship. He still turned to his gods to help him. Once more God spoke to him through Moses: "Let my people go, that they may serve me. For I will send all my plagues upon thine heart. . . ." If God's plagues came on the hearts of Pharaoh and his people, they would be humble before the Lord and know that there is none like Jehovah in all the earth. Didn't Pharaoh know that yet? Yes, but he would not confess it. He still thought he was fighting with God.

   2. Before this plague, Moses gave Pharaoh a warning. A terrible hailstorm, such as Egypt had never seen, would come tomorrow. He gave Pharaoh and his servants warnings to get their animals in from the fields before they were killed by the storm. Those of Pharaoh's servants who feared the Word of the Lord listened, and put their animals in shelters. We do not know whether these servants feared the Lord in love, or whether they were terrified, and obeyed. The other servants left their cattle in the fields.

   3. Moses stretched out his rod toward heaven, and the Lord sent rain and thunder and hail, and fire that ran along the ground. It was a dreadful,

terrifying storm, which destroyed crops and trees and men and beasts, for it was the voice of God's anger. There was no storm in the land of Goshen.

4. Pharaoh could not stand the storm. He called for Moses and said, "I have sinned this time." Notice carefully what he said next: "The Lord is righteous and I and my people are wicked." Pharaoh glorified God! Did he change? No. He admitted he sinned this time, and he covered up all the rest of his sins. He confessed that the Lord is righteous in order to make a bargain with the Lord: if Pharaoh admitted that he was wrong, the Lord would stop the storm. Pharaoh's repentance was false.

5. Read verse 30. Moses knew Pharaoh would not fear the Lord. But he went out of the city, stretched out his hands, and the storm stopped. Pharaoh hardened his heart.

C. The Eighth Plague — Locusts

1. Before Jehovah sent this plague, He talked with Moses. Moses' task in Egypt was so very difficult and disappointing, and he must not be discouraged. So God told him in chapter 10:1 that He had hardened Pharaoh's heart. Why?

    a. To teach Moses and his children, all his descendants, and to teach us, too, His signs, because He is Jehovah.

    b. God had more wonders to show Pharaoh, until his heart was so hard that he was ready for God's judgment. Then God would drop him to the bottom of the Red Sea.

2. Once more Moses said the words of the Lord to Pharaoh: "Let my people go, that they may serve me." If Pharaoh refused, tomorrow the Lord would send locusts — grasshoppers. They would eat everything in Egypt:

    a. what the hail did not destroy,

    b. every tree and every green crop in the fields.

3. This time Pharaoh's servants spoke up. They were afraid. They asked (in verse 7), "How long shall this man be a snare* unto us?" Notice that the servants blamed Moses, not Pharaoh! Next they asked, "Knowest thou not yet that Egypt is destroyed?" Of course, Pharaoh knew it. He was to blame for Egypt's destruction because he would not bow before the Lord.

4. The servants made Pharaoh afraid. He knew their words were true. But he did not want to take the blame. He called Moses back so that he could show the servants that Moses was to blame.

    a. He said, "Go, serve the Lord your God."

b.   But he added: "Wait a minute. Who are to go?"

c.   When Moses said that everyone, with all their animals, must leave, Pharaoh raved at him in anger and chased Moses and Aaron away from his presence.

Read Exodus 10:12-20

5.   Moses used the rod of God, and God sent a strong east wind all day and all night. Then the grasshoppers came. God had called them to Egypt from a far country. Locusts come in swarms, making the sky black, and they destroy everything in their path. Their path was the whole land of Egypt. The locusts laid their eggs, which hatched into caterpillars. These caterpillars ate every living thing. Egypt became a desert.

Discuss in class Psalm 105:34, 35 and Psalm 78:46.

6.   In a great hurry, Pharaoh called for Moses and Aaron and said, "I have sinned against the Lord your God and against you." It seemed as if Pharaoh had at last confessed his sin. But, no, he didn't. He admitted that he had sinned, but he was not sorry. All he wanted was that the locusts go away.

7.   The Lord made a strong west wind blow every one of the locusts into the Red Sea. And the Lord hardened Pharaoh's heart.

Read Exodus 10:21-29

D. The Ninth Plague — Darkness for Three Days

1.   Many of the animals and people had died. There was nothing left to eat in the land. Then came the ninth plague without any warning. The Lord told Moses to stretch his hand toward heaven, and when Moses obeyed, the Lord sent a thick darkness into Egypt for three days and three nights.

2.   What kind of darkness was it?

a.   Verse 22 calls it a "thick darkness." No one left his home in these three days. Why did they not use a light or make a cozy fire?

b.   They could not, for no light would pass through the awful darkness.

c.   Remember that God created light on Day One and put it in light-holders on Day Four. Now He took away the gift of light from the Egyptians. Through the whole land was the darkness of death and hell — cold, black, thick darkness. It must have been terrifying.

3.   What made it more frightening to the Egyptians was that the Israelites had light in their houses. The Bible does not say, "in the land of Goshen," but, "in their dwellings." It was God's sign to them that the light of His love and grace was shining on His people, but His anger was over the Egyptians.

159

4. After three days the Lord lifted the darkness and let light return. Pharaoh called Moses. He wanted to make one more bargain with him: go and serve the Lord, but leave your cattle here. When Moses refused, Pharaoh's heart was hardened, and he spoke his last words to Moses: "See my face no more." If he ever saw Moses again, he would kill him. Calmly, Moses answered, "I will see thy face again no more."

DO NOT FORGET that we have studied much about hard hearts. As God's children, we remember what a soft heart, a heart touched by God's grace, says. It says, "I am sorry. God be merciful to me, a sinner."

WORD STUDIES
snare — a trap, anything by which one is entangled

LESSON 46
Israel Leaves Egypt
Exodus 11, 12

BEFORE WE BEGIN, in order to understand the last plague, we must know that almost all of chapter 11 happened before Moses left the palace of Pharaoh. Therefore, in the first part of our lesson we will go back to the palace.

Read Exodus 11:4-8

LESSON OUTLINE

A. Moses Announces the Tenth Plague

1. While Moses was still standing before Pharaoh, he said once more, "Thus saith the Lord. . . ." He told Pharaoh that about midnight God would kill the firstborn, the oldest of every family in Egypt, from Pharaoh's firstborn child to the firstborn child of the lowliest servant in his land, and also the firstborn of all the animals.

2. It would not happen at midnight that night, but Pharaoh had to wait in suspense, until it was God's time.

3. No danger would come to the Israelites. God did not let even a dog move its tongue against them.

4. Moses told Pharaoh that after the Lord had killed all the firstborn in the land, Pharaoh and his servants would tell Moses and the children of Israel to hurry out of the land. After he gave his message to Pharaoh, Moses left him and never saw that wicked king again.

Read Exodus 12:1-5

B. The Israelites Get Ready

1. It was the beginning of our month of April. In verse 2 God told them that this month, which they called Abib (or Nisan), was to be the first month of the year for them.

2. On the tenth day of that month, they must take a perfect lamb of a year old and separate it from the rest of the animals.

Read verses 6-13

3. On the fourteenth day of the month, in the evening, they must kill the lamb, sprinkle its blood on the sides and the tops of the doors of their houses, and prepare to leave. They must roast the lamb whole over a fire and eat it with unleavened* bread and bitter herbs*.

161

4. Moses told the people the words of the Lord: eat it in haste, verse 11. They could not take time to sit down, but had to be dressed, with sandals on their feet, and their staffs in their hands, ready to go. It was their last night in Egypt, for tonight the Lord was coming to send death to all the firstborn in Egypt. It was a night of wonder.

5. It was also a night full of meaning for the Israelites and for us. Both the Israelites and we must know what God did on the night of the fourteenth day of the first month.

    a. He called His son out of Egypt. Even before Moses had come to Egypt, God had told him to say to Pharaoh (in Exodus 4:22): "Israel is my son, even my firstborn: Let my son go, that he may serve me: if thou refuse to let him go, I will slay thy son, even thy firstborn."

    b. Israel was God's firstborn son because God gave the Israelites the promise that they had God's inheritance — God's blessings, just as God gave Abraham, Isaac, and Jacob His promise that He would be their Friend and bless them. Israel was a type of God's Son, Whom He called out of Egypt. See Matthew 2:15.

    c. Now God was ready to take His firstborn children out of the land of Egypt, the land of sin and slavery.

    d. It was a sign of God taking Israel out of the darkness of sin in Egypt to perfect life forever in the Canaan of heaven, a picture of their salvation from sin.

6. God gave the Israelites something they could see. When each family killed a lamb and sprinkled its blood on their doors, they listened to what God was saying: "When I see the blood, I will pass over you." That is why the meal they were ready to eat was called the feast of the passover.

    a. The flat, unleavened bread was a sign of cleaning out the yeast of sin rising inside them, and of becoming holy to the Lord.

    b. The bitter sauce reminded them of their hard lives as slaves, and of their bitter repentance for the sins they had committed in Egypt.

    c. The lamb was a picture of the Lamb of God, Whose blood on the cross took away all their sins.

Read Exodus 12:29-33

C. The Tenth Plague — All the Firstborn in Egypt Killed

1. At midnight the Lord killed all the firstborn children in Egypt. Think of the crying and the shock in the families of Egypt. They were terrified. At

162

least one person was dead in every family. Every household was preparing for a funeral. Pharaoh's oldest son died, too.

2. The frightened people thought this was only a beginning of their death. Soon they would all be dead, they thought, verse 33. They almost pushed the Israelites out of the land.

3. Even stubborn Pharaoh told them to take everything and be gone, and to bless him.

Read verses 35 and 38

D. Israel Leaves Egypt

1. God told the Israelites to take all kinds of treasures from the Egyptians. The words "borrowed" and "lent" really mean "asked" and "gave," so that the Israelites asked the Egyptians for treasures, and they gave them.

2. The Egyptians were left poor, and the Israelites went out with silver, gold, and beautiful clothes.

Discuss in class why God told the Israelites to take the rich gifts of Egypt.

3. Six hundred thousand men left Egypt. With their families, we can estimate that at least two million people left Egypt that night. They marched in orderly rows of five people. In Exodus 13:18 harnassed means five people in a rank, next to one another.

4. Verse 40 tells us that they had been in Egypt four hundred thirty years.

5. It was a night of great wonder, a night to be remembered and celebrated. Verse 42 tells that all the generations of the Israelites will observe* this night of wonder.

DO NOT FORGET that the passover feast was a meal for the Israelites. It was a picture of sitting down in friendship with their God. Because we live in New Testament times, we do not celebrate the passover, but we also sit at a meal with our God. When you are older, you will celebrate the Lord's Supper, because you believe that His body was broken and His blood was shed for your salvation.

WORD STUDIES

1. unleavened — flat bread, without yeast
2. herbs — plants used for seasonings or medicines
3. observe — to take notice of, to look back to

LESSON 47
Through the Red Sea
Exodus 13:17-15:21

BEFORE WE BEGIN, we will notice that the people of Israel took the bones of Joseph with them. They kept their solemn promise made to Joseph hundreds of years earlier that they would carry his bones along with them and bury them in Canaan.

Read Exodus 13:17-22

LESSON OUTLINE

A. The Israelites Leave Egypt

   1. In this lesson we will use the map on our worksheet for Lessons 46 to 48. Remember, the Israelites did not just travel to Canaan. The Lord led them. He could have led them the short, easy way by going north along the shore of the Great Sea directly into Canaan. But God did not lead them that way. Why not?

      a. If they went that way, they would soon meet the Philistines, who would fight them; and the Israelites were not ready for war.

      b. It was not time for them to fight the heathen people in Canaan, because the measure of the Canaanites' sin was not yet full in God's cup. We know that Egypt's measure was full. God destroyed them.

      c. In God's perfect plan, Pharaoh and his army must follow the Israelites and be drowned in the Red Sea.

      d. Israel had to learn, by being trapped at the Red Sea, that salvation is of the Lord. Only He can save them.

   2. The Israelites went harnessed, in an orderly march in rows of five.

   3. On your maps, follow the route they traveled:

      a. From Rameses (also called Raamses) to Succoth, where they probably gathered as one great host of people.

      b. From Succoth they went south to Etham, which was on the edge of the desert, and camped there.

      c. From Etham they turned toward the Red Sea and camped at Pihahiroth.

      d. Then they came to Baalzephon, and there they camped close to the Red Sea.

   4. Each day the Lord led them by a pillar of cloud and each night by a pillar of fire. The Israelites always saw their Leader.

Read Exodus 14:1-8

B. Pharaoh Chases the Israelites

1. God was leading Israel into a trap, into a place from which they could not possibly escape if they would have to flee.

2. Then, in verses 3 and 4, He told Moses that Pharaoh knew that Israel was closed in between the mountains, the desert, and the sea, with no possible way of escape. He told Moses that Pharaoh was preparing to follow them, to bring them back to Egypt.

3. Why did the Lord box in His people in such a dangerous spot? To teach His people to cry to Him for help. They must learn that no escape is impossible with God, and they must learn to give Him all their thanks and praise.

4. Pharaoh was getting ready. He took all the chariots in Egypt plus six hundred chosen chariots, along with his horsemen and his army.

5. How did the people of Israel react?

   a. They were terrified! They took their eyes away from the Pillar of Strength Who was leading them and looked at the horses and chariots of Pharaoh.

   b. They rebelled. They used evil words against Moses. Weren't there graves in Egypt for us? Do we have to die in the desert? Those were words of unbelieving people. Not all the people complained, for some trusted Jehovah; but those who had their hearts in Egypt rebelled.

6. Moses gave these complaining people a beautiful answer: "Fear ye not, stand still, and see the salvation of the Lord." He promised them that they would never see the Egyptians again, for the Lord would fight for them.

7. But Moses needed God's help. He must have cried to God, for in verse 15 the Lord said to him, "Wherefore criest thou unto me? Speak unto the children of Israel, that they go forward." If they went forward, they were following the Lord!

Read verses 19-31

C. Pharaoh and His Army are Drowned

1. Do you understand the danger of the people of Israel? The Red Sea was directly ahead of them, the high mountains on either side of them, and the Egyptian army behind them.

2. They need not fear, for God was there to rescue them. He moved the pillar of cloud so that it stood between them and the Egyptians. Through a wonder, the side of the pillar facing the Israelites was light. The side toward the Egyptians was totally dark.

3.   God worked this wonder to save His people. These two million people, besides thousands of animals, had to cross the Red Sea. Without God's help, Pharaoh's chariots would have overtaken them and brought them back to Egypt. The pillar shining on the Israelites was a picture of the Angel of the Lord, of Christ, shining His goodness and salvation on them.

4.   God's next wonder was a strong east wind which blew all that night. The wind came when Moses stretched out his rod, the rod of God's power, for the Israelites to see. The wind was God's servant, to blow the waters away, to pile them into strong walls on either side of the Israelites, and to make the bottom of the sea dry. Usually it takes days for even a small puddle to become completely dry. God made the huge sea dry immediately.

5.   God's rod and His east wind and His walls of water were God's salvation for Israel. Weren't the Israelites afraid to go forward? What if the walls of water fell down? The people were not afraid, for God gave them faith to believe Him.

   a.   When God's people walked through the Red Sea, they were being saved from Egypt, a type of their slavery to sin. They were on their way to Canaan, the type of the perfect kingdom of heaven.

   b.   Of what was the Red Sea a type? Of baptism. The Israelites were separated from the Egyptians by the waters of the Red Sea, just as you were separated from the evil world when you were baptized as babies.

   Discuss in class how baptism makes us separate from the world.

6.   Pharaoh should have been afraid of those walls of water, but he was blind with the foolishness of sin. He rushed into the sea after the Israelites.

7.   The God of the wonder bothered the chariot wheels of the Egyptians. They were stuck in the middle of the sea. It was too late to escape, for God told Moses to stretch out his rod. The walls of water rolled over the Egyptians, drowning them.

8.   God's people were safe on the other side of the Red Sea. There they sang a song praising their mighty God for their salvation. Moses' sister Miriam and the other women accompanied them with musical instruments, chapter 15:20, 21. Suggestion: read the Song of Moses in chapter 15 for devotions at noon hour.

DO NOT FORGET that we have a Pillar Who leads us, too. He is the same Savior, our Lord Jesus Christ, Who saved the Israelites, Who loves us and pities us and carries us in His arms. Isaiah 63:9 tells us about Him.

LESSON 48
Water, Quails, and Manna
Exodus 15:22-16:36

BEFORE WE BEGIN, we are ready to start another period in the history of the Israelites. This is the period of the journeys in the wilderness. Before we study this history, we will remember that their journey through the wilderness is a type of our journey through this world. We, too, travel from the "Red Sea" of our baptism, through the "wilderness" of our sins, to the "Canaan" of our perfect rest in heaven.

Read Exodus 15:22-27

LESSON OUTLINE

A. Marah

1. The Israelites traveled south to Marah. Find it on your map. They were traveling in the triangle-shaped piece of land called the Sinai Peninsula*. On their left was the Gulf of Suez and on their far right was the Gulf of Akaba. These two bodies of water are two forks of the Red Sea. On the right side of the people were hills of limestone*, called the Wilderness of Shur (or The Wall).

2. Do not picture the people of Israel walking on smooth beach sand. The land was rocky and bare, filled with dried river beds. It was hard for the people to walk because the ground was so uneven. At times huge mountains rose up alongside them, bare, frightening, and lonely.

3. The Wilderness of Shur at times was beautiful, too. The Israelites saw richly colored red sandstone and a green kind of stone called prophyry. Very few plants grew in the sandstone, but the trees and plants that did grow were colorful and fragrant.

4. Did the Israelites think their troubles were over now that they had crossed the Red Sea? Did they think they would have a lovely walk through the wilderness to Canaan? We do not know. But God knew, for He planned their pathway in the desert. It was not a smooth, easy path. He planned that path to be a type of the lives of His people, a type of our lives, too. It is a life of trouble and loneliness and hardship, with joy and happiness coming just when we need it.

Discuss how Israel's journey through the desert
is like our journey through life.

167

5. Verse 22 tells us that they came to Marah in three days. It was a journey of thirty-three miles. The huge host of two million people, with their animals, traveled about eleven miles a day. They had made good time traveling in the heat of the desert, but all the water they had taken from Egypt was gone. At Marah they found water, but it was bitter. They could not drink it. They could not live without water! What did they do? They murmured* against Moses.

6. Moses brought the problem to the Lord, Who told him to cut down a tree and throw it into the water. Suddenly the waters were sweet and good.

    a. Why a tree? The tree lived near that bitter water. It could drink the bitter water and use it to grow fresh, sweet leaves.

    b. It was another one of God's pictures: just as God gave the tree power to change the bitter to the sweet, God can change the bitter waters of sin in us into the sweet waters of life with Jesus. In this picture, God was showing the blessing of His grace to His people.

    c. Verse 25 says that God made a statute* and an ordinance*. God made it a rule to heal and save them by His wonders. God also made it a rule that they be obedient to Him. They must listen to God and keep His commandments.

7. At Elim they found twelve wells of water and seventy palm trees. The people stayed there and rested, perhaps about a month. The Lord gave His people rest and refreshment there.

Read Exodus 16:1-8

B. The Wilderness of Sin

1. When the Israelites left Elim they kept close to the shore of the Red Sea as they traveled south. They were now in the Wilderness of Sin. Find it on your maps. It was a lonely and fearful wilderness.

2. The food they had taken with them from Egypt was gone. There was no food in this dreadful desert of chalk-white hills. What did the people of Israel do?

    a. They murmured against Moses and Aaron and said very evil and cruel words to them: "We wish we had died in Egypt, for you brought us into this wilderness to kill us."

    b. Moses scolded the people. He told them they were not murmuring against him, but against God, Who brought them to this wilderness.

    c. Not all the people complained. Those who feared the Lord prayed and asked God for food. Psalm 105:40 tells us about them.

3. The Lord is good, even when His people complain. He sent them two wonders.

    a. In the evening He sent them quails*, enough to feed two million people.

    b. In the morning He gave them round white kernels: bread from heaven. It was a perfect food, with everything they needed to keep their bodies strong and healthy. The Israelites asked, "Manna?" which means, "What is it?"

4. Why did the Lord choose to feed the Israelites in this special way?

    a. In verse 4 God said, "that I may prove them, whether they will walk in my law, or no." God tested their faith in Him.

    b. He took away all their food. Now they must eat every day from His hand. Would they trust Him?

5. God showed His people that the manna was a great wonder, for His bright glory appeared in the cloud, verse 10.

Read verses 16-21

6. Before God sent the manna, He gave them rules.

    a. Each morning the Lord gave just enough manna for everyone for that day. They must eat the manna they gathered that day.

    b. If they saved any, it was full of worms the next day.

    c. On the sixth day they must gather twice as much, enough for the seventh day. On the seventh day the manna they saved would not be wormy.

7. Did the Israelites have faith to walk in God's law and obey His rules? Many of them were wicked and did not. Those to whom God gave His grace obeyed Him.

8. When Jehovah gave His people manna and took care of their bodies every day, He was teaching them a greater truth: that "man doth not live by bread only, but by every word that proceedeth out of the mouth of the Lord," Deuteronomy 8:3.

DO NOT FORGET that the manna was a picture of Christ, Who said, "I am the Bread of life." He fed the Israelites and He feeds us with the new life of walking with Him in faith.

WORD STUDIES

1. peninsula — a piece of land nearly surrounded by water
2. limestone — white rock
3. murmur — to complain, grumble, mutter
4. statute — a law
5. ordinance — a rule, a command
6. quail — a bird similar to a partridge, with a short tail

LESSON 49
Rephidim
Exodus 17

BEFORE WE BEGIN, Jehovah gave one more instruction about the manna. Moses told Aaron to put some in a pot and keep it for many generations, for their children. When these children looked at the pot of manna, they would see how Jehovah fed His people in the desert, and thank Him.

Read Exodus 17:1-4

LESSON OUTLINE

A. The People Murmur

1. The people of Israel turned from the Wilderness of Sin toward the east and traveled three days until they came to Rephidim. Find it on the map for Lessons 46 to 48.

2. It was a journey of three days under the hot desert sun. When they came to Rephidim, they were tired and thirsty; and all they found there was a large, bare rock towering over the vast, empty desert.

3. The people reacted two ways. Most of them sinned.

   a. One of their sins was a lack of patience. As soon as they came to the rock and saw no water, they said these unholy words: "Give us water that we may drink." They hated this wilderness because their hearts were still in Egypt. They really meant to say to Moses: "You brought us here. Now take care of us."

   b. Another of their sins was rebellion. First they rebelled with their mouths: they asked Moses whether he brought them out of Egypt to kill them and their children. Then they rebelled with their hands. They were either looking for stones or holding stones, ready to kill Moses.

   c. Most of the Israelites sinned. A few prayed. God tells us in Hebrews 3:16 that not all the Israelites rebelled. Psalm 105 tells that some asked — they prayed — God for water.

4. Moses called the name of the place Massah and Meribah because the people tempted the Lord. They asked an evil question: "Is the Lord among us or not?" They asked this question after all the great wonders Jehovah had just done for them: the crossing of the Red Sea, giving water at Marah, the quails, and the manna. Besides, the Lord, by His pillar, brought them to this

huge, dry rock. Why did they ask whether God was among them? Because they were proud, wicked men who wanted God to be their servant.

Read verses 5-7

B. Water From the Rock

    1. God did not leave His people, even though they deserved to be left alone. He told Moses what to do.

        a. Moses must call all the people together and take the elders of Israel with him.

        b. With the rod of God in his hand he must strike the rock before the eyes of all the people. Why? So that the wicked Israelites would know and understand that when Moses struck the rock and water gushed out, it was God Who performed the miracle!

        c. Jehovah promised in verse 6 that He would stand on top of the rock. Most likely He came in His glory in the pillar of cloud. When they saw the bright cloud, the ungodly Israelites would have no excuse to doubt God's wonder.

    2. I Corinthians 10:4 says about the Israelites: "And did all drink the same spiritual drink; for they drank of that spiritual Rock that followed them: and that Rock was Christ." The Lord is not telling us here that the huge rock followed them by rolling behind them as they traveled through the desert. That cannot be. For it was a spiritual Rock, and the Rock was Christ. It means that:

        a. wherever the Israelites traveled in the hot, dry desert, Christ, their Rock, was following them, to give them water from rocks;

        b. when the text says that they drank spiritual water, it means that the water which came out of the rock was water to quench their thirst, water such as you and I drink. How, then, was it spiritual water? It was a sign of the water of life. When the people drank it, they knew that they were thirsty for righteousness, and that when they drank it they knew that by faith they were drinking in the blessings of salvation from Jesus.

Read verses 8-16

C. Victory Over the Amalekites

    1. Suddenly, Amalekites were there. Who were the people of Amalek?

        a. Amalek was a grandson of Esau and his wife Adah. Esau hated his brother Jacob, and Jacob's descendants, who were the Israelites.

        b. Amalek's grandmother, Adah, was the daughter of Heth, a Canaanite who came from Ham, who hated God, and whom God had cursed.

172

2. Amalek learned from his grandparents to hate the Israelites, and Amalek's descendants, the Amalekites, were enemies of Israel. The Israelites hated the Amalekites, for they were rough, wandering people who did not fear the Lord.

3. The Amalekites had heard about God's wonders in Egypt and in the Red Sea. They knew the nation of Israel was marching to Canaan. They did not want the Israelites in Canaan! So they came to Rephidim to stop the Israelites and destroy them. These wicked servants of Satan were there to prevent God's people from getting to Canaan.

4. There is another reason Amalek came, the most important reason, which we may never forget. God wanted to show His people Israel (and the wicked Amalekites, too) the power of His wonder, when He fought for His people.

5. The Amalekites were not clean fighters. They were sneaking cowards. Deuteronomy 25:17, 18 tells that they attacked those who were near the end of the line to get water from the rock. These people were weary and faint from lack of water, and the enemy pounced on them.

6. The Israelites had given them no reason to attack them. It was a mean, hateful attack on God's people. The Israelites were not ready for war.

    a. Spiritually they were not ready. Many of them had just rebelled and spoken angry words about Jehovah.

    b. Physically they were tired and weak and not ready for battle.

    c. It was the first time God called them to be active, to fight the battles of the Lord. It was different from their crossing of the Red Sea, where God had said, "Stand still!"

7. In verse 10 we meet Joshua for the first time. He was the captain who led the battle with the Amalekites.

8. God called Moses to the top of a hill. Aaron and Hur went with him. Hur may have been the husband of Miriam, Moses' sister. Moses held the rod of God toward heaven, and the Israelites began to win the battle.

    a. The Israelites fought, but they did not win because of their own power.

    b. They won because of their faith. The rod pointed to Jehovah, Who gave them the victory.

    c. When Moses' arms were tired and he lowered the rod of God, Amalek gained the upper hand in the battle. The position of Moses' hands decided who would win the battle.

9. The rod was not some sort of magic charm, but it was the sign of the power of the Lord. The battle was the Lord's, and the victory was the Lord's. Moses and the Israelites were fighting by faith! Aaron and Hur helped Moses, each on one side, to hold his hands with the rod pointing to heaven.

10. Moses wrote about it in a book. Then he built an altar and called it Jehovah-Nissi, which means, "Jehovah is my Banner*."

DO NOT FORGET that Jehovah-Nissi is our banner, too. We fight all our lives. We fight against sin and we fight for the cause of God and His people. We do it by faith, for when we carry Jehovah's banner, we always win the victory.

WORD STUDIES

banner — a flag or standard of an army

LESSON 50

The Israelites Come to Sinai

Exodus 18 and 19

BEFORE WE BEGIN, we may wonder about Moses' wife and their two sons. We have not heard about them since Moses went to Egypt. Very likely Moses sent them back to Jethro their father after they had gone only part of the way with him in the desert. Moses' life in Egypt was probably too hard for them to share. Now Jethro was coming to meet Moses, with his wife and two sons.

Read Exodus 18:1-12

LESSON OUTLINE

A. Jethro Visits Moses

1. You will remember that Jethro, Moses' father-in-law, a descendant from Abraham and Keturah, was a God-fearing priest. He lived near the mountains of Sinai, and it was easy for him to go to meet Moses. Perhaps Jethro was already looking for Moses, for when Moses was still living with Jethro, God had given him a promise. Do you remember it? When God met him at the burning bush, He promised that Moses would come back to this mountain with the people of Israel, to worship.

2. Moses and Jethro met each other differently from how we would meet our relatives. They bowed formally to one another, kissed, and then talked; for they lived according to the customs of the Eastern countries. Moses must have been extremely happy to have his family with him again.

3. Moses did the talking, for he had so much to tell:

   a. He told what Jehovah had done to Pharaoh and to Egypt, and he told how the Lord had saved this huge nation of people from their bondage in Egypt and from their troubles in the desert.

   b. We do not read that Moses spoke any words of complaining about his hard life, nor any words about the murmurings of the people. Moses was a kind and patient shepherd of the Israelites, a type of our Good Shepherd Who is kind and patient with us.

4. Moses' telling of all God's wonders must have been a wonderful story for his family and his father-in-law to hear. Jethro's response was: "Now I know that the Lord is greater than all gods." Didn't Jethro know it all his life? Yes, he did, but when he heard Moses tell how God is so far above all idol gods, Jethro's faith was made stronger, and he praised the Lord.

Discuss in class what Bible story you love,
which makes your faith stronger.
Read verses 13-17

B. Jethro's Advice

1. The next day Moses was busy from morning until night helping the people with their troubles and problems. In this large nation of Israel, there were many problems, and Moses could not finish his work, even though he worked all day.

2. Jethro watched. He saw how busy Moses was and he saw that one man could not possibly handle the problems of all the people. He asked Moses why he did the work all alone.

3. Moses gave a simple answer: "Because the people come unto me to inquire of God." What else could he do but help them?

4. Jethro gave Moses a surprising answer: "The thing that thou doest is not good." Then Jethro gave his advice.

a. Moses must measure his strength and use it wisely, or he would wear out. This task was not for one man.

b. Jethro did not say that Moses was doing it all wrong. No, it was a good system, but he needed help. Just as only one ray of the sun gives only one ray of sunlight, and many rays make the earth bright, so one man can give a little advice, and many men can give much advice. Jethro advised that Moses still speak the Word of God to the people, but that he have many helpers.

c. Jethro told Moses to choose able men who feared God, who were truthful, and who were not greedy, as his helpers. Moses appointed helpers over groups of people, from small family groups to large communities of people: helpers over groups of tens, fifties, hundreds, and thousands. They decided the cases, and only the very hard cases went to Moses.

d. Jethro ended his advice by saying that then the Israelites could go in peace to their place (the promised land), verse 23.

5. Moses, the ruler of the greatest nation on earth, the nation of God's own people, was not proud. He listened humbly to his wise old father-in-law and took his advice.

Read Exodus 19:1, 2

C. At Mount Sinai

1. It was now three months since the Israelites left Egypt. They came to

Mount Sinai, **the central mountain of a group of mountains called Horeb.**

2. The Israelites came to Mount Sinai to receive the law from God. They had to learn what the relationship between God and His people is. God told Moses to tell the people:

a. that His people are God's precious possession. They are so precious to God that He made a word-picture of carrying them as baby eagles on His eagles' wings, verse 4.

b. In verse 6, God called His people a kingdom of priests. Kings rule. Priests serve in love. God's people were going to rule and to serve in love. In order to rule, they needed laws. God was ready to give them the laws now.

3. Moses spoke all God's words to the people, and they answered, "All that the Lord hath spoken, we will do." They gave that answer in faith, but they did not yet understand what they must do. Do you think they could obey all God's laws? Oh, no!

4. God had to teach them that they could not keep His law. This is the way God taught them:

a. God came to them in a thick cloud, verse 9. That cloud showed that He was too holy to be seen. He was separate from His people.

b. God spoke to them through Moses' mouth. Moses was a mediator*, one who stood in their place, who would stand between them and God.

5. God's people must get ready to listen to God. To show that their hearts were spiritually clean, they washed their clothes and did not come, with their sinful bodies, near to the holy mountain, verse 14.

6. Why did they stand back from God? Because God came to them as their Judge. Read verse 16. He kept His people at a distance. They were too sinful to come close to His holiness. God showed Himself as a fire, ready to burn the wicked. The people were afraid. They trembled and stood afar off.

7. How could they come close to God? Only when their sins were covered. From these very people standing here at the Mount, Jesus would be born. He would cover their sins with His blood and make them friends with God.

DO NOT FORGET that Moses the mediator was a type of Jesus, our Mediator, Whom God gave to stand in our place and take our punishment for us.

WORD STUDIES

mediator — one who is given by God and goes between God and His people

177

LESSON 51
God Meets with His People
Exodus 20:1-20 and Exodus 24

BEFORE WE BEGIN, immediately after God appeared to the Israelites in the thick cloud, with thunders and lightnings, He spoke the words of the ten commandments to them. In these lessons, we will not study the ten commandments, for we are studying Bible history this year.

LESSON OUTLINE
A. God Gives the Law

   1. The people who were camped at the foot of the mountain saw all the signs of God's power and holiness. They saw the thunder, lightning, the thick cloud, and they heard the sound of the trumpet. They heard God's voice saying the words of the ten commandments, and were frightened.

   2. They asked Moses to be a mediator, a go-between, to tell them God's words. They were so filled with fear at God's holy majesty that they thought they would die.

   3. Moses went up the mountain alone (chapter 19:20). While the people waited in fear and reverence below, God gave Moses many laws for the lives of the Israelites. We find these laws in chapters 21, 22, and 23. We will not study these laws at this time, but go on to chapter 24.

Read Exodus 24:1-8

   4. When Moses came down from the mountain, he told the Israelites all the laws God had given him, and then he wrote them in a book. The people, filled with awe and fear, listened to the laws, and said, "All the words which the Lord hath said will we do," verse 3.

B. The Blood-Sprinkled Altar

   1. Next, Moses built an altar of stone, with twelve pillars around it. The altar in the Old Testament times was the place where God met His people and lived with them and blessed them. It was the place where they stood in God's presence.

Discuss in class where we go to stand in God's presence
and ask His blessings.

   2. The altar with an animal for a sacrifice on it was a type of the sacrifice of Christ on the cross. When the Israelites saw the blood of the innocent

animal which had been killed, they knew it was a promise that Christ, Who was the Innocent One, was coming, and would pay for their sins with His blood.

3. The twelve pillars around the altar represented* the twelve tribes of Israel. They were signs that Israel stood close to God. God chose, not the priests, but young men from the nation of Israel to make the sacrifice.

4. Moses took half the blood of the animal which was killed and sprinkled it on the altar before the face of God. The other half of the blood he sprinkled on the twelve pillars which stood for the twelve tribes of Israel. He most likely did not sprinkle the people themselves. This ceremony meant that God's people were clean from their sins through Jesus' blood, the Jesus Whom God had promised to send.

5. God was continuing His covenant of friendship which He had made with His friends Adam, Noah, Abraham, Isaac, Jacob, and all His other friends. God lived with His people on this altar. It is important for us to remember that this is the meaning of all the sacrifices of God's people in Old Testament times.

6. After the sacrifice, Moses read and explained the words of the book of the covenant to the people, verse 7.

    a. He read laws about the lives of the people with one another: laws about their families, neighbors, and property.

    b. He read laws about serving God, giving gifts to Him, and celebrating His feasts.

Read verses 9-18

C. Into the Mount

1. God called Moses, Aaron, Nadab, Abihu, and seventy elders of the people to go up the mountain with him. Nadab and Abihu, sons of Aaron, would be priests in the future, after Aaron died.

2. On the mountain they ate and drank with God. This time they did not see God as their Judge, but as their Friend. Verse 10 gives us beautiful words about what they saw. Moses wrote about this heavenly sight in earthly words. They are the only words our minds can understand. We cannot imagine what the vision looked like, but will have to wait until we get to heaven to understand.

3. After they ate in friendship with God, they all came down the mountain again. Aaron and Hur were to be the rulers of the people while Moses went

179

back up the mountain once more. This time he took Joshua with him as his servant. Moses stayed at the top of the mountain forty days and forty nights.

DO NOT FORGET that when we come into God's presence, we come to the Holy One. When we remember His holiness and majesty, whether we come to pray to Him or to worship Him, we will come in deep reverence.

WORD STUDIES
represent — to stand for, to serve as a type

LESSON 52
The Tabernacle and its Meaning
Exodus 25-30

BEFORE WE BEGIN this lesson, have the worksheet for this lesson on your desks. Following the instructions God gave Moses on the mountain, we can learn just what the tabernacle was like.

Read Exodus 24:12-15

LESSON OUTLINE

A. God Talks to Moses

1. In our last lesson, we left Moses and Aaron and the seventy elders of Israel on the mountain-top. After they ate and drank with God, they went down again to the camp of Israel.

2. Very soon, God called Moses up to the mountain again. This time Joshua went part of the way up the mountain with him, while Aaron and Hur stayed down to rule the Israelites.

3. For forty days and nights, as long as a person can survive without food and water, Moses stayed on the mountain with God. We do not know how God appeared to him, but we know that God spoke to him face to face. It was a great wonder. Moses was the most blest of all men because he spoke directly with God on the mountain.

4. During these forty days God gave Moses:

a. the ten commandments;

b. many more rules teaching the Israelites how to live;

c. the instructions for the tabernacle.

B. God Gives Instructions for the Tabernacle

1. Why did God want His people to have a tabernacle? It was a place where God would meet His people and have friendship with them, and where God's people might see God's glory and live holy lives with Him. Read Exodus 29:43 and 45.

2. The Bible also calls the tabernacle the tent of meeting and the tent of witness*. God witnessed that He is holy and His people witnessed that they were sinful and could be saved only by the blood of their Savior.

3. In this lesson we will study the tabernacle and learn about its beauty, and understand what this beautiful tabernacle means.

181

C. The Courtyard

1. God told Moses to use the wood of the acacia, or shittim tree for all the wooden parts of the tabernacle. It was a hard wood which would not rot, with a beautiful, polished look. The pillars of the court were made from this wood. Between them hung curtains of fine white linen, fastened with hooks to the wooden pillars. The doorway of the court faced east, toward the rising sun, and was covered with a beautiful curtain embroidered in red, blue, and purple. The walls of the courtyard were made of curtains so that it could easily be picked up and carried with the Israelites as they travelled. The desert sand was always the floor of God's house.

2. The altar of burnt offering was covered with a grill so that the priests could sacrifice the animals the people brought. The altar was not beautiful, but it was very important. When the priests sacrificed the animals, and the altar ran with blood, the people looked ahead to the promise that some day Jesus' blood would cover all their sins. Read Hebrews 10:4 and 10.

3. The laver, filled with water, was necessary for the priests to wash the animals for the sacrifices and to wash their hands and their feet, Exodus 40:31. It was a picture of having clean hearts before God. Read Psalm 24:3, 4.

Discuss in class what having clean hands
meant for the Israelites and what it means for us.

D. The Tabernacle

1. The tabernacle proper stood at the far end of the courtyard. It, too, was made from acacia wood and covered with gold. The roof was made of fine linen. Embroidered in colors of blue, red, and purple were figures of cherubim, God's holy, guarding angels. On top of the linen was a covering of goat's hair, then one of ram's skins dyed red, and finally one of badger's or seal's skins. The covering probably extended down the walls of the tabernacle, to protect it from the weather. At the entrance curtains embroidered with cherubim were between five pillars covered with gold.

2. Again, the holy place was a picture of God living with His people under one roof. Nearest to the holy of holies stood the altar of incense. The priests took coals of fire from the altar of burnt offering and lit the sweet-smelling incense on the altar with these coals. Then the holy place was filled with a refreshing and fragrant odor. The smoke of the incense rising in the holy place was a picture of the prayers of God's people, which are sweet to God.

Notice that this sweet-smelling incense could be lit only by the coals covered with blood from the altar of burnt offering. God was teaching the people of Israel, and us, that we can never pray to Him unless we are covered by the blood of Jesus, and pray in His name. Read Psalm 141:1, 2.

3. On the right side of the altar of incense was the table of showbread. On it were twelve small loaves of bread, which were replaced every sabbath day. Aaron and his sons sat down and ate the bread each sabbath day before they replaced the loaves. What was the meaning of that? It was a promise from Jehovah that He would always feed His people, also when they came to the land of Canaan. It meant, too, that God's people could not live by bread alone. Read what Jesus said in Matthew 4:4. The words from God's mouth are the Bread of Life. The Israelites (through the priests) prayed at the altar of incense, and God fed their souls at the table of showbread with the Bread of Life, Who is Jesus.

4. The priests filled the seven bowls of the lampstand with oil. Oil in the Bible is a picture of the light of the Holy Spirit in the hearts of His people. The lampstand told the Israelites that God's people are the light of the world!

5. The holy of holies was the place where God lived in all His glory. The two tables of the law were in the ark of the covenant. On top of the ark were two golden cherubim, looking down on the pure, golden mercy seat. Once a year the high priest sprinkled blood on the mercy seat, a picture which looked forward to the day when Jesus would shed His blood for the forgiveness of the sins of all His people.

DO NOT FORGET that, although we live many years after Jesus' death, the pictures and signs of the Old Testament tabernacle are beautiful reminders of the wonderful way that God saves us.

WORD STUDIES
witness — that which gives proof or evidence; or the person who gives proof

LESSON 53
The Golden Calf
Exodus 32:1-28

BEFORE WE BEGIN, we know that while Moses was on the mountain top for forty days and nights, he was in the presence of the holy God. The people of Israel, at the foot of the mountain, knew it, too. God was in the thick cloud. They had already heard God's words and they trembled with fear. The mountain was still smoking and quaking and thundering with God's great holiness. They were all in the presence of God!

Read Exodus 32:1-6

LESSON OUTLINE

A. The Terrible Sin

1. The people of Israel came to Aaron complaining that they did not know what happened to this man, Moses, who brought them out of Egypt. Those were very wicked words. They were lies, for

a. it was God, not Moses, Who brought them out of Egypt;

b. they did know where Moses was: with God on the mountain top.

2. They demanded of Aaron: "Up, make us gods, which shall go before us." The Israelites had just heard the first commandment, "Thou shalt have no other gods before me," but they would not listen. They rejected* the God of heaven and earth and begged for an idol. They did not believe God and would not worship Him. Read I Corinthians 10:7.

3. The people asked Aaron to make them gods (or a god). They wanted to worship an idol they could see. Aaron was their leader while Moses was on the mountain. God had called him to lead Israel in obedience to Him. Do you think Aaron was angry and refused their request? No, he gave in. He asked for their golden jewelry and agreed to make a god for them. Why?

a. He was weak and afraid. What if all these people turned against him?

b. He probably thought if he asked for their treasures, they would refuse to part with them.

4. But the people gladly gave up their valuable jewelry if it would help them sin. They insisted they must have a god they could see.

5. They brought their gold, and Aaron melted it down and made a calf. He made the shape of a calf, most likely of the ox Apis, the god the Egyptians

worshipped, and then covered it with gold. When it was finished, Aaron presented it to the people by saying, "These be thy gods which brought thee up out of the land of Egypt."

6. The people had another reason for wanting a golden calf. They wanted to have a wild, evil celebration, with dancing and eating and drinking, the kind of parties they had with the wicked Egyptians.

7. Why did the people do this? They had just lived through all the wonders God had showed them: He drowned the Egyptians in the Red Sea, gave them water from the rock, manna from heaven, and quails in abundance, and He was leading them to the promised land. The answer is that they did not believe in and love this God of the wonder. With hard hearts they would not serve Him.

> Discuss in class how it is possible
> to know that God rules over all things,
> but to refuse to believe in Him.

8. Not all the Israelites wanted the golden calf. God had His own children in Israel who were shocked and sad at all the evil around them. But most of Israel at this time was wicked.

> Read verses 7-14

B. Jehovah's Anger

1. God told Moses everything that was happening on the mountain side below them. In His great anger, He said that He would destroy the Israelites and make a nation from Moses' seed.

2. Moses begged the Lord not to destroy the people whom He had just saved from Pharaoh's armies. What would the wicked Egyptians say? And what about God's promise to Abraham, Isaac, and Jacob, to make of them a great nation? Moses begged God to turn away from His fierce anger.

3. And then we read in verse 14 that "Jehovah repented of the evil that he thought to do unto his people." Did God change His mind? No, that is not possible. God is unchangeable. The answer is that God was terribly angry with the ungodly Israelites, but He had endless mercy for His own chosen people, who loved and obeyed Him. Remember: the nation of Israel was not one, but two — the elect and the reprobate. For the sake of His elect people, whom He saved before the world was, Jehovah would not destroy the nation of Israel. When God does not destroy Israel for the sake of those He loves, we say that God repented.

C. Moses and Joshua Come Down

1. Joshua, who was probably a little farther down the mountain while Moses talked with God, thought the noise in the camp of Israel was the sound of war. Moses knew better. It was the sound of the evil shouting of an idolatrous feast.

2. As soon as Moses and Joshua came down to the people, Moses threw down and broke the two tables of stone on which God had written the law. It was a sign that Israel had broken God's law and His covenant of friendship.

3. Next he broke the golden calf, ground it to powder, put it in their drinking water, and made the people drink it. This was a sign that their sin came down over their own heads, and made every part of them unclean.

4. Then Moses scolded Aaron, verse 21. Aaron did not really admit his sin. He made the excuse that the people were filled with mischief, verse 22; and he lied when he said that after he threw the gold into the fire, a calf "came out."

5. All this time the wicked Israelites were continuing their noisy, idolatrous feast. The whole nation was in an uproar. Moses knew what he must do: he must separate God's true children from the idol-worshippers.

   a. He called out, "Who is on the Lord's side?"

   b. The men of Levi, Moses' tribe, came out to Moses.

6. God told the Levites to kill the revelers* in Israel. The revelers were the neighbors of the Levites, and possibly their relatives. Must the Levites fight and kill them? Does it seem that God ordered too harsh a punishment?

   a. No, for there was no other way to restore order and peace to Israel.

   b. It was the Lord Who said the sinners must have the punishment of death and hell to get rid of the evil idolatry in Israel.

DO NOT FORGET that we do not live on a playground in this life. The sinners in Israel thought so. We live on a battle field and fight a war that is never finished in our lifetimes. We fight the battle against sin. Our weapons are the shield of faith and the sword of the Spirit, and we fight by God's grace.

WORD STUDIES

1. reject — to refuse to accept or recognize or believe
2. revelers — those who make a noisy or boisterous uproar.

Moses Pleads for the People

Exodus 32:28 - Exodus 34

BEFORE WE BEGIN, we will try to imagine how angry Moses must have felt after he found out the terrible sin of the Israelites; and how sad he must have been when God ordered war. Some of the men from God's chosen nation must kill other men from God's chosen nation.

Read Exodus 32:28-35

LESSON OUTLINE

A. Moses Intercedes* for Israel

1. You will remember that in yesterday's lesson Moses prayed for the Israelites when God said He would destroy them and make a nation from Moses' seed. Moses acted as a mediator, a go-between, when he begged God not to destroy His people.

2. Even after God punished many of the sinners with death, Moses knew that the relation between God and His people was not yet healed. That horrible sin was in the way. When Moses spoke to the people, he told them, "Ye have sinned a great sin." They had rejected their God!

3. In verse 30 Moses told the Israelites that perhaps he would make an atonement for them. What is an atonement? It is a payment or satisfaction for sin, by someone else, someone who is a substitute. Maybe Moses could give his life for their sins.

4. Moses went to the Lord with his problem. Would the Lord forgive this great sin? If not, Moses asked God to blot him out of His book. God's book is His record of those whom He chose to be His own, those who will live in heaven with Him forever. Moses knew that his name was in that book. Moses was asking that if the Lord could not forgive the Israelites, he would have his name taken from God's book, and would go to hell to pay for the people's sins.

5. What was God's answer? "Whosoever hath sinned against me, him will I blot out of my book," verse 33. Moses' blood was not the perfect atonement. He was a sinner himself. He could not pay for their sins. Only Jesus' blood is the perfect atonement for sin.

Discuss in class how we know
that our names are written in God's book.

187

6. Moses thought that all the Israelites were God's true children. Now God was teaching him that those whose names were not in His book would die in their sins.

Read Exodus 33:1-8

B. The People's Reaction

1. God instructed Moses to speak to the people. He told them four things:

    a. that God will punish their sins;

    b. that they must continue their journey to Canaan;

    c. that He will not go before them, but will send an angel, verse 2;

    d. that they must take off all their ornaments and mourn for their sins.

2. Moses went out to the tent of meeting to meet with God (the tabernacle was not built yet) and all the people stood at their tent doors and watched him and mourned for their sins and worshipped.

3. While the people looked on, Moses prayed. He asked God, "Show me thy way," verse 13. He was not satisfied that an angel would lead the people to Canaan. They needed their God to lead them. Read God's answer in verse 14.

4. That is a beautiful verse, for the Israelites and for us. But Moses wanted more than this from God. Would God go with them in His grace and love and mercy? He prayed a special prayer: "Show me thy glory," verse 18.

Read verses 19-23

C. God Shows His Goodness

1. No one on this earth can see God's face and live. It is too holy for mere men to see. Only when we get to heaven, and when we are perfect, heavenly beings, will we see God's face, through Jesus.

2. Because Moses was God's special Old Testament prophet, God promised to show him a little bit of His glory. He promised to put Moses in a cleft* of a rock and cover his face with His hands. The Lord's face would be turned away from Moses. After His face was past, His glory would shine from His back. We cannot imagine the wonder of the glory that God promised Moses.

3. When did Moses see God's glory? Chapter 34 tells us that God called him back into the mountain to give him two more tables of stone with the law written on them, to replace those which Moses had smashed.

4. While Moses was on the mountain top, God caused all His goodness to pass before Moses. Moses was hidden in the cleft of the rock, with God's hand covering him. Jehovah passed by him, saying His name, chapter 34:5, 6.

188

His name is merciful, gracious, longsuffering, goodness, and truth.

5. Moses, the only man on this earth who saw all God's goodness pass by him, bowed and worshipped. God promised to lead His people to the promised land.

Read Exodus 34:29-35

D. Moses Comes Down From the Mount

1. Because Moses had seen all God's goodness and glory, his face shone. It shone because God had showed him the light of the coming of Christ, Who is the Light of the world. The brightness of the salvation from sin shone from Moses' face. Moses' face reflected Jesus!

2. The Israelites were afraid when they saw Moses. They asked him to put a veil over his face. They could see the two tables of stones with the law written on them in Moses' hands, but they would not look at the reflection of Jesus in his face, the Jesus Who would come to save them when they sinned and broke the law. They asked Moses to cover the glory of Christ's grace and mercy and salvation.

3. Moses kept his shining face the rest of his life. It is possible that the shining brightness may have faded at times, but each time he went to speak with God, his face shone with the brightness of God's goodness. Then he covered it when he met the people. Read and discuss II Corinthians 3:13-15.

DO NOT FORGET that the Israelites sinned when they refused to see the light of Christ in Moses' face. We, too, see the light of Christ, not in Moses' face, but in God's Book. Ask God never to let you close your eyes to that Bible, but to look into it and see Jesus, the Light of the world.

WORD STUDIES

1. intercede — to come between two parties; to plead for others
2. cleft — an opening, a crevice

LESSON 55

The Tabernacle is Built and Feasts are Celebrated

Exodus 35:30-35; Exodus 36; Leviticus 23

BEFORE WE BEGIN, do you know that God gave the men who were in charge of building the tabernacle special gifts? Exodus 35:31 tells us that God filled them with the spirit of God, in wisdom and in understanding. God prepared men, not only with clever brains and nimble fingers, but with a deep understanding of the greatness of this holy work they were doing for God's people.

Read Exodus 35:30-35

LESSON OUTLINE

A. The Construction of the Tabernacle

1. The Lord appointed Bazaleel, the grandson of Hur, from the tribe of Judah, and Aholiab from the tribe of Dan to build the tabernacle. These talented men were experts in working with gold, silver, brass, in cutting stone, and in carving wood. Besides that, they were good teachers for those who helped them.

2. God put into the hearts of many of the Israelites to give gifts of gold and silver and precious stones; and He stirred up their hearts to work on carving wood, or with embroidery, or with gold and silver.

3. They also made the robes and the breastplates, with twelve precious stones in them, for the priests. The Lord gave special instructions for the robes of the priests, for they were God's ministers who served Him and sacrificed the offerings to Him in holiness; and their robes were pictures of the holiness of their duties.

4. Just a year after the Israelites left Egypt, the tabernacle was finished. The workers had finished it in six months. When the tabernacle was ready, God kept His promise. He came to live in His house. He came in a thick cloud, which stood above the tabernacle, and His glory filled the tabernacle. All the people could see God's Presence with them. Read about it in Exodus 40:34, 35. Do you remember that the Lord promised that His Presence would go before His people? Now the people could see Him keeping His promise.

5. As soon as Israel left Sinai, Jehovah would guide them in their travels:

a. If the cloud of His Presence stayed over the tabernacle, the Israelites did not travel.

b. If the cloud was taken up from the tabernacle, it was God's sign that they must move on.

Read Leviticus 23:4-12

B. The Passover

1. It was the fourteenth day of the first month. The tabernacle was finished and the Israelites were still at Mount Sinai. Do you remember that this was the day they were to celebrate the passover each year? Review in class how they had celebrated the passover in Egypt just a year ago. This year they did not eat the passover standing up. They did not have to hurry. They already were in the desert. And this year they had the tabernacle. This year the priests offered a perfect lamb to God on the altar in the courtyard.

2. At the end of the celebration, the Lord told the people that when they arrived in Canaan and started their farms, they must take a stem of grain (barley, which was ripe at passover time), and wave it before the Lord. Why? By holding that stem of grain before the Lord, they confessed that the crops and also their daily bread came from the hand of Jehovah. They said that God was in charge of the harvest!

C. The Feast of Firstfruits

1. The feast of the passover took place on the fourteenth day of our month of April. After seven weeks passed (49 days), on the fiftieth day God told the Israelites to celebrate the feast of firstfruits. When would that day be on our calendars?

2. At this feast the people were to bring gifts of the crops they harvested, after they had arrived in Canaan. They must wave them before the Lord, and then offer a lamb on the altar. God told them to bake loaves of bread with the grain they harvested, and wave loaves of bread before Him at the tabernacle, and praise Him, for the harvest was completed. They thanked the Lord, for He gave them their crops and their daily bread.

3. Next came the burnt offerings: a goat for a sin offering and two lambs for peace offerings. In these sacrifices, His people told the Lord that they were asking forgiveness for their sins and thanking Him for the blessing of the harvest. They were happy, for they lived at peace with God.

4. Do these feasts have anything to do with us?

a. The passover is a type of the death of Jesus for our sins. Near the end of the passover, the Israelites waved the firstfruits of grain. Paul in I Corinthians 15:20 calls Jesus' resurrection the firstfruits. Read it. The

191

feast of the passover looked forward to Jesus' death and resurrection, which we, too, celebrate in April.

b. What comes fifty days later? Pentecost, the day that God poured out His Spirit on His people. Pentecost is the New Testament feast of first-fruits. At the feast of firstfruits, the harvest in Israel was finished. At Pentecost, we celebrate the full harvest of salvation. How? We believe that Jesus died and rose for us; and at Pentecost, He gave His Spirit so we can understand it all.

Discuss in class how the Old Testament feasts
were types of our New Testament celebrations.

D. The Day of Atonement

1. On the tenth day of the seventh month (our month of October) the people stopped their work and were sad.

2. The priest put on pure white garments, a picture of holiness, and offered a ram and an ox (or bullock) for his own sins and the sins of his family. The priest then took some of the blood, some hot coals from the altar, and sweet-smelling incense. He went into the most holy place and with his fingers sprinkled the blood on the mercy seat of the ark.

3. Next, the priest cast lots between the two goats. One was chosen to be sacrificed, a type of the sacrifice of Jesus which covers all our sins.

4. The priest chose a man to lead the other goat to the desert. Before the man led the goat away, the priest laid his hand on the goat. It was a sign before all the people that they confessed their sins and laid them all on the scape goat. The goat went away, carrying the sins into the desert, just as some day Jesus would come and take away all their sins, and ours, forever. Read Leviticus 16:21, 22.

Read Leviticus 23:39-44

E. The Feast of Tabernacles

1. This feast came five days later, on the fifteenth day of the seventh month. God told the Israelites to find good trees, to cut some of their branches, and to make booths (huts) to live in for seven days for a feast of thanksgiving.

2. In the desert, while they lived in booths, the Israelites thanked the Lord for manna and quails and water. When they came to Canaan, the Israelites remembered the care and protection of God in the wilderness.

3. It was a feast of rejoicing and thanksgiving. They said the words of Deuteronomy 8:16 and 18. Read them.

DO NOT FORGET that these feasts with all their beautiful details, tell us the story of our salvation. The passover tells us how Jesus died and rose for us; the feast of firstfruits tells us that He gives His Spirit in our hearts; the day of atonement tells us that Jesus has taken away all our sins; and the feast of tabernacles tells us to thank Him and live in happiness as His children.

LESSON 56

The End of the Stay at Sinai

Leviticus 10:1-7; 24:10-16; Numbers 1:1-4

BEFORE WE BEGIN, it was almost time to leave Sinai and travel to Canaan. This lesson tells the details of the end of Israel's stay at Mt. Sinai.

Read Leviticus 10:1-7

LESSON OUTLINE

A. The Sin of Nadab and Abihu

1. Nadab and Abihu must have sinned on the very first day that the Israelites used the tabernacle. Just before this, in chapter 8, the Lord had told Moses to anoint Aaron and his sons with oil and wash them with water, and then to put on them their new priestly garments. They were ready to take over their duties as priests in the tabernacle. Moses took Aaron to the tabernacle and presented him to the Lord.

2. Aaron had offered his first sacrifice of an ox to the Lord while all the people watched. Leviticus 9:24 tells us that a special fire from the Lord burned that offering; and all the people shouted and fell on their faces because of the wonder.

3. Nadab and Abihu, Aaron's sons, helped him with the sacrifices on this special day, a day of joy and wonder! Their duty was to go into the holy place to offer incense. God's rule was that they take fiery coals from the altar of burnt offering to light the incense. Nadab and Abihu knew the rules, but they took their own fire to light the incense; and they lit the incense at the wrong time of day. God's rules were morning and evening only.

4. Nadab and Abihu ignored God's commands. They burned the incense their own way. In their hearts they were like Cain. They did not want to offer the right kind of sacrifice. They knew that the fiery coals with the blood on them were a type of the blood of Jesus; but they did not want to be covered with Jesus' blood. Just as Cain did, they came with their own ideas and their own works to God's holy place. Their sin was the sin of pride. They thought they knew better than God.

5. Remember that the altar of incense was very near to the doorway of the holy of holies. See your worksheets for Lessons 52 to 54. That is where Nadab and Abihu were standing. Jehovah in all His glory lived in the holy of holies. Suddenly the fire of the Presence of the Lord came out and burned

194

them. They were not burned to ashes, for Moses asked two young men to carry out their bodies, verse 4.

6. God sent two fires on the first day that Israel used the tabernacle:

    a. He sent the first fire in His mercy. He accepted the sacrifice which was a picture of Christ.

    b. He sent the second fire in His anger because Nadab and Abihu disobeyed Him.

7. Aaron and his two living sons might not mourn because Nadab and Abihu died. They had to take God's side, not the side of their flesh and blood sons, who hated God.

8. The Israelites were allowed to mourn, to show their sorrow, and to repent.

Read Leviticus 24:10-14

B. The Sin of the Blaspheming* Young Man

1. The Israelites were still at Mt. Sinai and Moses was still teaching them more of the laws which God had given him, when a second great sin took place.

2. Remember that some of the Egyptians had come with the Israelites out of Egypt, and some of the Israelites had married them. Those were called mixed marriages because believers married unbelievers. There were many of these mixed marriages. The Bible calls these people and their families "the mixed multitude." God told Moses that these people must live outside the camp of Israel.

3. One of the women from the tribe of Dan, Shelomith the daughter of Dibri, had married an Egyptian. When she did this, she lost her place in the camp of Israel. Their son was a mongrel*. He not only was a mixture of Egyptian and Israelite, but he was brought up in a home which was a mixture of faith and unbelief, of the church and the world.

Discuss in class the kind of life this young man had.

4. The son of this mixed marriage came into the camp and started a quarrel. It may be that he insisted that he had a right to live in the camp of Dan because his mother was a Danite. When the Danites refused, the young man committed two grievous sins.

    a. He blasphemed the name. The name is Jehovah, the covenant God of His people. In this verse the meaning of the word blaspheme is "to stab." He stabbed at Jehovah.

    b. He cursed Jehovah's people, who worshipped the name of Jehovah, particularly the men with whom he was arguing.

195

5. Jehovah gave the punishment. All who heard the young mongrel curse laid their hands on his head. The people of Israel, who were on the Lord's side, were commanded to stone him. The Lord gave a severe punishment for a serious sin. Death was the only way to get rid of this cursing mongrel, and it was a warning to the rest of Israel. Nowadays we do not stone a cursing sinner, but if he does not repent, the church excommunicates him.

C. The Marching Orders

1. Moses was finished teaching the people at Mount Sinai. It was the first day of the second month, about two weeks after they had celebrated the passover. Now God told Moses to number all the Israelites.

   a. They probably numbered the people by using Jethro's plan. Do you remember it? He suggested to divide Israel into groups of tens, fifties, hundreds, and thousands, each with a leader. It was an orderly way to count the people and report to the head of each tribe whom Moses had appointed.

   b. The Levites were numbered separately. They were the tribe who served in God's house, and they were excused from going to war. They were also arranged into three groups of priests: the sons of Gershom, of Kohath, and of Merari, and each group had its own special duties in the tabernacle. We will hear more of these priests later.

   c. The number of men over twenty years old totalled 603,550. We can estimate that the whole nation of Israel at this time numbered more than two million people.

2. Some of the princes, important men in Israel, brought gifts to Moses; six covered wagons and twelve oxen to pull the wagons. They asked Moses to give the wagons to the Levites to use to transport the tabernacle and its furnishings when they started their travels.

3. On the twentieth day of the second month, the Israelites left Mount Sinai. Moses gave them their marching orders, which are found in Numbers 10. You will find them explained on the worksheet for Lessons 55-57.

DO NOT FORGET that when Israel came to Sinai, they were an unorganized mob of people. When they left, they were an orderly nation, living according to the laws God gave them.

WORD STUDIES

1. blaspheme — to speak in an evil and irreverant manner about God or holy things
2. mongrel — someone of mixed parents; a mixed breed

LESSON 57
The Rebellion at Taberah
Numbers 10, 11

BEFORE WE BEGIN this lesson, we will picture the ceremony which took place when Israel left Mount Sinai. Jehovah lifted the cloud from the tabernacle. Then the priests blew their silver trumpets to call the people to their places for the march. When the ark of the Lord started to move, Moses said, "Rise up, Jehovah, and let thine enemies be scattered; and let them that hate thee flee before thee." At the end of each journey, Moses said, "Return, O Jehovah, unto the many thousands of Israel," chapter 10:35, 36.

Read Numbers 10:29-32

LESSON OUTLINE

A. Hobab Helps the Israelites

1. The Israelites travelled north toward Kadesh-Barnea, which was a journey of eleven days (Deut. 1:2). Find it on the map for Lessons 58 to 60.

2. Hobab, the son of Jethro (and Moses' brother-in-law), was with the Israelites at this time. He planned to go home, but Moses begged him to go to Canaan with Israel. Moses wanted his brother-in-law to help him. He used the argument that they would show Hobab the goodness which God had given to the Israelites. Why did Moses want Hobab to go with them? Because Hobab was an expert in the knowledge of the wilderness which the Israelites were ready to travel.

3. But didn't God promise to lead His people? Yes, Jehovah led them by His Presence in the cloud. But God did not tell them every detail of the strange and frightening wilderness. Hobab knew how to help the people find paths and springs of water and pastures for their animals in the desert.

4. Hobab went to the land of Canaan with the Israelites, and settled there. Later we will read about his descendants in Canaan.

Read Numbers 11:1-3

B. The First Complaint

1. While the Israelites were at Sinai, they did not complain to the Lord. Perhaps they were afraid of God's holy presence on the top of the mountain.

2. Now they were three days' journey away from the mount (about 35 to 45 miles) and they were already complaining. The Bible does not tell us what

197

they complained about. It is likely that the heat of the desert and the hardships of travelling in a rough, wild desert were the reasons for their complaints.

3. Suddenly, without warning, a fire from the Lord came down and burned some of the people. Verse 1 says it was those "that were in the uttermost parts of the camp." That is where the mixed multitude lived, those who were half Egyptians and half Israelites. These people started the complaint.

4. The people cried to Moses, and Moses prayed to the Lord, and the Lord stopped the fire. Moses named the place Taberah, which means burning.

Read verses 4-10

C. The Second Complaint

1. Instead of paying attention to God's warning, and repenting, the Israelites almost immediately started a second round of complaints. Verse 4 tells us it started again with the mixed multitude. These were the people who came along from Egypt, not because they loved the Lord, but because they thought they would be better off with the Israelites. The complaining soon spread to all Israel. Remember, there were three kinds of Israelites here in the desert:

    a. the mixed multitude who did not care about the Lord;

    b. The Israelites who were not God's chosen children, who hated the Lord;

    c. the Israelites who were God's children, who loved the Lord, but who were still sinners.

2. They complained about the food. They wanted the good foods of Egypt: fish, cucumbers, melons, leeks, onions, and garlic. They wanted these foods so badly that they stood weeping in the doorways of their tents.

3. Read once more the names of the foods the Israelites wanted (verse 5). All these good-tasting things had very little food value. The Israelites craved foods that tasted good: sweet, sour, strong, or bitter. The people lusted* for these foods, verse 4.

4. Then the Israelites sinned even more. They compared these tasty foods from Egypt with what they called "this manna." They hated and despised the manna, and they lied about it when they said, "But now our soul is dried away."

5. The truth about the manna is that it was:

    a. a wholesome, nourishing, healthful food;

    b. a tasty food — verses 7 and 8 tell us the many ways to eat it;

198

c. the bread from heaven.

6. The manna was a type of Jesus, Who says, "I am the Bread of life," John 6:35. When the Israelites despised the manna, they despised Christ. When they wanted the foods from Egypt, they wanted foods which are types of all the sinful pleasures in the evil world: the good times, and the enjoyment of their senses, not their souls.

7. The complaining of the Israelites was foolish. There were not fish to be caught in the desert. They could not grow the cucumbers, nor melons, nor the rest of the foods in the desert. These were not desert foods. Besides, they forgot that God was feeding them with the bread from heaven on their way to Canaan.

8. Do you know that the complaining of the Israelites speaks to us? The onions and garlic and leeks and melons are types of the worldly lives of ungodly men. Ungodly people lust for things which please themselves: riches, possessions, amusements, and fun. They live for the tastes of this life, and do not want to think of God.

9. The manna is a type of what God's children want more than anything, through their whole lives, for the manna is the Bread of life.

Discuss what the Bread of life does to your lives.
Read verses 11-15

D. Moses' Reaction

1. Moses was displeased. He thought the Lord should give the people meat to eat. He asked why Jehovah afflicted him. He asked why he had all the burden of this people. He complained that he could not bear it all alone. And he asked God to kill him now and take him out of his misery. Moses felt that he could not be Israel's leader any longer.

2. Moses did have great responsibilities, but what Moses said was not all true. He was exaggerating. Moses was not bearing all the burden of the Israelites. God was. Moses did not have to give the people meat to eat. God would. God was not slowly killing Moses. He was with him every minute in His love. To show His care for Moses, God gave him seventy helpers from the elders of Israel; and God gave these men the spirit of Moses so they could learn from Moses and then teach the people.

Read verses 31-35

E. God Sends Quails

1. God sent a southeast wind, which brought quails to the people, enough

199

quails to last two million people for a month. These quails stood three feet high all around the camp. For two days and a night they gathered the quails. Those who gathered the least gathered about fifty bushels.

2. Then the people ate, without thanking the Lord, and without repenting. They had quails in their stomachs and unbelief in their hearts. God had sent the quails in His anger, and in His anger He sent a plague, which killed many of the Israelites. Moses called the place Kibroth-hattaavah, which means "graves of lust."

DO NOT FORGET that I Corinthians 10:11 tells us: "Now all these things happened unto them for examples: and they are written for our admonition* upon whom the ends of the world are come."

WORD STUDIES
1. lust — a strong, overwhelming desire or need
2. admonition — a warning, advice, or caution against danger

LESSON 58
Miriam Rebels
Numbers 12

BEFORE WE BEGIN, we will find the next stop of the Israelites on the map for Lessons 58 to 60. They travelled to Hazeroth and camped there. We do not know exactly where Hazeroth was, but we know it was north of Taberah.

Read Numbers 12:1-3

LESSON OUTLINE

A. The Occasion for Miriam's Sin

1. Before we learn about the sin of Miriam (and Aaron), we must keep in our minds that they knew that Moses was called to be the leader of the Israelites. God had given Moses the signs and wonders in Egypt, and when they stayed at Mount Sinai, God chose Moses to go to the top of the mountain to hear His Words.

2. The title of this lesson is Miriam Rebels. Aaron rebelled, too. But Miriam started the sin. Miriam spoke, and Miriam was punished. We already know that Aaron had a weak character. He went along with Miriam in his weakness.

3. Miriam and Aaron complained to Moses because he had married an Ethiopian woman. Ethiopia at that time was a rather large area in Africa, southeast of Egypt. We think of Ethiopia as being the home of black people; but many of the Ethiopians at that time were not. We also know from Bible history that there were God-fearing people in Ethiopia. But that is not so important. The question is: why did Moses marry an Ethiopian?

a. He had a wife: Zipporah. Did he have two wives now? No, for then God would have scolded him for marrying the Ethiopian. Zipporah must have died.

b. Why did he not marry an Israelite woman? Probably because other Israelite women would be jealous of the one Moses chose to be his wife. Moses was a very important man in Israel, somewhat like the president in our country. Verse 3 tells us also that Moses was very meek. To avoid trouble, he was humble and married this Ethiopian.

4. God did not object to Moses' marriage. Miriam did. Moses was already more than eighty years old (Miriam was ninety) and he could take care of himself. It was really none of Miriam's business.

B. The Sin of Miriam and Aaron

1. Miriam talked to Aaron about it. Aaron listened and went with her to speak to Moses. When they complained to Moses, the real reason came out. It is in verse 2. Read that verse once more.

2. We already know that Miriam was a very talented woman. She was a quick thinker and a leader. She led the people in song after they crossed the Red Sea. In Exodus 15:20 she is called a prophetess. She was also a God-fearing woman.

3. But Miriam sinned. Her sin (and Aaron's) was really three sins bound together in one great sin:

   a. Miriam was proud. She was puffed up with her own importance. She did not want to listen to Moses anymore. She really wanted three leaders, each ruling separately. Miriam was thinking of her own honor, not of the glory of God and the good of His people.

   b. Miriam was bold. She did not have respect for the leadership of Moses, the leadership the Lord gave him.

   c. Miriam was rebellious. She wanted to split the people and take charge of some of them herself.

4. Moses was meek (verse 3). He did not answer. Yet he must have been shocked and hurt by Miriam's harsh words. Moses' meekness was a gift from God, and it was a type of the meekness of Jesus, Who said, "I am meek and lowly of heart," Matthew 11:29.

Read verses 4-9

C. Jehovah's Answer

1. Moses did not answer Miriam and Aaron because he was not the judge. He was waiting for the Lord. We read at the end of verse 2: "And the Lord heard it." Miriam and Aaron may have forgotten God for the moment, but Moses knew He would come to help him in his trouble.

2. God called Moses, Miriam, and Aaron to go to the tabernacle. Then Jehovah came down in a pillar of cloud and stood in the doorway of the tabernacle while Moses, Miriam, and Aaron were at the entrance to the courtyard.

3. God gave Miriam and Aaron two reasons why Moses was a special prophet, above all the other prophets of the Lord.

   a. The first reason is that Moses was God's faithful servant over the whole house of God. What is the "whole house of God"? It is the whole history of the Old Testament, with the prophets, priests, and kings, the sacrifices, and the laws for His people. God calls that His house. Moses laid down the rules for it. God had just given him the rules on Mt. Sinai, and Moses had written them and told them to the people. God calls it the foundation of His house. Other prophets in the Old Testament built on the foundation of Moses' laws and showed us more of the beauties of God's house. We know it was God's house because Hebrews 3:5 tells us that Moses was a servant in that house, but Christ was a Son in His own house.

Discuss in class how, after all these hundreds of years,
we still live in the same house in New Testament times.

b.   The second reason why Moses was a special prophet was that God spoke to Moses mouth to mouth. To other prophets in the Old Testament God had spoken in dreams or visions. He gave them symbols and signs and parables; and often He spoke in dark sayings they could not fully understand. But God spoke to Moses openly. It means that:

1)   Moses is the only prophet who saw a part of God.

2)   God spoke to Moses mouth to mouth, in Moses' language; and Moses could speak to God. They held conversations!

3)   God did not speak to Moses in dark sayings, hard to understand, but openly and clearly.

4.   Miriam and Aaron saw their sins:

a.   they knew they were trying to build a foundation for another house — not God's house and Moses' house — but a house built on pride and selfishness.

b.   they had refused to listen to Moses, God's true prophet, but wanted to be prophets who spoke their own words. We call them false prophets.

Read verses 10-16

D. Miriam's Leprosy

1.   Jehovah left the tabernacle in the cloud: and Miriam was covered with leprosy. With this punishment, the Lord showed her that the evil pride in her heart was like the stinking leprosy of her body.

2.   Aaron confessed his sin and begged that Miriam be healed.

3.   Moses asked the Lord to heal her, and He answered that she must be humbled for seven days. Then she would be healed.

DO NOT FORGET that pride is a horrible sin. To cure Miriam's pride, God humbled her greatly. He "spit in her face." That is what verse 14 means. God told us this story so that when we are proud, we will remember Miriam, and repent.

203

LESSON 59
The Spies are Sent Out
Numbers 13 and 14

BEFORE WE BEGIN, we will learn in this lesson that the Israelites were close to the land of Canaan, almost ready to enter it. Before they went farther, God had one more test for them. Our lesson will tell whether they passed or failed the test.

Read Numbers 13:3, 17-20

LESSON OUTLINE

A. The Spies Are Sent Out

1. From Hazeroth, the Israelites travelled to Kadesh. Find it on the map on your worksheet. Kadesh is southwest of Canaan, but the exact spot is not known.

2. Moses told the people not to be afraid, for it was time to get ready to possess the land of Canaan. The people, however, asked whether they might first send spies to learn more about the land of Canaan. Read Deuteronomy 1:20 - 22.

3. It was not wrong to send out spies. It would help the Israelites to know what the land looked like and how strong their enemies were. But we must remember, through this whole lesson, that most of the Israelites were unbelievers, who did not want to go to Canaan; and they were afraid because they did not trust in the Lord.

4. Moses agreed to send out twelve spies. He chose one man from each tribe except the tribe of Levi. He gave the spies two duties:

a. to report on the kind of land they found: rich or poor, good or bad, and to bring back some of the fruits of the land;

b. to report whether the people were strong or weak, few or many, and whether they lived in strong, walled cities.

Read verses 21-33

B. The Spies Are Sent Out

1. The spies did a thorough job. They went from the south, through Hebron, to Hamath in the north. Find these places on your maps. They stayed in Canaan for forty days. They took back with them fruits of the land: the cluster of grapes which two men carried, besides figs and pomegranates*.

2. All the people of Israel came together to hear their reports: for they came back with two reports. Ten spies brought back the majority report; and two spies, Joshua and Caleb, brought the minority report.

3. The majority spoke first. They said two things:

    a. It was a land flowing with milk and honey, which means that it was a good land, a fertile country, with bountiful harvests.

    b. There were many strong men in the land. All the powerful Canaanites lived there, even giants; and their cities had very strong walls.

4. These ten spies should have turned their report around and said, "The land is filled with strong enemies, but the land is good and worth fighting for."

5. Caleb interrupted the report of the ten spies, and said the words of verse 30. Read them.

6. Then the ten spies showed the real purpose of their report: in verse 31 they said, "We be not able to go up against the people." They changed their report, too, and exaggerated in two ways. Now they said:

    a. The land eats up the people, meaning that it does not yield enough food for the people. That was a lie. They had just said the opposite.

    b. All the people are tall giants, and we felt like grasshoppers. The people of the land saw us as grasshoppers, too!

7. Why was this report so evil?

    a. The majority (the ten spies) looked around them at the people, and at their strength. They did not look up to the God of the wonder.

    b. They were filled with unbelief. They forgot the victories in Egypt and in the desert, which God had given them; and they said, "We be not able to go up against the people."

Read chapter 14:1-10

C. The Reaction of the People of Israel

1. Most of the Israelites were God's people in name only. In their hearts they did not love Him, and they did not want to obey Him. Most of the people felt just like the ten spies felt. They, too, were filled with unbelief.

2. The unbelieving Israelites banded together, discussed the report of the spies, murmured against Moses, and said they wished they had died in Egypt. Then they stood weeping in the doors of their tents. They were not sad, but angry and rebellious. They cried so that Moses and Aaron and the rest of Israel would hear them.

3. They wept in self-pity, to get the sympathy of the rest of Israel. Why? They did not want to go to the promised land, the picture of heaven. They were not interested in serving Jehovah, and they hated His strict laws. They wanted to return to Egypt, verse 3. They said in verse 2, "Would God that we had died in the land of Egypt." Anything was better than serving God. They would rather go to hell with the Egyptians.

4. They put all the blame on Moses and suggested getting for themselves a new captain to take them back to Egypt, verse 4. By saying this, they showed that they despised the prophet Moses, whom God had given them.

5. Not all of the people accepted the majority report. God's children listened to the minority report of Joshua and Caleb, and believed them. These two spies were so sad and disappointed with the majority report that they tore their clothes and spoke to Israel. They told the people exactly the opposite of the majority report, for they spoke to the people with faith in their hearts:

    a. they said that the land was very good;

    b. that the Canaanites lived without strong defenses and could easily be conquered;

    c. if the Lord took delight in them, He would give them the land;

    d. they warned the people not to rebel and not to be afraid, for the Lord was with them.

6. What did the majority of Israel do? They tried to stone Joshua and Caleb. They wanted to kill God's servants because they did not want to hear the truth.

7. Jehovah heard the rebellious words of the wicked people and He asked Moses two questions. Read them in verse 11.

Read verses 13-16

D. Once Again Moses Intercedes for the People

1. In anger God told Moses He would kill the people with a plague and make a great nation of Moses.

2. Moses understood that most of the people had sinned, but would God really destroy all His people, the whole nation of Israel? That meant that God would destroy His church. God could not destroy His church!

3. Moses pleaded with the Lord in this way:

    a. The Egyptians will hear about it and tell all the countries that Jehovah was not able to bring His people to Canaan, that the sinners were more powerful than God. Moses begged God to show His glory to all the world, and bring Israel to Canaan by His power.

b. He asked Jehovah to forgive His people who had sinned. Moses begged God for mercy.

4. God answered Moses.

a. He promised to pardon the sins of His own children;

b. He promised to judge and destroy the wicked majority of Israel, who had tempted him ten times and who would not fear Him.

E. The Result for the Israelites

1. God told Israel that He would give them their wish — that they could die in this wilderness (verse 33). The Israelites would not go into Canaan, but wander in the wilderness for forty years, one year for each day the spies were gone.

2. Everyone older than twenty years would die in the desert (verse 29), even those who feared the Lord, except Joshua and Caleb.

> Discuss in class how God's people
> often must suffer with the ungodly.
> Give some examples.

3. God showed to Israel that His justice would not let the evil spies live. He sent a plague which killed the ten spies. But God-fearing Joshua and Caleb were spared, verses 37, 38.

DO NOT FORGET that in the nation of Israel the people who loved the Lord, who were His true church, were few; and the worldly Israelites far outnumbered them. In all the history of the world, in the time in which we live, too, the church is small and weak, and evil men are strong and powerful in this world.

WORD STUDIES

pomegranate — a reddish fruit about the size of an orange. Inside is red pulp with many seeds.

LESSON 60
Korah, Dathan, and Abiram Rebel
Numbers 14:40-45; 16:1-35

BEFORE WE BEGIN, when ungodly men discover the consequences of their sins, they are quick to say, "We have sinned," Numbers 14:40. These men knew they were wrong, but they were not sorry for their sins. This lesson will show us how they still followed their stubborn ways.

Read Numbers 14:40-45

LESSON OUTLINE
A. Another Unsuccessful Rebellion

1. After Jehovah told the rebels to turn around and wander in the wilderness, they decided that they wanted to go to fight the Amalekites and the Canaanites after all. They were ready to go to the land the Lord had promised. But these were wicked men, and the Lord had not promised the land to them!

2. Moses warned them that they would be defeated and killed by their enemies, for the Lord was not with them.

3. They went anyway, and the Amalekites (the same tribe they fought at Rephidim) and the Canaanites defeated them and pursued them to Hormah, which was twenty-five miles north of Kadesh.

Read chapter 16:1-3

B. Korah, Dathan, and Abiram Come to Moses

1. Jehovah had told the people to leave Kadesh and start marching toward the Red. Sea. The people did not want to obey, and most likely stayed right there at Kadesh. (Read Deuteronomy 1:45, 46.) It was probably while the Israelites were still wandering around Kadesh that the rebellion of Korah, Dathan, and Abiram broke out.

2. Korah was a Levite and Dathan and Abiram were Reubenites. These men had been stirring up a rebellion for some time, for they already had two hundred fifty princes, leaders in the tribes of Israel, and a large number of the people who followed them.

3. When Korah, Dathan, and Abiram said to Moses and Aaron, "Ye take too much upon you" (verse 3), they had two reasons for their complaint:

    a. Especially Dathan and Abiram wanted the right to rule. They had enough of the leadership of Moses, whom God had chosen.

b. Korah, a Levite, wanted to take Aaron's place as priest.

4. Their reason was that "all the congregation are holy," verse 3. They did not believe that God spoke only through Moses. They said they were God's people, too; and they wanted to go to Canaan, the promised land. They paid no attention to the fact that now God forbade them to go, and they accused Moses of being stubborn. These three rebels were filled with an unholy pride.

Read verses 4-15

C. Moses' Answer

1. Moses fell on his face when he heard the rebellious words. Then he spoke to Korah and all the men who were with him. Tomorrow Jehovah would choose who was holy.

2. He told Korah and his fellow Levites to take their censers*. These Levites must already have burned incense at the tabernacle, as helpers to the priests, but not in the holy place, at the altar of incense; for only Aaron and his sons might go into the holy place. That is why Korah and his men wanted to get rid of Aaron. They wanted to burn incense in the holy place where the Lord lives. They all wanted to be priests!

3. When Moses called Dathan and Abiram, they refused to come. They gave these reasons:

a. Moses had brought them out of a land flowing with milk and honey. That was the land of Egypt, the land of Pharaoh, the land of sin and idol-worship. What Dathan and Abiram were saying was that Egypt was the promised land.

b. Moses brought them into the desert to kill them.

c. Moses failed as a leader. He did not bring them into Canaan, as he had promised.

Discuss why Dathan and Abiram said
the opposite of the truth in verses 13 and 14.

Read verses 16-30

D. The Test

1. When Moses heard the proud words of these men, he prayed to Jehovah, and he did two things:

a. He asked God not to accept the offerings of these men.

b. He told Korah and his men to come to the tabernacle the next day and take with them their censers with incense in them. This rebellion must end, for the Lord would choose, before all the people, the men whom He had chosen to be His holy priests. Aaron must come, too.

2. The next day Korah and his two hundred fifty princes came with their censers to the tabernacle. They came, not to obey Moses, but to show that they were equal to Aaron. They were priests, too! The fire which burned the incense did not come from the altar of burnt offering, as God had commanded. They brought their own fire. Their sin was the sin of Nadab and Abihu all over again.

3. Verse 19 tells us that the congregation joined Korah and his princes. He had a large following in Israel. Dathan and Abiram did not come. They would not accept Moses as their leader, nor come to put Moses' leadership to a test. They ignored his command.

4. Now the wicked rebels stood at the door of the tabernacle with Moses and Aaron. Suddenly the glory of the Lord appeared. He told Moses and Aaron to separate themselves from the congregation of the rebels, for He would destroy them in His holy anger. Once more Moses interceded for the people, and told Jehovah that it was after all the sin of one man, Korah.

5. Jehovah heard Moses' prayer. He told Moses and the congregation to stay away from the tents of Korah, Dathan, and Abiram. By moving away from these rebels, the congregation was showing that they did not stand with the rebels, but that they hated their wickedness.

6. Next, Moses went to Dathan and Abiram because they would not come to him at the tabernacle. With the elders following him, he went to their tents and told these men that the judgment of the Lord was coming.

7. The people obeyed Moses and left the rebels. Why were they ready to obey?

    a. The people were afraid. They had seen the glory of the Lord and they knew judgment was coming.

    b. Dathan and Abiram and their families stood at their tent doors in pride and hatred and unbelief, ready to show that Moses was wrong.

8. Now Moses was ready to announce the test. Read it in verses 29 and 30.

Read verses 31-35

E. The Punishment

1. Korah, Dathan, and Abiram and their households were buried alive, a horrible, frightening death. As they went down into the depths of the earth, the Lord was giving His people a sign that they were going to the depth of hell forever.

210

2. A fire, the symbol of God's hot anger, burned the two hundred fifty princes in the sight of all Israel. The punishment for these sins shows us what a terrible evil it is to sin against God's holiness.

DO NOT FORGET that when God commanded His people to separate themselves from these ungodly men, He tells us that we must do the same. We can never have friends who are not God's children. We cannot be friends with the world and be saved with God's people.

WORD STUDIES

censer — a small pan for burning incense

LESSON 61

The Blossoming of Aaron's Rod

Numbers 16:36 - 17:13

BEFORE WE BEGIN, can you imagine how horrified the people of Israel were to see three families drop down into the earth, and two hundred fifty princes burn to death by the fire of the Lord's anger? In today's lesson, we will learn that the Lord made a memorial, so Israel would always remember this day.

Read Numbers 16:36-40

LESSON OUTLINE

A. The Memorial

1. The Lord told Moses that Eleazar, Aaron's son, was to pick up the two hundred fifty censers from the fire which had destroyed the princes. They were holy censers, for incense had been offered in them to the Lord.

2. God instructed Eleazar to use the brass of these censers for a covering for the altar, so that the Israelites would always remember that no stranger, but only Aaron and his seed might offer incense before the Lord in His tabernacle.

Read verses 41-45

B. The People Murmur

1. Suddenly the congregation of Israel made this astonishing statement to Moses: "Ye have killed the people of the Lord." They said it immediately after they had seen God's wonders.

2. That statement was a double lie:

    a. They charged Moses and Aaron with killing these men. They knew better, for Moses had called on the Lord to open the earth, verse 30.

    b. They called the rebels the people of God.

3. Didn't the people know any better? Of course, they did. The reason for all their rebellion was that they did not want to obey the Lord and go back to their journeys in the desert. They knew the truth: that Moses was God's chosen leader; but they did not want the truth. They did not want the truth because they did not want God.

Discuss in class how the ungodly people in our day
show that they do not want God in their lives.
Give examples.

Read verses 41-50

C. The Plague

1. All the murmurings of the people took place near the tabernacle. As they stood there, something at the tabernacle drew their attention. The cloud of Jehovah's glory which usually rested above the tabernacle now covered it. And through the cloud the glory of the Lord shone, verse 42.

2. Jehovah called Moses and Aaron to separate themselves from the people, for without warning, a plague from the Lord had begun. We do not know what kind of plague it was.

3. Moses told Aaron to go quickly and get fire from the altar, and his censer, and burn incense on it, in the middle of the people who were dying from the plague. Why?

    a. Because Moses had faith that Jehovah would not kill all His people, His church. He had faith that God would not kill him nor Aaron when they went into the middle of the plague.

    b. Because the incense was a picture of praying to God for mercy.

    c. Because the fire for the incense, with the blood of the sacrifice in it, was a type of the blood of Jesus, which covered the sins of His people.

4. Aaron hurried. It could not have taken more than a few minutes to get his censer. But when he went into the congregation of Israel, he stood between the living and the dead. Already 14,700 people had died.

5. God accepted the prayers of Moses and Aaron and the blood which was a type of the blood of Christ, and He stopped the plague in His mercy to His people.

Read Numbers 17:1-9

D. The Sign of the Blossoming Rod

1. The Lord had already given the Israelites a sign which showed them that only Aaron and his seed were called to be priests. The sign was the brass covering for the altar made from the two hundred fifty brass censers. But the people paid no attention to it.

2. This time the Lord chose a more vivid sign, a sign which the congregation of Israel could not ignore. The Lord instructed Moses to ask each of the twelve princes, who were leaders of the twelve tribes, to take a rod to the tabernacle. Each prince must write the name of his tribe on his rod, and Aaron must put his own name on the rod of the tribe of Levi, because Aaron was God's chosen priest. These rods were very likely sceptres which each prince used when he ruled his tribe.

3. God told Moses to put the rods in the most holy place (or the holy of holies), where God met with His people, verse 4. The next day, when Moses went into the holy of holies, he saw a wonder. Aaron's rod had not only sprouted buds, but blossoms, and fruit — almonds. This wonder happened overnight. All the other rods were still dead sticks.

E. The Lesson of the Blossoming Rod

1. Why did God choose this sign to teach the people that He chose only Aaron to be priest? Remember that the question was: "Can't we all be priests?" What did it really mean to be a priest? A priest gave himself with his whole being to the Lord, in love. He was consecrated* to God. The rebels could not be priests. They were consecrated to themselves!

2. By the sign of Aaron's blossoming rod, God was teaching all His people, also the wicked rebels, what it meant to be a priest of God. The rod told the beautiful story of salvation. Pay attention to both parts of a, b, and c.

a. Once Aaron's rod was alive, when it was a branch of a tree.
Once Adam was alive to God, without any sin.

b. Then Aaron's rod was cut off the tree and became a dead stick.
Then Adam fell into sin, died, and all his seed died with him.

c. By a wonder, God made Aaron's rod live again, and bear fruit.
By a wonder, God made His dead sinners alive again, and able to bear the fruits of righteousness.

3. By the wonder of the blossoming of Aaron's rod, God showed the people of Israel that without His grace, they were just like the dead sticks which Moses laid before the Lord in the tabernacle. The Lord taught them that there was only one way to become alive again: only by the wonder of God's grace, the wonder of Jesus Christ, Who was coming to earth to die and to wash away their sins.

4. But there is still a question. Did not Jesus die for all His chosen people? Yes, He did. Why then could only the priests offer incense in the tabernacle? The answer is that in Old Testament times, God chose Aaron and his seed to be types of God's great High Priest, Jesus Christ. Only Aaron and his sons could offer the sacrifices which were types of Jesus making His people alive and bearing fruits of good works, as Aaron's rod bore fruits.

Read verses 10-13

F. The Effect of the Blossoming Rod

1. The people came to Moses in great fear. They said that whoever came to

the tabernacle would die. That was a lie. Only the wicked who came with their own good works would die.

2.   These evil people ended by asking a hopeless question: "Shall we all die?" The answer is: "Not if you repent." But they did not want to repent. They would rather be consumed by dying. All unbelievers, who do not have God's grace, choose eternal death, as the evil Israelites did.

DO NOT FORGET that after Jesus came and died, all the types of the Old Testament were finished. Now Jesus lives by His Spirit in our hearts, and His Spirit guides us so that we want to live consecrated lives in His service.

WORD STUDIES

consecrate — to set apart as holy, to dedicate

LESSON 62
Forty Years of Wandering
Numbers 20:1-13

BEFORE WE BEGIN to study the next event which happened in the wilderness, we will take a look at the Israelites as they wandered in the desert for forty years.

LESSON OUTLINE
A. The Wanderings

1. After the Israelites had left Mt. Sinai, had arrived at Kadesh and sent out the spies, they had been in the desert one year and a half. At that time, because of their sin of rebellion, God told them they must wander forty years in the desert until everyone over twenty years old had died. It meant that they had thirty-eight and a half years left for the rest of their desert wanderings.

2. They wandered back and forth, without any purpose, between Kadesh and Ezion-Geber. Find these places on your map on the worksheet for Lessons 61 to 63. The Lord tells us of only one event during those forty years: the rebellion of Korah, Dathan, and Abiram, which we already studied. Numbers 33:18-36 gives us the names of the places at which they camped, but we know nothing more about these places. Take a look at the list of names. These places tell us the story of a dreadful time of hardship, sadness, and death.

3. At last the wanderings ended. Almost all the people who were twenty years or older at the time that the spies were sent out were dead. Joshua and Caleb, the two spies who brought the good report, and Moses, Aaron, and Miriam had not died. God promised Joshua and Caleb that they would enter Canaan.

4. Read chapter 20:1. "The first month" was the first month of the fortieth year of their wanderings, and the Israelites were back at Kadesh. The forty years were at last over. Just as the people were ready to start out for Canaan, Miriam died and was buried. Now only Moses and Aaron were left as leaders.
Read Numbers 20:2-9

B. Israel Murmurs

1. A great change had taken place in the congregation of Israel. Almost all the people older than twenty years old had died. The small children who had

come out of Egypt were now grown up, and were the leaders in Israel. These grown-up children and young people were God's church in the desert. Were they different from their complaining, murmuring parents? No.

2. Verse two informs us that they had no water. This is what they did:

   a. They came together to murmur against Moses and Aaron.

   b. They used the same words their parents had used.

   1) We wish we had died in the desert, as our relatives died.

   2) Why did you bring us to this evil place?

   3) There is nothing good to eat here, no figs nor pomegranates.

   4) We have no water.

3. Moses and Aaron went to the door of the tabernacle and fell on their faces. Jehovah's glory came to them, and the Lord told Moses to take his rod, which was probably kept in the tabernacle, and to get the congregation together at a rock close by. When they all arrived at the rock, God told Moses he must speak to that rock, and He promised that abundant water would flow from it, enough for all the people and their animals.

Read verses 10-13

C. Moses' Fall Into Sin

1. Moses took the rod, as the Lord had told him. He and Aaron gathered the people before the rock. That is as far as Moses' obedience went.

2. Then he disobeyed the Lord by doing two things:

   a. He spoke angrily to the people: "Hear now, ye rebels; must we fetch you water out of the rock?"

   b. He struck the rock twice instead of speaking to it.

3. Did Moses do this because he misunderstood the Lord? No. Moses, the man who had been meek and patient with the Israelites for forty years, was disappointed, bitter, and angry. He was so angry that he called God's people rebels. Read what Psalm 106:32, 33 says about him.

4. Why was Moses so angry? Because Moses was guilty of the sin of unbelief. God says it in verse 12: "Because ye believed me not." What was Moses' unbelief?

   a. His unbelief was not that God did not have the power to give the people water from the rock,

   b. but that God would not give water to these rebels because they did not deserve it.

5. Moses' second sin was that he refused to sanctify God in the sight of the

217

people of Israel, verse 12. What does that mean? It means that Moses refused to give God the glory of His holiness; for God, through Moses, would show His holiness by giving His people water and by making the rebels ashamed.

6. Moses did not understand why God wanted to give the people water. He was so bitterly disappointed with the people that he thought God's cause was hopeless. All he saw in Israel were rebels. That is why he said, "Must we fetch you water out of the rock?" Moses meant to say that he would never give God's people water. He would rather let God's people die. That was a great sin. But Moses thought that God's true church in the wilderness was lost. He thought that all God's children had died. That is also why he struck the rock twice in his anger: not to bring water, but to show the Israelites that God would not give water to rebels.

Discuss in class why this was a serious sin.
Did not Moses have good reasons to be angry with the rebels?

7. Moses could not see, at that moment, that he was speaking in anger to God's covenant seed. They were there in the desert, alongside the rebels. And Moses did not act as a mediator, a go-between for God and His people.

D. The Punishment

1. Because of his sin, Moses was not allowed to lead Israel into the land of promise. Moses himself was not allowed to enter Canaan, but, worse still, God took away his leadership. Someone else would lead Israel into Canaan.

2. Why was this such a serious sin? Because Moses failed as a mediator. He did not pray for God's people and did not beg God to forgive them. He almost brought them into Canaan. Then, because of his sin, he failed.

DO NOT FORGET that Moses was a type of Christ, but a very imperfect type. God's people needed a better mediator than Moses. Soon Joshua would be their leader. Joshua was also a type of Jesus, Who takes His people into the perfect promised land. He paid the perfect price for His people, the price of dying for them, and He will never fail them.

LESSON 63
Israel Goes Around Edom
Numbers 20:14-21:9

BEFORE WE BEGIN, we left Israel at Kadesh, at the waters of Meribah. Meribah means striving or arguing — with God. The name of the place continually reminded them of their sin.

Read Numbers 20:14-21

LESSON OUTLINE

A. Moses Sends Messengers to Edom

   1. In order to understand this lesson, you will first do the map work on your worksheet. Have your finished map on your desks. You have drawn two lines showing the routes the Israelites could take to Canaan. There is also a third choice: straight north from Kadesh, right into Canaan. That would be an easy way. But in His wisdom God chose to lead Israel around the east side of the Dead Sea.

   2. The way around the Dead Sea presented a problem for the Israelites. The land of Edom was in their way. They had two choices:

       a. to get permission to travel through Edom;

       b. or to go the long way around Edom.

   3. Moses sent messengers to Edom to try to get permission to march through their land.

B. The Message

   1. Before we follow the messengers to Edom, remember that the Lord led His people into this difficult situation. Remember, too, that He was ruling His people during these hard times.

   2. Moses told his messengers to ask the king of Edom a simple and a reasonable question: May we pass through your country?

   3. The messengers showed the king why he did not have to hesitate to say yes.

       a. They promised to walk only on the highways. They would not trample the fields and vineyards, and they would do no damage.

       b. If they needed water, they would pay for it.

       c. Besides, Moses instructed the messengers to start their request by saying, "Thus saith thy brother Israel." Edom and Israel were twin

219

brothers, descendants of the twins, Jacob and Esau. Surely Edom would help its twin-brother-nation of Israel. In fact, they might even welcome Israel by giving them some of the fruits from their fields.

d. Another reason was that Edom would feel sorry for the Israelites. The messengers told the king of Edom about all the hardships they lived through in Egypt and the wilderness. Now they would welcome some kind treatment.

e. They told the king of Edom that Jehovah had led them in all their hardships. They were the people of Jehovah, the Lord of heaven and earth. Surely Edom would help Jehovah's chosen people!

4. The question of the messengers of Moses is a type of the question of God's church today. We, as the members of God's church, are pilgrims wandering to heaven, just as the Israelites were. On our way we must pass through the wicked Edom of this world. Wicked people in this world surround us; and we must ask them for room to pass through. How do we do that? We ask for freedom to worship Jehovah, for freedom to learn God's fear in separate Christian schools. We tell them the reason: we are God's chosen people, just passing through this world.

C. The Answer

1. Read the king's answer in verse 18. It was a flat no, with a threat that he would use weapons of war. After the messengers emphasized once more that they would only pass through and do no harm, the king of Edom gathered his soldiers and came out against Israel. He showed Israel that he would enforce his refusal with war. And Israel turned back.

2. Why did the king of Edom refuse? Because he and his people hated God's people. There was no place for Israel in wicked Edom.

3. Edom was a picture of the evil world all through history. The purpose of the world always is to destroy God's church by persecuting, torturing, and killing His people, just as Edom wanted to do to Israel. All through the Old Testament, the wicked nations hated Israel. When Jesus finally came, the world said, "We will not let You pass through. We will kill You." They killed Him in their awful hatred of God.

Discuss in class why it is the best way for Israel and for us
to travel through the hatred and persecution of the evil world.

Read verses 22-29

D. Aaron Dies

1. The Israelites were at the border of Edom, at the foot of Mount Hor. Although it is on your map, no one is exactly sure just where it was.

2. The Lord told Moses and Aaron that it was time for Aaron to die; and He told them just what they must do:

    a. Aaron must die in the desert. Because he had sinned with Moses at the waters of Meribah, he was not allowed to enter Canaan. God did not even let him see the land.

    b. God told Moses, Aaron, and Eleazar to go up the mountain together. In the sight of the people, Moses took off Aaron's priestly robes and put them on Eleazar. Then Aaron died. God does not give us the details of how he died or was buried. Moses and Eleazar came down the mountain alone.

    c. Aaron died. But the priesthood continued. When Moses went up Mt. Hor, he went up with the high priest Aaron. He came down with the high priest Eleazar. He was showing Israel that Aaron and Eleazar were weak and sinful types of the great High Priest, Jesus Christ, Who will always live with His people.

Read Numbers 21:4-9

E. The Serpent of Brass

1. The Israelites started their long, hot journey through the great and terrible wilderness around the country of Edom. Verse 4 tells us that they went by the way of the Red Sea, for the Gulf of Akaba was a fork of the Red Sea. They may have been past Ezion-Geber (find it on your maps) and starting north toward Canaan; for in that area many serpents are found.

2. Try to understand how the people felt:

    a. They were disappointed because they were not allowed to march the easy way through Edom.

    b. They were discouraged because of the hardships of living for so many years in the wild and dangerous wilderness.

    c. They had no food other than the manna, and they said, "Our soul loatheth (hates) this light bread." There was no water.

    d. They did not believe that God would bring them to the land of Canaan. They rebelled and said that Moses brought them into the wilderness to die.

3. The Lord sent an immediate punishment. He sent fiery serpents. This was a land of serpents, and now the Lord sent them in large numbers. The

serpents were fiery because their poisonous bites burned, and caused many of the people to die.

4.   The burning poison of the snake bites was a symbol of the burning poison of sin in their hearts. The Israelites knew that their hearts were full of the deadly poison of sin, and they repented and were sorry and asked God to take away the serpents.

5.   God heard them and gave them a sign. He told Moses to make a serpent of brass and put it on a pole. Those who looked at the serpent were healed. Some, who looked without faith, were healed only in their bodies. God's people, who looked at the brass serpent by faith, were healed from their sins, too.

6.   Read John 3:14, 15. Now you know that the serpent on the pole was a picture of Jesus on the cross. How was the serpent a type of Jesus?

   a.   The serpent, who was a type of the power of sin, was lifted up. Jesus, Who took away the curse of sin, had to be lifted up on the cross to take away those sins.

   b.   The brass serpent was a symbol of the serpent's power to kill. Jesus on the cross took away the serpent's power to kill God's children.

   c.   The brass serpent shone brightly in the camp. It meant life to those who looked at it. Jesus, the Light of the World, gave us life through His death on the cross.

DO NOT FORGET that the Israelites were saved by faith. When they looked at the brass serpent with a look of faith, they were healed. When we look at our Savior with a look of faith, we are healed from our sins.

LESSON 64
On the East Side of the Jordan River
Numbers 21:21-22:20

BEFORE WE BEGIN, the Israelites had traveled around the country of Edom and were at last very close to the land of Canaan. Do the map work for Lessons 64 to 66 before you start this lesson.

Read Numbers 21:21-26

LESSON OUTLINE

A. The Battles With the Amorites

1. In your map work, you showed that the Israelites marched around the country of Moab, crossed the River Arnon, and avoided the territory* of the Ammonites. So far, they did not have to fight any enemies. But when they came to the territory of the powerful Amorites, the descendants of Canaan, the son of Ham, they came to strong armies and fortified* cities. Deuteronomy 3:5 tells us that "All these cities were fenced with high walls, gates, and bars." The Amorites had taken much land away from the Moabites and the Ammonites.

2. Before the Israelites entered the land of the Amorites, they sent messengers to Sihon, king of the Amorites. Read the message in verse 22. It was God's message to Sihon, for God was speaking to him through the mouths of the messengers.

3. Sihon did not listen to the messengers. In Deuteronomy 2:30 we read that "the Lord hardened his spirit, and made his heart obstinate." God wanted Sihon to say no, because He wanted Israel to fight and to win. Before they started a battle with Sihon, God told them that, "I have given into thy hand Sihon the Amorite, king of Heshbon," Deuteronomy 2:24. Their victory was a gift from God and was already won in God's counsel*.

Read verses 33-35

4. On your maps, find Edrei. The Israelites travelled north, conquering many cities, until they came to Edrei. There they conquered Og, king of Bashan, and fought until no more people were alive.

5. These were not ordinary battles in an ordinary war. The victories of the Israelites were wonders of the goodness and grace of Jehovah for His covenant people. Jehovah gave them these victories because:

a. He wanted to put the "fear of thee upon the nations that are under the whole heaven," Deuteronomy 2:25. He wanted the heathen nations to fear, not Israel, but Israel's God.

b. He wanted the nations to know that He is the God of the wonder. That is why He gave the Israelites victories with amazing speed.

c. He wanted to encourage the Israelites. They would have many more battles to fight, and these victories would spur them on.

d. He wanted the land on this side of the Jordan River conquered; for later this land would be the home of two and a half tribes of Israel.

Read Numbers 22:1-6

B. Balak is Afraid

1. Suddenly, the whole territory on the east of the Jordan belonged to Israel; and Balak, the king of Moab, was filled with fear when he saw that Israel had easily conquered the Amorites, the strongest nation on this side of Jordan.

2. Balak saw that the Israelites were camped in the Plain of Moab (which had formerly belonged to Moab) and were ready to cross the Jordan River to go into Canaan.

3. Read verse 4 once more. Balak needed the help of Midian, not to fight the Israelites, for they knew they could not win, but to curse Israel.

4. These two nations sent messengers to Balaam the son of Beor. Before we follow them, we will learn what kind of man Balaam was.

a. His name means destroyer, and probably came from the fact that people thought that he had the power to curse, and that his curses came true. The heathen in those days believed in the power of magic spells and magic charms.

b. He lived in Pethor, by the river. The river was most likely the great River Euphrates in Mesopotamia, the land from which Abraham came. We do not know whether he was a descendant of Abraham, but we do know that some of the people there still had some knowledge of Jehovah, probably handed down from father to son. And they may have heard of the wonders of Jehovah in Egypt and in the wilderness. Balaam knew about God.

c. But he did not love God. II Peter 2:15 says that he "loved the wages of unrighteousness," and Revelation 2:14 tells us that he "cast a stumbling block before the children of Israel." He was an evil man.

d. Balaam was a prophet. He spoke about God. But he was a false prophet and a hypocrite*.

224

Discuss in class what a hypocrite is
and whether it is possible to know if someone is a hypocrite.

5.   King Balak knew that the Israelites were God's people and that their God loved them and gave them great victories. But his idea was to tell Balaam to ask God to change His mind and curse His people.

Read verses 7-14

C. The Messengers Go To Balaam

1.   The messengers came with great rewards to persuade Balaam to curse God's people. They wanted Balaam to change God's mind by praying to Him. If he succeeded, he would get paid with great riches for cursing God's people.

2.   Balaam was flattered and honored by the visit of the high officials of the governments of Midian and Moab, and he did not mind using prayer to God to get rich.

3.   When Balaam heard their request that he curse the people whom God had blessed, he should have told the messengers that they had asked the impossible. He should have refused to listen and said good-bye.

4.   Instead, Balaam asked for a little more time. If the messengers stayed over night, he said he would ask permission of the Lord. Didn't Balaam know what the Lord's answer would be? Certainly, he did. He knew he could not even say to Jehovah, "Let me curse Thy people."

5.   Balaam never intended to ask God's permission. His words were just an excuse. He wanted some time to think, for he had a problem:

   a.   He wanted the riches the messengers had taken for him;

   b.   But he was afraid of the anger of Jehovah. He must have known that God always blesses His people, and only His people, and curses all the wicked who hate His people.

   c.   He could not choose both the riches of Moab and the blessing of God. What would he do?

6.   God solved the problem. He came to Balaam during the night and said the words of verse 12. Read it.

7.   Balaam told the messengers, "The Lord refuseth to give me leave to go with you." He meant, "I would really like to go with you, but I may not." So the messengers went home to report to King Balak.

Read verses 15-20

D. The Messengers Go to Balaam a Second Time

1.   King Balak thought that Balaam refused because he wanted more money

and more honor. This time Balak sent more important men and more riches.

2.　Balaam knew that Jehovah always blessed Israel and that He would never let them be cursed. That is why he said to the second group of messengers, "I cannot go beyond the word of the Lord my God," verse 18. What Balaam meant was, "But I wish I could!"

3.　Again the messengers stayed over night, and again God came to Balaam. Read the words God spoke to Balaam in verse 20.

DO NOT FORGET that sometimes the Lord allows the wicked to go on in their sin and to walk right into the hot anger of God. This is what Balaam was doing. We will learn the consequences of Balaam's stubborn sin in our next lesson.

WORD STUDIES

1.　territory — a tract of land, over which there usually is a ruler
2.　fortified — strengthened against attacks of enemies
3.　counsel — God's plan which He made from eternity, and which God sees as already finished
4.　hypocrite — one who pretends to be honest, sincere, and godly, but is not

LESSON 65

Balaam Blesses Israel

parts of Numbers 22, 23, 24

BEFORE WE BEGIN, we know, and Balaam knew, that God always blesses His people. Jehovah said about Israel, "They are blessed." But Balaam set out to curse the people whom Jehovah blessed. Why? He knew better, but he wanted to sin. He was foolish in his sin. Sin is always foolish.

Read Numbers 22:21-35

LESSON OUTLINE

A. Balaam Goes Along with the Messengers

1. God could have forbidden Balaam to go with the messengers to curse Israel. But it was God's will that Balaam go his foolish way and walk right into His anger. It was His purpose, through Balaam's words, to show His glory to all the nations.

2. From Balaam's point of view, he was willing to curse God's people. He foolishly made himself think that Jehovah had given him permission to curse Israel, and he left that impression with the messengers. Spiritually, his eyes were blinded by his greed for riches and honor. He had eyes only for earthly treasures. In his heart, he had no thought or love for God.

3. He took his donkey and went with the princes of Moab. The Lord let him start out on his journey. Why? It was the Lord's purpose to humble Balaam and to show him that he was blinder and more foolish than his ass. In His anger, God used the donkey to teach him what a fool he was before the living God.

4. The Angel of Jehovah stood before the ass. This Angel was not an ordinary angel, but the Christ of the Old Testament. You will remember that the Angel of Jehovah showed Himself in Old Testament times. He came to His people to encourage them. (Think of Abraham.) And sometimes He appeared in His hot anger to evil men who hate Jehovah. Three times the Angel of Jehovah appeared to the ass:

   a. the first time near an open field, where the donkey could step aside. Balaam whipped her back onto the path;

   b. the second time in a narrow place with walls on both sides, where she pushed against the wall and crushed Balaam's foot, and again Balaam whipped her;

227

c.   the third time in a place with no room to move, and the ass lay down under him; and once more Balaam beat his animal.

5.   Balaam still did not see the Angel and he did not see that he was riding his ass into the path of the awful wrath of God. Only the donkey saw it.

6.   To humble Balaam more, the Lord gave the ass the gift of speech. It was a wonder! God gave the ass eyes to see the Angel of Jehovah and a mouth to speak words of warning to his master. Read verse 30.

7.   The surprising part of this happening is that Balaam did not seem at all surprised when his animal spoke human words. Balaam did not see the great wonder of it. The Lord used the words his animal spoke to show Balaam that he was more foolish than his donkey. He used the donkey to bring Balaam to his senses. The donkey was trying to tell him, "Don't you think there was a reason for my actions?"

8.   Then God opened Balaam's eyes and he saw the Angel of Jehovah.

Discuss in class
how Balaam must have felt at that moment.

9.   Balaam was so afraid of the Angel of Jehovah that he did three things:

a.   He fell on his face to the ground.

b.   He said to the Angel of Jehovah, "I have sinned;" but he did not say, "I repent. I am sorry."

c.   He offered to turn around and go home if the Lord was displeased with him, verse 34.

10.   But now the Lord insisted that Balaam go on with the men, verse 35. The Lord had prepared words for Balaam to speak, and He insisted that Balaam speak them. Now Balaam knew that he would never curse Israel, even though his wicked heart had not changed. He still wished he could.

Read Numbers 23:1-6

B. Balaam's Parables

1.   Balak, king of Moab, went out to meet Balaam, and offered sacrifices, probably to the God of Israel, chapter 22:40. Together they went to a high place where they could view the camp of Israel. For how could Balaam curse Israel if he could not see them?

2.   Now Balaam offered sacrifices on seven altars. He was still trying to gain the favor of God, so that God would let him curse Israel. At the same time, he went away by himself to use his magic charms and enchantments, verse 3. But Jehovah met him and put a word in his mouth.

3. You have just read some beautiful words which came from the mouth of Balaam. It is hard for us to understand how Balaam could prophesy as he did:

    a.   Because he spoke against his own will. He did not want to bless Israel.

    b.   Yet he spoke some of the most beautiful prophecies in the Bible.

    c.   Was he just God's "talking machine," repeating words he did not understand? Oh, no. He even uttered a wish (in the last part of verse 10): "Let me die the death of the righteous, and let my last end be like his!"

4. Balaam spoke three parables:

    a.   The first time he emphasized that the people of Israel "shall dwell alone." Only the Israelites were blessed. They might never mix with the heathen nations, for God's people and the devil's children cannot mix. Verse 10 tells us that God would make the Israelites a great multitude. This multitude was God's church, which He would take to glory.

    b.   Balak was very displeased with Balaam. If they moved to a place where they could see only a little part of the camp of Israel, the nation would look so poor and small that Balaam might be able to curse them. But again Jehovah put His Word into Balaam's mouth. In this prophecy God, through Balaam, told of His great mercies over His people. Read verse 21.

    c.   By this time Balak was disgusted, and said, "Neither bless them at all, nor curse them at all," verse 25. He was ready to send Balaam home again. But he changed his mind and took Balaam to a third place. This time Balaam did not even try to use his enchantments (chapter 24:1). This time the Lord gave him a vision. He not only spoke the words God put in his mouth, but he saw what would happen to Israel. Read verses 5 to 7.

5. Balaam ended his parable by saying about Israel, "Blessed is he that blesseth thee, and cursed is he that curseth thee," verse 9. King Balak was angry and clapped his hands together. He had tried to curse Israel, and now he knew that God would curse him. Balak told Balaam to say no more and to go back home.

6. God would not allow him to go home yet. Balaam must speak once more. God gave him another vision, and the Holy Spirit gave him words to say. This time in his vision Balaam saw the Star Who was to come from Jacob. Read verse 17.

DO NOT FORGET that Balaam's first three parables were building up toward the fourth one. In his first parable he did not refer to Jesus. In the second, Balaam heard "the shout of a king among them." In the third, he saw a king, "higher than Agag." All these kings pointed to the King, the Star of Jacob, our Lord Jesus, Who has the victory over all His enemies.

LESSON 66

The End of the Wanderings

parts of Numbers 25, 26, 27

BEFORE WE BEGIN, you may wonder whether the Lord put the beautiful words which Balaam spoke into his heart. He did not. Balaam left the camp of Israel with devilish hatred in his heart; and he set out to get revenge against Israel because the Lord did not let him earn his rich rewards.

LESSON OUTLINE

A. Israel's Sin

1. Balaam did not immediately go home to Mesopotamia. He first stopped at Moab to see King Balak, for he had a plan, an evil plot, to bring a curse on Israel another way. This is the way Balaam organized his plan:

    a. He described his plot to King Balak.

    b. Balak asked his princes and leaders in Moab to help.

    c. The princes went to the people of Moab to get them to cooperate in this evil plot.

2. Balaam's plan was not to fight another war with Israel. He knew that Moab would not win. Instead, he advised the king and the princes to send the most beautiful young women from Moab into the camp of Israel. These heathen women would tempt the young men to marry them, and after they lived in Israel, they would teach the Israelites the beauties of their idol worship. Balaam's plot was to make God's people turn away from Him. When they turned to idols, God would no longer bless His people, and Balaam's wish to curse Israel would come true after all! And if God did not bless His people, they would not win any more battles. This evil plot came straight from the devil. Read Numbers 31:16 and Revelation 2:14.

Read Numbers 25:6-9

3. At first, Balaam's evil plot seemed to work. The men of Israel were attracted to the women of Moab and took them into their tents. They did not even try to do it secretly, but sinned openly in the sight of all the people. Zimri, a Simeonite, was boldly proud of his sin, verse 14. He took Cozbi, the daughter of a Moabite prince, to live in his tent.

4. The results of Balaam's plan were that Israel disobeyed two important commandments of the law:

231

a. They committed adultery by taking heathen wives along with their own wives.

b. Then they learned about idol-worship from their Moabite wives, and began to worship and to sacrifice to heathen gods.

5. The Lord was angry with Israel and punished them:

a. First, He punished the leaders, who should have been examples, and were not, verse 4;

b. Then the Lord sent a plague which killed twenty-four thousand of the people.

6. In all of this trouble and sin, God was still blessing His people. Those whom He loved were weeping at the door of the tabernacle. They were filled with sorrow because of the wickedness in the camp of Israel.

Discuss in class what we do
when there is serious sin in our churches.

Read Numbers 26:1-4

B. The Second Census*

1. Soon after the sin of Israel, the Lord told Moses and Eleazar to take a census of the people of Israel from twenty years and older, of all the men who were able to go to war. The first census, you remember, took place at Mt. Sinai. The second census took place in the Plains of Moab, where Israel was still camped.

2. No one who was over twenty years old when they left Egypt was alive anymore, except Joshua and Caleb.

3. After studying the history of Israel in the desert, we know why they were not allowed to enter Canaan. It was because of their unbelief. Most of the unbelievers died by the special judgments of God in the desert. We must not think that all the people who died in the desert perished in hell, but God says that "with most of them he was displeased."

4. Moses and Eleazar were taking a census of God's church. Now it had all new members. The old generation of the church in the wilderness was dead. The number of members in the new church was almost the same. At Sinai the people numbered 603,550. At the Plains of Moab they numbered 601,730. The nation of Israel was a little smaller.

5. God had a reason for taking the census at exactly this time. He wanted everyone to register his name, family, and tribe; for soon they would be in Canaan and God would assign each tribe to a certain area in Canaan. God would give each family and tribe its own place in the promised land.

C. Moses Dies

1. Jehovah gave Moses many more instructions for the people before they went across the Jordan River into Canaan. Because he sinned at the waters of Meribah, Moses was not allowed to lead the people into the promised land.

2. Moses was very sad. He had endured so much in the desert, and now he could not even see the land. He asked the Lord whether he might see "the good land that is beyond Jordan." Moses added a little bit to his question. In Deuteronomy 3:24, he said he had begun to see God's mighty works when Israel had defeated Sihon and Og. Moses really was asking, "Please let me finish the work in Canaan, so the heathen may see God's glory." What do you think of Moses' prayer?

3. God was angry with him. At the waters of Meribah Moses had refused to give water to the people whom God loves. He was ready to see God's people die. By committing this great sin, Moses failed. He did not act as the mediator between God and His people. He was an imperfect type of Jesus, the Mediator. Now Joshua, whose name means Jehovah-Salvation, would take Israel into the promised land.

4. Jehovah said, "Let it suffice thee." It means, "Rest in my grace and goodness." He told Moses, "Speak to me no more of this matter." Moses' work was finished.

5. It was time for Moses to go, all alone, to Mt. Nebo, one of the peaks of Mt. Pisgah. From Mt. Nebo, the Lord showed him the whole land of Canaan. Through a wonder, God increased the power of Moses' eyes, and he saw the whole land. He could not enter the earthly land of promise, but it was time for God to take him to the heavenly promised land.

6. Moses died and was buried without a funeral, without his people Israel surrounding him. All we know is that God buried him. God wanted Moses to be prepared for a special resurrection. Michael and his angels prepared a special heavenly resurrection body for Moses. While they were preparing Moses, the devil came and claimed that Moses' body belonged to him, (Jude 9). But God took Moses to the glory of heaven with his resurrection body.

DO NOT FORGET that two other saints in heaven already have their resurrection bodies. They are Enoch and Elijah. The rest of us will receive our new bodies at the end of the world.

WORD STUDIES

census — a count, by the government, of the people of a nation

LESSON 67
Two Spies Go to Jericho
Joshua 1, 2

BEFORE WE BEGIN, we should know that we have just finished studying one long period in the history of the Israelites, the period in which the Lord delivered His people from Egypt and led them for forty years in the desert toward the promised land. This lesson starts a new period of Old Testament history: Israel's entry into the promised land.

Read Joshua 1:1-7

LESSON OUTLINE

A. Jehovah's Instructions to Joshua

1. We have already met Joshua in our lessons. Through the wanderings in the desert, he was Moses' helper. We met him at Rephidim when he led Israel's army to fight the Amalekites while Moses held his hands up. He was also one of the spies who brought a good report. His name means "Jehovah is Salvation." It is the same name as Jesus in the New Testament.

2. The Lord chose Joshua to be the new leader of Israel. Before Moses died, God told him to lay his hands on Joshua, and God gave Joshua a spirit of wisdom; and the people of Israel listened to him.

3. In the verses we have read, God told Joshua about all the boundaries of the land. It was Joshua's task to capture all the land inside those boundaries. Remember that the land of Canaan was not empty. The Israelites could not move into it as we move into a vacant house. They would meet strong nations and they would have to fight. The responsibility would fall on Joshua. It was a huge task.

4. Therefore Jehovah said to him, "Be strong and of a good courage." Do you know how often Jehovah said it? Four times: twice through the mouth of Moses, in Deuteronomy 31:7 and 23; and twice Jehovah spoke the words to Joshua, in Joshua 1:9 and 18. Joshua needed courage. But the Lord did not merely tell him, "Have courage, Joshua!" God's Words are powerful, and His Words gave him strength and courage to claim for Israel all the promised land.

5. God told Joshua to do two more things:

    a. to keep and obey God's law, verse 7;

234

b.   to trust Him, for God said, "I will not fail thee, nor forsake thee," verse 5.

6.   Then Joshua told the officers of Israel to command the people to prepare food for the trip into Canaan, for in three days they would leave.

7.   The tribes of Reuben, Gad, and half the tribe of Manasseh wanted to live on the east side of the Jordan. Moses had given them permission, but insisted that their men must go over the Jordan River to help the rest of the Israelites fight. Now Joshua reminded them of their promise. Read chapter 1:14, 15. About 40,000 soldiers joined Joshua's army. The rest of the men of the two and one half tribes stayed on the other side of the Jordan to protect their families and to care for their animals.

B.   Two Spies Are Sent Out

1.   Joshua did not send the spies over the River Jordan because he was afraid, or because he did not trust in the Lord, nor to find the right place to attack Jericho. The spies were sent out with a special purpose — God's purpose. God must have told Joshua to send them out, and He had two reasons:

a.   He wanted His people to know about the trembling fear in the hearts of the people of Jericho;

b.   He wanted the spies to meet Rahab.

2.   Who was Rahab? She was a Canaanite citizen of one of the strongest cities in the land. Jericho was the key city to the whole land of Canaan. It was a very wicked city, so wicked that the Lord said it was ready for His judgment.

3.   As a citizen of Jericho, Rahab joined in all the sins of that city. In fact, she was known in that city as an evil woman, a harlot who had no husband, but lived with many men.

4.   Lately Rahab had changed. The astonishing news of Israel's passing through the Red Sea and their victories over Sihon and Og had reached the citizens of Jericho. Rahab knew that God had given those victories. In verses 9 to 11, she told the spies how the terror of Jehovah fell on all the people of Jericho.

5.   But Rahab was not frightened. She believed. Because her heart was changed, she changed the way she lived, and was no longer a harlot. She did not belong in the city of Jericho anymore, and she knew it. God had given Rahab the gift of His grace so that she had faith to believe in Israel's God.

C.   Rahab Receives the Spies

1. The Bible does not tell us how the spies found Rahab's house. We do know that she lived on the wall of the city and could see long distances into the countryside. She must have been on the lookout for the Israelites, hoping to escape to the people of Jehovah. Then the spies came, and she took them into her house, not in fear, but in faith.

2. Rahab helped the spies, not by showing them how to fight a war against Jericho, for in verse 9 she said to the spies, "I know that the Lord hath given you the land." She told the spies that because the citizens of Jericho heard of the wonders of Jehovah, their hearts melted, and they lost all their courage. That is what the spies needed to know: that Jehovah had struck terror into their hearts.

3. News traveled fast in Jericho. The king heard that spies had come to Rahab's house; and he demanded that Rahab hand them over to him. What was Rahab's answer?

   a. A lie: "The men were here, but they have left."
   b. Meanwhile, she hid them under the drying flax* on her roof.
   c. She urged the king's men to chase the spies.

4. What must we think of Rahab's lie?

   a. It was wrong. A lie is always wrong. She could have told the truth and trusted Jehovah.
   b. But Rahab was a new believer, and her faith was not yet strong.
   c. The Bible does not say anything about her lie. Read what Hebrews 11:31 and James 2:25 say about Rahab.

Discuss in class what you think of Rahab's lie.

Read verses 12-18

D. The Spies Make a Promise

1. Rahab made the spies promise to save her family from death when they came back to conquer Jericho; and the spies promised. They told her to leave a scarlet cord in her window as a sign, so they could find her.

2. Then Rahab let them down the wall of the city by a rope through a window, and told them to hide three days before they went back to Joshua.

DO NOT FORGET that Joshua is a type of Jesus. In this lesson, Rahab put her trust in Joshua for mercy, just as we look to Jesus for mercy.

WORD STUDIES

flax — a plant from whose stem linen is made

LESSON 68
The Israelites Cross the Jordan
Joshua 3, 4

BEFORE WE BEGIN, we will see that this lesson is also a beginning. It is the beginning of the fulfillment of God's promise that Israel will live in the land of Canaan, the land God had prepared for His people. Soon they would take their first steps into that land.

Read Joshua 3:1-8

LESSON OUTLINE

A. Joshua's Instructions

1. Joshua and the people moved from Shittim in the Plains of Moab to the shore of the Jordan River. There they stayed for three days.

2. Then Joshua gave the people these orders:

a. They must be ready to march when the priests carried the ark forward.

b. They must leave a space of about 3,000 feet between themselves and the ark. Why? Verse 4 says, "for ye have not passed this way before." It does not mean, "for you have never crossed the Jordan before," but "you have never traveled the path of this wonder."

c. Joshua said to the people, "Sanctify* yourselves." They must be ready to meet the Lord of great wonders.

3. The priests received their orders next. They must take the ark of the covenant from the holy of holies in the tabernacle and walk to the edge of the water and stand still as soon as their feet touched the water. Then all the people were to pass by the front of the ark as they crossed the river. Why?

a. When the people started across the Jordan, they knew they could not go through the mighty waters by themselves, to get into the promised land.

b. As they were walking, they were making a picture of their lives. They could not go through the river of death and get to heaven, the promised land, all by themselves, either. First the Lord had to forgive their sins and make them pure and holy. That is where the ark comes in.

c. You remember that on the top of the ark was the mercy seat, on which the high priest sprinkled blood once a year. The blood was a type of Jesus' blood, which makes His people clean from their sins.

d. When the Israelites walked past the ark through the water, they knew they were going to a promised land on the other shore. It was a type of what happens to all of God's children. We all go through the Jordan of death on our way to the promised land of heaven, because Jesus has prepared the way by washing our sins away with His blood. The Israelites were walking the way of salvation.

Read verses 12-17

B. Through the Jordan River

1. Find the Jordan River on the map for Lessons 64 to 66. It is about sixty-five miles long and averages about ninety feet wide. At this season (the first month, which was harvest time) the river overflowed its banks and was much wider, verse 15. Especially at this time of the year, the swiftly flowing waters made the current very strong, and the waters were about twelve feet deep.

2. It was impossible for the Israelites to cross this mighty river. Strong men and women, small children and babies, household goods and all their animals had to cross the Jordan. They could not have done it without a wonder. And God gave them a great wonder. He opened the way by piling up the waters fifteen miles upstream near the city of Adam. It must have looked as if an invisible dam was holding the waters back. The rest of the water flowed away and Israel was ready to walk over a dry riverbed. All the Israelites walked past the ark which the priests were carrying and they walked on dry ground through the wonder.

Read Joshua 4:1-9

C. The Memorial

1. Before the people of Israel started to cross the river, the Lord told Joshua to appoint twelve men, one from each tribe, to pick up a large stone from the place where the priests stood on the east side of the Jordan. God told each of them to carry the stone on his shoulder through the riverbed to the other side (the west side). There they set up the stones as a pillar.

2. Meanwhile, Joshua went back to the east side, where the priests stood, and set up twelve stones as a pillar on that side, too. Now there was a pillar on both sides of the river, and verse 9 says, "and they are there to this day." This day means that the stones were still standing when the author of the Book of Joshua was writing this history. We do not know who wrote the Book of Joshua.

3. Why did God instruct Joshua to set up the memorial?

a. Because after the Israelites crossed the Jordan, their crossing was finished. It belonged to history, and it could easily be forgotten. God did not want His people to forget. Therefore He ordered a memorial, a double memorial, one on each side of the river. It was something the people could see.

Discuss in class whether we in our churches
have signs (memorials) which we can see as we worship.

b. There is another reason. In later years, when their children asked, "What mean these stones?" their parents would tell them about the wonder of the crossing of the Jordan. But they could not stop there. They would tell the story of God's leading them out of the bondage of Egypt, through the desert, to Canaan. The story was a picture of their salvation. Jehovah always wants His people to teach their children about the God Who saves them.

c. There is one more reason: that all the people on the earth may know that the Lord is mighty.

DO NOT FORGET the last part of the last verse of chapter 4: "that ye might fear the Lord your God forever." God spoke those words, not only to the Israelites, but also to us. When we fear the Lord, we love Him. We love Him for His wonders, the wonders we study every day in our lessons, and most of all for the wonder that He chose us to be His children and sent Jesus to save us.

WORD STUDIES

sanctify — to purify, to make holy

LESSON 69
The Walls of Jericho Fall
Joshua 5, 6

BEFORE WE BEGIN, can you imagine how frightened all the kings of the Canaanites and Amorites were? "Their hearts melted," and their courage was gone because they saw the wonders of God as He fought for Israel. Read chapter 5:1.

Read Joshua 5:10-15

LESSON OUTLINE

A. The Israelites Camp at Gilgal

1. On the tenth day of the first month, just forty years after they left the land of Egypt, the Israelites crossed the Jordan River. On the fourteenth day of the first month they celebrated the passover. For forty years in the desert they had not celebrated it, but now in the promised land they celebrated how God had delivered them from Egypt. The day after the passover God stopped sending manna, for now the people could eat the food of the land of Canaan.

2. What were the people of Israel to do next? They must start to conquer Canaan. Joshua, as their leader, had all the responsibility. The strong city of Jericho lay just ahead. How would they be able to take the city? Verse 13 says that Joshua was by Jericho. With his thoughts, he was in Jericho, trying to decide what the next move of the Israelites should be; and he must have asked Jehovah to guide him. Jericho was fortified with thick walls and gates. It was shut up tight. The people of Jericho were not ready to surrender. They were ready to fight. Yet the Israelites must conquer this city first, for it was the gateway into the rest of Canaan.

3. As the leader of God's people, surrounded by enemies and unbelievers, Joshua felt helpless. He knew that their enemies would destroy God's people if they could. But they couldn't, because God always works to save His people, His church in the world.

4. Suddenly, when Joshua looked up, he saw a man, a stranger, with a drawn sword in his hand, and he asked, "Art thou for us, or for our adversaries*? He meant: friend or enemy? The stranger answered, "Nay." Who was the stranger?

    a. He was not a man, but Captain of the host of Jehovah.

b. The Captain was the Angel of Jehovah, the Christ of the Old Testament, Whom we have met several times already in our lessons.

c. He told Joshua that He is Captain of the host* of Jehovah, the host of all of God's creation, and of all God's creatures.

d. The Captain of Jehovah's host showed Joshua that He came ready for a battle, for He held a sword in His hand. Do you think that Christ fights with a sword of steel? No, the sword was only a picture that Christ, as the Captain of Jehovah's host, could use all the weapons of creation to save His people. As we study the victories of Israel in Canaan, remember that Israel's Captain used all the powers of nature — storms, hail, fire, and even the sun, moon, and stars — to fight for His people.

Read Joshua 6:1-5

B. The Fall of Jericho

1. In these verses, the Captain of the host of Jehovah was still speaking to Joshua. He said, "I have given into thy hand Jericho." But Israel had not even started to fight! In His plan, before He created the world, Jehovah had already given the city of Jericho to His people. In God's plan, the Israelites had won the victory over Jericho and already had the city in their possession.

2. What kind of city was Jericho? It was a beautiful and great city built on a fertile plain near the Jordan River. Although it was surrounded by strong walls which kept their enemies out, it was not a very large city, for the Israelites could walk around it seven times in one day.

3. God instructed His people to march around the city once each day for six days and then return to their camp. This was the order of their march:

a. The armed men (soldiers) of Israel were to lead.

b. Seven priests, carrying trumpets of rams' horns, followed. The priests were to blow their trumpets as they marched. The priests who carried the ark followed them.

c. The rest of the people followed the priests. God told the people to walk in silence. They were not to shout nor make noise. They might not even talk. Only the sound of the trumpets was to be heard.

3. On the seventh day, the Israelites were to start their march at dawn and march around the city seven times. Read verse 15.

Read verse 16 and 20-27

4. Joshua and the people of Israel obeyed Jehovah's command. Once a day for six days the whole nation of Israel marched around the strong city in complete silence, except for the priests blowing the trumpets. The people of

Jericho had never seen a war fought in this way. It either struck terror into their hearts, or they laughed with hard hearts at the foolishness of the Israelites; for the marching seemed so foolish to these wicked men.

5.   On the seventh day, the people in Jericho must have become more and more uneasy as Israel kept marching in silence seven times around the city until, after the seventh time, the priests blew their trumpets and Joshua said, "Shout, for the Lord hath given you the victory!" The people shouted with a great shout and the walls, the strong, thick walls with houses on them, fell down like a house built of match sticks.

6.   Verse 20 says that "the people went up into the city, every man straight before him." Suddenly there were no walls. Wherever an Israelite soldier was standing, he could go right in and take the city.

7.   The spies brought out Rahab and her family and saved them, as they had promised. The rest of the city they destroyed with fire, verse 24.

C.   The Wonder

1.   Can we explain how the walls fell down, except for the part where Rahab lived, and how the Israelites had a victory without fighting? No, for the Almighty God gave it to them as a free gift of His grace. While He gave them the victory, He used some earthly signs to teach His people.

    a.   The trumpets. In Scripture, trumpets are signs of God's judgments over the wicked and His salvation for His people.

    b.   The ark of the covenant. It was a sign of Jehovah living with His people, even in battle.

    c.   The number seven. It was a sign of God's finished work. God used these signs to teach them that God is always for His people.

2.   Read Hebrews 11:30. Does this verse mean that the faith of the people of Israel destroyed the walls of Jericho? No: God destroyed the walls. But He put faith in the hearts of His people and saved them through the power of their faith.

Discuss in class how you know that you are saved.

DO NOT FORGET that just as God saved Israel by His gift of grace, He saves us by the same gift of grace. He simply gives salvation to us because He loves us. And He gives us faith to believe that we are saved.

WORD STUDIES
1.   adversary — an opponent or enemy
2.   host — a large number of men or things; an army

LESSON 70
Achan Sins
Joshua 7

BEFORE WE BEGIN, we have three verses in chapter six to read and understand before we can study this lesson about Achan's sin. Read Joshua 6:17, 18, and 21.

LESSON OUTLINE
A. Jehovah's Command About Jericho

   1. The Lord gave Joshua and the people a different command about the city of Jericho than the commands He had given them in the wars between Sihon and Og. When they fought Sihon and Og, God told the Israelites to kill all the people, but He allowed them to keep the animals and the spoil and the good possessions they found in the cities. However, God commanded everything in Jericho to be destroyed, and even burned with fire, verse 24.

   2. The Lord told them to put the precious things, silver and gold, into the treasury of the tabernacle. The precious things belonged to God.

   3. Why were God's commands about Jericho different?

   a. Because Jericho was the first city in Canaan which Jehovah had given to His people by a wonder.

   b. The Israelites devoted* it to the Lord. Because God is the Holy One, He cursed everything in the wicked city of Jericho. When God's curse was on everything in Jericho, God was telling Israel not to take for themselves the treasures of the evil world. They must give the treasures of evil to God, and He would destroy them.

   c. When the people destroyed the wicked Canaanites and everything they had, and saved only the silver and gold and precious things to be holy before the Lord, they were saying that everything in the city belonged to Jehovah, verse 19.

   e. The Lord gave a warning, too. If anyone disobeyed, he was cursed of God. Read verse 18 once more.

   4. The Lord gave Joshua one more command. Read verse 26. Anyone who rebuilt the city of Jericho with walls and gates would be cursed. All his sons would die: the oldest when he laid the foundations, down to the youngest when he finished the gates.

Read Joshua 7:1-12

243

B. Israel's Defeat

1. Joshua, as captain of Israel, was ready to go on to capture the next city, a small city about ten miles west of Jericho, called Ai. Find it on your map. He sent out spies, who reported that two or three thousand soldiers were enough to conquer this city of about 12,000 people.

2. Joshua sent 3,000 soldiers, but the soldiers of Ai chased the Israelites and killed thirty-six men. The Israelites were defeated! Joshua had been sure that Israel would win. Jehovah had promised them victories. But, remember, He had promised victory only if Israel was obedient. It must not have entered Joshua's mind that Israel was at fault because of disobedience.

3. Joshua was totally miserable. He tore his clothes and fell on his face to the ground before Jehovah's ark and prayed. Read his prayer in verse 7. He almost asked whether Jehovah was betraying His people, and destroying them.

4. There was a hint of a scolding in Jehovah's answer, when He said, "Get thee up; wherefore liest thou thus on thy face?" Then God explained to him that the defeat at Ai was Israel's fault, for Israel had sinned. He gave Joshua instructions what to do.

    a. He told Joshua that there was a cursed thing in Israel.

    b. In the morning Joshua must gather all the people together.

    c. God would show them who had committed the sin.

Read verses 14-26

C. The Great Sin

1. The next morning, the tribes passed before Joshua, and the Lord chose the tribe of the guilty man. By casting lots (we do not know how they cast lots) the tribe of Judah was chosen. Then the family of the Zarhites and the household of Zabdi were chosen. Achan, the son of Zabdi, was finally chosen as the sinner who had troubled Israel.

2. Achan's name means troubler. He troubled Israel by taking three things: a Babylonish garment, 200 shekels of silver, and a wedge of gold of 50 shekel's weight. (We do not know the value of these shekels.) This sin caused Israel to lose a battle and thirty-six men to be killed. Why was taking those things such a serious sin?

    a. Because Jehovah had said: Devote everything in Jericho to Me; this city is set apart for Me. Jehovah told Israel how to set it apart for Him. They must destroy everything in the city except the silver and gold, which they were to put in the treasury of God's house.

244

b.   At the same time, Jehovah cursed everything that was in the city of Jericho, because He destroyed the city in His anger and judgment; for Jericho was a type of the wickedness of the whole land of Canaan and of the whole world.

c.   Therefore, Achan's sin was that he wanted the goods of the cursed city for himself, and refused to devote them to Jehovah. His sin showed that he loved the things of the evil city more than he cared about God's commandments.

d.   The tenth commandment tells us, "Thou shalt not covet." Achan's sin was covetousness. He wanted the good things of Jericho to please himself. He deliberately took them for himself in spite of Joshua's stern warning in verse 18. And when he hid them under the floor of his tent, he was sleeping on God's curse.

e.   Achan was the cause of Israel's losing the battle of Ai and thirty-six men of Israel being killed.

f.   Achan still kept his sin secret in his hard heart when Joshua cast lots and Jehovah, through the lots, chose him as the culprit. Achan knew he would soon be found, and he could have come forward and confessed his sin. But he kept silent.

g.   Even when God's lot fell on Achan, Joshua still had to pull the story of his sin out of him. All these were Achan's sin.

3.   But did you notice in verse 11 that God said to Joshua, "Israel hath sinned"? Didn't Achan sin? The reason is that God said that Achan's sin affected the whole nation of Israel. God told the whole nation of Israel to be obedient, to be totally devoted to Him if they were to conquer Canaan; and they could not go farther into the land of promise until the curse was taken away.

4.   Israel was troubled. They could not stand before God's enemies now, and they could not win a battle. Sin was in their camp.

> Discuss in class how your sins are not private, either,
> but affect your family, friends, and church.

5.   Achan's sin was great and his punishment was severe. The Lord commanded that he and his family be stoned to death. Why his family? They must have been guilty, too, and knew about Achan's sin, but kept it secret. For we know that the Lord never punishes innocent people. After the people of Israel stoned Achan and his family to death, they burned him and all his

possessions, even his animals, with fire. Then they piled a great heap of stones over them as a memorial which served as a warning to all those who saw it.

DO NOT FORGET that this memorial was far different from the memorial which Joshua set up in the Jordan River. This was a memorial of covetousness. It is not a pleasant memorial, but Jehovah wants us to remember it and flee from the sin of Achan.

WORD STUDIES
1. covet — to desire something belonging to another
2. devote — to give completely; to set apart

The Battle at Ai
Joshua 8

BEFORE WE BEGIN, in our last lesson we learned that God had once more taught His people that He would give them the land only in the way of holiness and obedience. In this lesson they obeyed Him and conquered Ai.

Read Joshua 8:1-5

LESSON OUTLINE
A. The Lord Gives Them a Plan

1. Joshua and the people were afraid and down-hearted because of their defeat at Ai. But in the first verse of this chapter, Jehovah comforted Joshua by saying, "Fear not, neither be thou dismayed." Now that the sinner was punished and God's people were obedient, they had no reason to be afraid, for their covenant God would surely keep His promises. He promised them the victory over Ai this time.

2. These were Jehovah's instructions for the battle:

a. God told Joshua to take all the people of war (the soldiers) to battle against this small city. Not all of them fought, for Joshua chose only 35,000 men from his army. God wanted the other soldiers to come to witness the way the Lord fought for Israel.

b. In case any of the soldiers was faint-hearted, Jehovah encouraged him by saying, "I have given into thy hand the king of Ai," verse 1. In God's plan, the battle was already won.

c. The soldiers were allowed to take the spoil and the animals from Ai for themselves.

3. Then Joshua told his soldiers the battle plan:

a. Five thousand soldiers were to travel at night to Ai, which was about ten miles from Jericho, and make an ambush* on the west side of the city, between Bethel and Ai.

b. Joshua would leave early the next morning with the main army of 30,000 men, and station themselves on the north side of Ai.

Read verses 9-22

B. The Battle With Ai

1. Early the next morning, the ambush of five thousand men was hiding on

the west side of Ai, toward Bethel, which was two or three miles away. Find these cities on the map on your worksheet for this lesson.

2. Joshua stationed his army on the north, with a valley between the army and the city.

3. Then Joshua stood between the two armies where he could be seen by the men of both armies.

4. When the men of Ai came out to attack, the main army of 30,000 men pretended to be defeated, and fled. As they fled, they drew the men of Ai out of their city in pursuit. They were so sure of defeating Israel again that they left their city open and unguarded. Verse 17 tells us that not a man was left in Bethel or Ai.

5. This was the moment Joshua was waiting for. The Lord told Joshua to give his 5,000 soldiers in the ambush the sign they were waiting for: he stretched out his spear. The soldiers rushed into the city of Ai and set it on fire.

6. When the soldiers of Ai saw that their city was burning, they knew they were trapped, for the 30,000 soldiers who were pretending to flee to the wilderness turned around and attacked. The 5,000 soldiers of the ambush were behind the men of Ai. They had nowhere to turn, for they were surrounded.

7. In obedience to the Lord's command, the Israelites killed all 12,000 people of Ai and burned the whole city; but they kept the animals and the spoil.

8. Where was Joshua all this time? He was standing between the two armies, stretching out his spear. The spear was not only a signal to the ambush to start to fight, but verse 26 says that "Joshua drew not his hand back." It was a sign from the Lord that His mighty power was with them during the whole battle, until they won the victory.

9. Read verse 29. This verse does not mean that Joshua killed the king by hanging him. God did not allow that kind of death in Israel. They killed him first and then hung his body on a tree until evening, a sign of the curse of God.

Read verses 30, 31

Mount Ebal and Mount Gerizim

1. The first word in verse 30 is "Then." It means that immediately after the victory at Ai, Joshua led the Israelites to Mt. Ebal and Mt. Gerizim. Find

them on the map on your worksheet for this lesson.

2. While Israel was in the desert, God had given instructions to Moses that they must go to these mountains. Now that Bethel and Ai were conquered, the way was open for them to go to Mt. Ebal and Mt. Gerizim.

3. The Israelites knew what to do there, for Moses (in Deuteronomy 27, 28) had told them:

a. Half of the tribes went up Mt. Ebal, the mountain of the cursing. They were Reuben, Gad, Asher, Zebulon, Dan, and Naphtali. The other six tribes went up Mt. Gerizim, the mountain of the blessing: Simeon, Levi, Judah, Issachar, Joseph, and Benjamin.

b. The priests with the ark of the covenant stood in the valley between, a picture of God coming into the midst of His people.

c. Before the blessings and the cursings started, the people took large stones, plastered them, and wrote the words of the law in the plaster, and put the stones on Mt. Ebal.

d. Then they built an altar on Mt. Ebal, the mountain of the curse, and offered burnt offerings to Jehovah.

1) Why was the copy of the law on Mt. Ebal? Because if God's people could not keep the law perfectly, they sinned and were under God's curse.

2) Why was the altar with a bloody sacrifice on Mt. Ebal? Because Jehovah showed His people a way out. Jesus was coming to shed His blood and take away the curse of their sins.

4. Then Joshua read the blessings: Blessed are you if you love the Lord, if you keep His law, if you love your neighbor. . . . And the people on Mt. Gerizim answered, "Amen."

5. Joshua read the curses: Cursed are you if you serve idols, if you steal from your neighbor, if you do not obey your parents. . . . And the people on Mt. Ebal answered, "Amen."

Discuss what kinds of curses and blessings God could say today.

6. Remember: God never curses His own covenant children. But we know that not everyone in Israel was a child of God, chosen before the world was made. If wicked Israel sinned, God would send the curse of plagues, drought*, and death.

7. For God's own children, who disobeyed Him and were sorry and repented, God forgave them and sent His blessings of covenant friendship.

249

DO NOT FORGET that the altar on Mt. Ebal was a picture of the cross of Christ planted there on the mountain. By His blood He took away the curse of the sin of all His people.

WORD STUDIES
1. ambush — a lying in wait to attack unawares
2. drought — long periods of dry weather, with no rain

The Trick of the Gibeonites
Joshua 9

BEFORE WE BEGIN, we will get acquainted with the seven nations, or tribes, of the Canaanites. These tribes were descended from Canaan, the son of Ham, the son of Noah, and are mentioned very often in the Bible. They are the Canaanites, Hittites, Hivites, Perizzites, Girgashites, Amorites, and Jebusites. Six of them are mentioned in the first verse of our chapter.

Read Joshua 9:1-13

LESSON OUTLINE

A. The Fear of the Canaanites

1. All the tribes of the Canaanites were watching Israel, and were eager for news of Israel's victories, not because it was pleasant news to them, but because they had to find ways to win battles with the Israelites.

a. They had heard the startling stories of Israel walking through the Jordan River on dry land and the fall of the walls of Jericho. Now they heard that Bethel and Ai were defeated.

b. The Israelites were already in the middle of Canaan. No one had stopped them.

2. Joshua had made his headquarters at Gilgal, and all Israel was camped there, verse 6. This was not the Gilgal which was near the Jordan where Israel had camped just after they had crossed the river. This Gilgal was near Mt. Ebal and Mt. Gerizim in the middle of the land of Canaan. You can find it on your map for Lessons 70 to 72.

3. What were the Canaanites to do about this powerful nation which easily won all its battles? They could have surrendered, but their hearts were hard and stubborn. There were two groups of Canaanites, one in the south and one in the north. Neither group was ready to surrender.

4. The Canaanites in the south joined their armies in an alliance*. These men were desperate! They were forced to fight for their lives. That is the reason they took the offensive and started this warfare. They thought if they prepared to attack Joshua and the Israelites, they might win the battle.

B. The Gibeonites

1. The Gibeonites were a tribe of Hivites who lived somewhat by themselves.

Near to the city of Gibeon were three smaller cities, which formed an alliance with Gibeon. These three cities are mentioned in verse 17. But Gibeon was "as one of the royal cities," and probably ruled the other three cities.

2. For the Israelites, Gibeon was an important city. It lay in the middle of the land. If Israel conquered Gibeon, their way to the south of Canaan was open. They could march straight south and conquer the Canaanites there.

3. The Gibeonites decided not to join the alliance of the Canaanite kings and not to fight Israel. They wanted to make peace. But God did not allow the Israelites to make peace treaties with their enemies. The Gibeonites knew that, too. But they decided there might be a way to make peace: by tricking the Israelites. This is what they did:

a. Some of the men of Gibeon came to Joshua and his princes wearing old, worn clothes and shoes that were very badly patched. They had bread with them. Some of it was dry and some was moldy. The wine bottles, made from skins of animals, were torn, and the torn parts were tied together. The men looked as if they had patched themselves up during a long trip.

b. They said they came from a far country and wanted to make a league with the Israelites, an agreement to be friends with Israel.

c. They told why they wanted to be friends. They had heard what the Lord had done for them in Egypt and on the east side of the Jordan; but they were careful not to tell anything more. For if the Gibeonites came from a far country, they could not have heard about Jericho and Bethel and Ai yet!

d. They told lies. Read what they said about their clothes and food in verses 12 and 13.

Discuss in class what you would have done
if you were one of the princes of Israel.

Read verse 15

C. The League

1. Joshua and the princes believed them and made a league with the men from Gibeon. They did not know that the Gibeonites were Hivites and were their neighbors, the people whom God had commanded them to destroy. But it was wrong of Joshua and the princes to make this agreement.

2. They were careless. In verse 7 they suggested that probably the men lived near them in Canaan, but when the Gibeonites lied and said, "No, we are

from a far country," Joshua and the princes did not ask the name or location of their country. They may have felt a bit proud and important, and carelessly decided to be friends with people they did not know.

3. Worse yet, they did not ask the Lord for guidance, but swore a careless oath in the name of the Lord that they would not destroy the people they were supposed to destroy.

Read verses 16-23

D. The Outcome

1. Three days later they found out that these men in old clothes were their neighbors. They realized they had been tricked.

2. The people of the congregation of Israel murmured against their leaders, and they had a right to complain. It was true that the Gibeonites had lied, but the leaders had made a hasty promise and there was no way for Israel to break their oath which they had sworn.

3. Now Joshua and the princes were in a serious predicament:

a. God commanded them to destroy all the Canaanites. They must obey that command.

b. They had promised with an oath which they might not break to save the Gibeonites alive. And they could not do both.

4. The princes decided to let them live and be slaves, to cut wood and draw water for the congregation of Israel, particularly for the tabernacle. From then on the Gibeonites were slaves in the house of the Lord.

DO NOT FORGET that God's Words always come true. In this lesson the words that He put in Noah's mouth many years before came true: "Cursed be Canaan; a servant of servants shall he be unto his brethren," Genesis 9:25.

WORD STUDIES

alliance — a union or an agreement between parties or nations

253

LESSON 73
The Battle with the Five Kings
Joshua 10

BEFORE WE BEGIN, you have already looked ahead and labeled the five cities of the kings in southern Canaan on the map in last week's worksheet. Have that map out on your desk, and do part one of your map work for Lessons 73 to 75 before you start this lesson.

Read Joshua 10:1-5

LESSON OUTLINE

A. The Five Kings Make Plans

    1. News of the victories of Joshua and his army travelled fast in the land of Canaan. The kings of the south heard how Jericho's walls had fallen down and how Ai was destroyed. The news made Adoni-zedek, king of Jerusalem, very afraid.

    2. On top of that, he heard the news about Gibeon, one of the royal cities, a city greater than Ai. They had not dared to fight, but made peace with Israel. That was the end of all hope for Adoni-zedek and his people because:

        a. The city of Gibeon blocked the way between Joshua and the cities of the south. Now Joshua controlled Gibeon, and nothing would stop him and his armies from marching straight south through the passes in the mountains which led directly to Jerusalem.

        b. We learned in our lesson last week that the five nations in the south made an alliance. Read their names in verse 3. But the alliance did not dare fight Joshua.

    3. The plan of Adoni-zedek and the other kings was to fight — not Joshua and the Israelites — but Gibeon. They had two reasons:

        a. to get revenge against Gibeon for making peace with Israel;

        b. to get control of the city and block the way south so Joshua could not reach them. In that way the five kings could defend themselves. They thought they could capture Gibeon.

Read verses 6-9

B. Gibeon Calls for Help

    1. The five kings marched north and camped near Gibeon, ready to destroy the city.

254

2. Quickly the Gibeonites sent messengers to Joshua and asked for help. The Israelites had made a league with them and were obliged to help them in their trouble. Joshua answered by traveling all night to Gibeon with his army.

3. Now a large, strong army of five tribes of the Canaanites from the south was ready to fight the one army of Jehovah. Was Joshua afraid? No, for he knew he had the victory. Jehovah had already delivered the enemies into his hand, verse 8.

Read verses 10-19

C. The Battle

1. Joshua and his soldiers went to battle, but the Lord fought for them, verse 10. It was not the strength and the weapons of Joshua's soldiers which killed their enemies, but the Lord "slew them with a great slaughter."

2. The soldiers of the five kings fled, and the Israelite soldiers pursued them. To understand how far the Israelites chased their enemies, follow the line on your map of last week, following the four cities of Part 1 of your worksheet, which you have already done.

3. It was when the armies of the five kings were fleeing to Beth-horon that Jehovah threw down great hailstones from heaven on His enemies and killed them. This was a great miracle of God, for none of the hailstones fell on the Israelites, but only on their enemies. Verse 11 tells us that "they were more which died with hailstones than they whom the children of Israel slew." God was fighting for His people!

4. The five kings of the Canaanites were cowards. They left their armies and hid in a cave at Makkedah. When Joshua heard it, he told his men to roll large stones against the mouth of the cave, trapping the kings inside.

Read verses 12 and 13 once more

D. The Great Wonder

1. Now we will go back in the battle to the time when they were still fighting near Gibeon. Joshua was standing between Gibeon and Ajalon. Print Ajalon on your map for last week. Joshua could see the sun high in the sky above Gibeon and he could still see the moon in the west, over Ajalon.

2. Joshua spoke to the sun and the moon in the name of Jehovah, and told them to stand still. For a little while, the Lord put Joshua above the sun and moon, and God made the sun and moon obey Joshua. They obeyed the voice of a man, and stood still! A whole day was added to that day, so that Israel had time to pursue their enemies.

3. We do not know how God accomplished this wonder. But we do know that He is Lord of the universe. Perhaps He stopped the earth's rotation for a whole day. We can only believe it with the faith that the Lord gives us.

Discuss in class whether this is a greater wonder
than God making the sun come up every morning.

E. God's Purpose

1. God gave Joshua the idea for the sun and moon to stand still and the faith to command them so that all the world would see His power and glory in that wonder. He wants us to see it, too.

2. God wanted the day to be longer so that Israel could finish the battle. Remember, this was not ordinary warfare, but God's people were fighting for God's kingdom in Canaan.

3. God had another purpose: He wanted to show the Israelites and us that Joshua was a type of Jesus. Remember, they had the same name. And it was Jesus, the Captain of Jehovah's host, Who fought through Joshua. Jehovah gave Joshua power over the sun and moon for just a day. Jesus has power over all His creation forever.

Read verses 22-27

F. The Slaying of the Five Kings

1. The Israelites were at Makkedah when Joshua ordered his men to take the five kings out of the cave, put their feet on the necks of the five kings, kill them, and hang their bodies on a tree.

2. Does it sound cruel to you? Remember, God told them to do this. When Joshua told his men to put their feet on the necks of the kings, he was once more a type of Jesus, Who also puts His feet on the necks of His enemies. Jehovah was encouraging Joshua to fight the battle of faith against the wickedness of His enemies.

DO NOT FORGET to read Psalm 110:1. This psalm is a picture of Jesus and His enemies. Also sing Psalter number 303:1 and 3.

LESSON 74

Israel Receives its Inheritance

Joshua 11 and parts of Joshua 13-19

BEFORE WE BEGIN, we can figure out from other passages of the Bible that the time it took the Israelites to conquer Canaan was six and a half to seven years. This includes the battles with Sihon and Og on the east side of the Jordan River. The Israelites fought on the west side of the Jordan about five years. Before you study this lesson, do Part 3 of your worksheet.

LESSON OUTLINE

A. The Battle Against the Kings of the North

1. Chapter 11, verse 1 tells us that Jabin, King of Hazor, organized a campaign with all the other tribes of northern Canaan to go to war against Israel. You will not have to read all those hard names in your Bibles.

   a. The armies came from as far north as the Sea of Chinnereth and Mt. Hermon to fight Israel. Find these places on your maps.

   b. Verse 4 says that "much people, even as the sand that is upon the seashore in multitude" came to fight Israel. It was the largest army the Israelites had faced, and their enemies far out-numbered Israel. These large armies also came with horses and chariots.

   c. Find the Waters of Merom once more on your maps. This is where the huge army camped. They were taking the offensive. Verse 5 says they came "to fight Israel."

2. Before the battle began, probably while the army of Israel was marching to battle, Jehovah came to Joshua once more and told him not to be afraid, for tomorrow at this time all their enemies would be killed. Read chapter 11:6.

3. Verse 7 tells us that Joshua came upon the enemy suddenly. Was it a surprise attack? We do not know. We do know that the Lord smote them (verse 8) and chased them in all directions: to the southwest, northwest, and the east. Israel's army houghed (pronounced hocked) the horses of the Canaanites. They did this by cutting the tendon of the joint in the horses' back legs, disabling them. The Canaanites had to flee on foot.

4. Again this battle was a wonder. The Israelites, no matter how strong and brave they were, could not have won the victory by their own power. Jehovah gave them the promised land.

5. Joshua came back from pursuing his enemies and destroyed the city of Hazor, the capital city where Jabin had ruled. Then Israel destroyed the rest of the northern cities, and kept the animals and spoil for themselves.

6. Read chapter 11:15. Already in the desert, the Lord had given Moses instructions about conquering the land. Moses instructed Joshua, and Joshua obeyed Jehovah to the last detail.

B. The Finished Work

1. Except for a narrow strip on the west coast, Israel possessed all the land of Canaan.

    a. Not a city made peace with Israel except Gibeon.

    b. Have you ever wondered why the Canaanites wanted to fight Israel when they knew they would lose? It was because the Lord hardened their hearts and made them foolish so that they would fight Israel and be destroyed. They knew that when they fought Israel they were fighting God, but in their wickedness they ran into God's anger, and were destroyed.

2. God was controlling Israel's enemies, and He made them fight, and He destroyed them so that Israel could live in safety in the promised land.

C. The Land is Divided

1. Read chapter 13:1. Joshua was old. He was Jehovah's worn-out warrior. But not every bit of the land of Canaan had yet been conquered. Besides the land on the seacoast, which was not conquered, there were small groups of Canaanites living in cities scattered through the land of Canaan. Israel had conquered the land, but not all the people in it.

2. Many years ago God had told Moses His reason for leaving some Canaanites in the land. Find it in Exodus 23:29, 30.

3. The Lord was teaching His people to go on fighting in faith. When they met enemies in their land, they had to say no to the enemies and yes to God. Little by little they had to fight the wickedness in their land and God would give them the victory. We are like the Israelites because we, too, are God's people. We fight evil in the world and in the church and in ourselves, too.

Discuss in class how we fight God's battles by faith,
little by little.

4. Before we learn how the land was divided, remember three things:

    a. The two and a half tribes, Reuben, Gad, and half the tribe of Manasseh, already had their land on the other side of the river.

b. The tribe of Levi received no land. They were workers in the tabernacle, and "the Lord was their inheritance," chapter 13:33.

c. Joseph had two portions in the land. Each of his two sons, Manasseh and Ephraim, had a portion.

5. Joshua and Eleazer, Aaron's third son, were in charge of assigning to each tribe the land which God had prepared for them. They used the method of casting lots to give each tribe its possession.

a. We call it casting lots (somewhat similar to the way we pull the longest straw). But never forget: the Lord controlled the lots and gave each tribe exactly the right land.

b. The Lord owned Canaan and He gave it to His people as a gift of His love and grace.

6. After each tribe received its piece of land from the Lord, each large clan in every tribe received its land by lot. Even the land for the individual families was chosen by lot. Everyone had an exact spot to live in Canaan.

7. The size of each tribe's inheritance depended on the size of the tribe. Benjamin, a small tribe, had a much smaller inheritance than Judah. On our worksheet we will study the division of the land more carefully.

DO NOT FORGET that although our lives as God's people are far different from the life in Old Testament times, we, too, receive our lands and homes and the places in our churches directly from God. He placed us in the family and home we live in, and He gives us everything we own. It is His gift of grace to us.

LESSON 75

The End of Joshua's Life

parts of Joshua 20 and 22-24

BEFORE WE BEGIN, one very important part of Israel still needed a home in Canaan: the tabernacle of Jehovah. The Lord chose Shiloh in the middle of the land as the place for His house. All Israel came to the ceremony of setting up the tabernacle at Shiloh, which means peace and rest, Joshua 8:1. Shiloh is one of the Bible's names for Jesus, Who gives us peace and rest.

Read Joshua 20:1-3

LESSON OUTLINE

A. The Cities of Refuge

1. Moses had given orders on the other side of the Jordan River about the cities of refuge. What was their purpose?

   a. If someone killed his neighbor accidentally, he could flee to one of these cities for safety, where none of the relatives of the dead person could take revenge.

   b. He had to tell his story of the accident to the elders of the city, and if his story was true, he might stay in the city of refuge and live.

   c. He had to stay until the death of the high priest. After that he was free to leave, and no one might harm him.

2. There were six cities of refuge, three on each side of the Jordan. Find them on your maps for this lesson.

3. Because the Levites had no land of their own in Canaan, Joshua gave them forty-eight cities, scattered throughout the land.

Read chapter 22:1-6 and 8

B. The Two and a Half Tribes Go Home

1. Now that the battles were over, the soldiers who had settled on the east side of Jordan could go home. For about five years they had fought with Israel's army and they had stayed until the land was divided.

2. Joshua called them and talked with them:

   a. He praised them for keeping their promise to Moses to help their brothers fight.

   b. He urged them to obey God's commandments and to love Him and serve Him with all their hearts.

260

c.   He instructed them to divide the riches which they had taken in battle with the men in their tribes who had stayed at home to take care of their families and animals. Verse 8 tells us that they went home with great riches.

d.   He blessed them and dismissed them.

Read verses 10-12

3.   At the Jordan River, before the men of the two and a half tribes crossed over, they built "a great altar to see to," verse 10, patterned after the altar of burnt offering in the tabernacle.

4.   When the rest of Israel heard about it, they were very angry. They made preparations to go to war with the two and a half tribes. But first they sent ten princes, one from each tribe, with Phinehas the son of Eleazar as their head, to talk with their brothers at the Jordan.

5.   Why were the Israelites so upset and angry with the men of the two and a half tribes? The Israelites thought their brothers were erecting an altar to an idol, and were forsaking the worship of Jehovah, as Balaam and Achan had done. They were worried! Read verse 16.

6.   This is the way the men of the two and a half tribes answered the men of Israel:

a.   We did not build this altar to turn away from Jehovah, nor to offer burnt sacrifices on it;

b.   but we built it as a witness — as a memorial — for our children and grandchildren and all our descendants. They will see that it is a pattern of the altar in the tabernacle, but it is not to be used for sacrifices. Read verses 26-28.

c.   We wanted our future generations to know that we fought on the west side of the Jordan until it was conquered.

Discuss in class what you think
about the building of this altar.

7.   The men of the two and a half tribes undoubtedly had a good motive in building the huge altar, but they should have remembered that Jehovah had commanded them to worship in one tabernacle and sacrifice on one altar only. An altar was a place of worship, and Jehovah had commanded them to have no other places of worship. If they had asked the Lord, He would have said no, and they knew it; but they wilfully went ahead anyway. It was really rebelling against God and His commands.

261

8. The rest of the Israelites, however, let themselves be persuaded that such an altar of witness was good, and they called the altar Ed. Read verses 33 and 34.

Read chapter 23:1-3

C. Joshua says Farewell to Israel

1. Many years had elapsed* between the time of the altar Ed and Joshua's farewell, about 20 to 25 years. Now Joshua was 110 years old and knew he was ready to die. The two great tasks to which the Lord called him were finished: the conquering of Canaan and the division of the land among the twelve tribes.

2. Now it was time for his farewell speech. He spoke to all Israel: that is, to their rulers and princes and the heads of tribes, clans, and families. This was Joshua's message to the people:

a. Do not stop driving out the Canaanites. Be strong and courageous to fight.

b. Jehovah your God will fight for you and drive them out of your sight, as He promised, verse 5.

c. Take care that you do not worship idols but "take good heed to yourselves, that ye love the Lord your God," verse 11.

d. If you marry heathen wives or husbands and worship their idols, they will trap you and be scourges (whips) in your sides and thorns in your eyes, and soon you will disappear from this good land, verse 13.

3. In Joshua's second farewell speech, he again called the elders of the people, this time to Shechem. His speech had two parts:

a. Starting with Abraham, he reviewed the history of God's chosen people (in chapter 24:1-13), teaching Israel once more that God fought for them from Abraham's time until now, when He had given them this wonderful land. Read verse 13.

b. Joshua ended his speech with the words of verses 14 and 15. Read them.

4. The people answered, "We will also serve the Lord; for he is our God."

5. Joshua's answer to them was amazing: "Ye cannot serve the Lord," verse 19. Joshua meant: "You are hopeless sinners, and God is the Holy One. You are not able to serve Him of yourselves. Only if God puts His love into your hearts will you be able to put away your idols and ask Jehovah for His grace and forgiveness so that you can serve Him."

262

DO NOT FORGET that Joshua's words to Israel were a warning not to serve Jehovah lightly. The Israelites had to know, and we must know that obedience to Jehovah is a life-long struggle, and that we serve Him only with His gifts of love, grace, and mercy.

WORD STUDIES

elapse — to slip away, to pass by

LESSON 76

Introduction to the Book of Judges

Parts of Judges 1 and 2

BEFORE WE BEGIN, the last verse of the Book of Joshua tells us that Joshua died when he was 110 years old, and was buried in the land of the tribe of Ephraim. At this time, the Israelites kept their promise made to Joseph in Egypt, and buried his bones in Shechem, also in the land of the tribe of Ephraim. Find Shechem on your map for this lesson.

LESSON OUTLINE

A. A New Period in Old Testament History

1. In the Book of Judges you will study part of the third period of Old Testament history. Remember, the first two periods were:

    a. the creation to the flood;

    b. the flood to the conquest* of Canaan.

2. The third period of Old Testament history extends from the rule of the judges through the reign of King Solomon. The period of the judges lasted about 350 years. Because the time of the Judges was a period of confusion, it is hard to figure out exactly when each judge began and ended his rule. It is also possible that the rule of some judges overlapped: that two judges ruled at the same time in different parts of the land of Canaan. You will find more details about this on your worksheets.

B. Life in the Days of the Judges

1. A new generation "which knew not the Lord, nor yet the works which he had done for Israel" grew up, Judges 2:10.

    a. The people who had seen God's wonders in the desert and in the conquering of Canaan had died. Their children were now the grown-up people of Israel.

    b. Chapter 2:10 does not mean that the Israelites did not know who God is, or did not know anything about Him, but they did not know Him as the God Who did wonders, and most of them did not want to worship Him.

    c. This new generation also liked the gods which the Canaanites worshipped. They served Baal and Ashtaroth. Baal was the sun-god, and Ashtaroth was Baal's female partner; and each heathen tribe had its own kind of idol for Baal and Ashtaroth, along with many evil and filthy ceremonies, when they worshipped their idols.

3. Many of the Israelites turned to the worship of Baal and Ashtaroth. They liked the gods of the Canaanites. They did not say that Jehovah was not God. No, they wanted to worship Jehovah and the heathen idols. They knew it was impossible, but they were disobedient and they did what was right in their own eyes. They started their own private ways of worshipping the gods they chose.

4. The Israelites at the time of the judges did not want to know or to hear about God's laws. They did not want God to be their King. The words of Judges 17:6 describe this dark period of history very accurately: "There was no king in Israel, and every man did that which was right in his own eyes." This text is a sort of motto for the Book of Judges.

Read Judges 1:1-5

C. Judah Tries to Obey the Lord

1. Soon after the death of Joshua, the Israelites asked Jehovah, "Which tribe shall fight the Canaanites first?" The Lord answered, "Judah." The tribe of Judah asked the tribe of Simeon, their neighbor on the south, to go with them to fight. The soldiers of these tribes conquered the Canaanites and the Perizzites who lived among them, and killed 10,000 men. These people were the enemies who lived in the hills and mountains. But the courage of Judah and Simeon gave out when they fought the men in the valley, for they were afraid of the chariots of iron with which their enemies fought.

2. The tribe of Benjamin fought against the Jebusites in Jerusalem, and partly destroyed them; but the unconquered Jebusites stayed in Jerusalem until the time of King David.

3. The rest of Judges 1 tells us about the half-hearted attempts of the other tribes to drive out the people of the land. Most of the Israelites let the heathen nations live in peace with them. And Israel settled down to farming and going about their business and cooperating with the idol-worshippers. This turning away from Jehovah and His commands happened in a very short time: between the death of Joshua and the rule of the first judge.

Read chapter 2:1-5

D. Bochim

1. The Angel of Jehovah came and spoke to Israel, probably to the rulers of the tribes. This Angel is the Christ Who appeared in Old Testament times,

and Whom we have met in many of our earlier lessons. It was God Who came down to talk with Israel.

2. The Angel came from Gilgal, next to the Jordan River, the place of the two memorial pillars of stones, the place where the manna had stopped, and the place where they had celebrated their first passover in the promised land. Had the Israelites forgotten all the joys of God's wonders and promises already?

Discuss in class how it was possible
for God's people to forget so soon.

3. The Angel of Jehovah told Who He was:
   a. the One Who brought them from Egypt;
   b. the One Who gave them the promised land;
   c. the One Who will never break His covenant of friendship with His people, Who is the God Who never changes.

4. The Angel rebuked Israel because:
   a. they made leagues and became friends with their heathen neighbors;
   b. they built altars and worshipped idols;
   c. they disobeyed God by not driving the heathen from the land.

5. The Angel of Jehovah told them that they would be chastised for their sins:
   a. Their heathen neighbors would become traps in which God's people would be caught, traps of sin and trouble and death.
   b. They would be scourges in their sides (or whips at their backs).
   c. Because they used their eyes to look to Jehovah, the heathen would be thorns in their eyes, so they could not look to Jehovah. God used these picture-words to teach His people that sin hurts!

6. When the Israelites heard the voice of the Angel, they wept. They wept true tears of repentance. For God always keeps a little flock of His own people for Himself. His own people are the ones who wept, and who carried God's message to the rest of the people of Israel. Therefore they named the place Bochim, which means weepers.

DO NOT FORGET that God never let all Israel become idol-worshippers and forsake Him. He had His little flock of weepers at Bochim. From their seed the Angel of Jehovah would some day come to earth again, to be born as Jesus; and God would pour out all His anger against the sins of His people on Him, at the

266

cross. In Canaan, His people had only a few victories over their enemies; but on the cross, Jesus won the great victory over all His enemies — over the devil, sin, and death.

WORD STUDIES

conquest — to overcome and subdue by force, as in war

LESSON 77
Micah and the Danites
Judges 17, 18

BEFORE WE BEGIN, you have probably noticed that we have jumped from Judges 2 to Judges 17 and 18. The history of the last four chapters of Judges took place before the history in chapter 3, and we will study it as it actually happened. Our lesson will explain how we know that our lesson for today took place before the first judge ruled in Israel.

LESSON OUTLINE
A. Sin and Idol-Worship in Israel

  1. We learned that very quickly after Joshua's death, Israel turned away from God. In chapters 17 and 18 the words which we read in our last lesson are often repeated: "In those days there was no king in Israel, but every man did that which was right in his own eyes." What happened when everyone did that which was right in his own eyes?

    a. The people — most of them — turned to all the idols of the heathen and worshipped them, almost immediately after Joshua's stern warning.

    b. Israel lived in anarchy*. They despised Jehovah's laws and the whole nation lived in lawless confusion, even in their homes.

    c. During this period, the people had no leader or ruler.

  2. God was the King of Israel, and the people knew it, but they did not want God, nor His rule.

Read Judges 17:1-6

C. Micah's Family

  1. Micah lived in the area of Mount Ephraim. Find it on your map for this lesson. His father is not mentioned in the story. His mother ruled in their home.

  2. His family must have been rather wealthy, for Micah stole eleven hundred shekels of silver from his mother. We do not know how much money that would be today.

  3. When Micah's mother missed the money, she called down a curse on the thief. The members of Micah's family heard her curse. Probably she suspected that someone in the household had stolen it. The curse made Micah afraid, and he admitted that he had taken the money.

268

4. His mother did not tell Micah how sinful his stealing was. She did not scold him. She blessed him in the name of Jehovah!

5. These were her plans:

   a. to dedicate the silver to Jehovah to make images. A graven image is a carved image, and a molten image is one that is melted down and shaped.

> Discuss in class how Micah's mother
> could dedicate the images to Jehovah
> if she knew the second commandment.

   b. Micah gave back the eleven hundred shekels he had stolen, but he did not seem to want the task of making the images. His mother took two hundred of the shekels to give to the silversmith, who made the idols for her.

6. Micah and his mother most likely used the rest of the eleven hundred shekels to pay for the upkeep of Micah's house of gods. Verse 5 tells us that he also had an ephod*, terraphim*, and now he had an image of Jehovah, probably of a calf. Micah had already made one of his sons to be the priest. It is no wonder that this section of the story ends with the words of verse 6. Read it.

Read verses 7-13

C. The Levite

1. When we read of the Levites in the Bible, we think of those who live close to God's Word and His law, and who faithfully obey it. The Levite who came to visit Micah was not an obedient, God-fearing young man. This is what he did:

   a. He had lived in the city of Bethlehem in Judah. In Lesson 75 you learned that Jehovah had given the Levites forty-eight cities through the land of Israel in which to live. Bethlehem was not one of them. This Levite should have lived in his own city and taken his turn to serve at the tabernacle at Shiloh.

   b. Now the disobedient Levite was traveling through the country to seek his fortune, to find a place which would please him. He did not care what the Lord said. This is another example of the anarchy in the land.

2. When he came to the mountains of Ephraim and stopped at Micah's house, Micah welcomed him. Why?

   a. In his house of gods Micah wanted a real priest, from the tribe of

269

Levi, who would make his idol worship seem to be the worship of Jehovah. This is the reason he welcomed the wandering priest and paid him ten shekels a year besides his room and board.

    b. Now that he had a Levite, he thought he could get Jehovah to cooperate with him in his worship of an image of Jehovah.

3. In chapter 18:30 God tells us that the Levite was Jonathan, the son of Gershom, the son of Moses. (The verse says Manasseh, but the King James Version does not translate the name correctly.) Can you imagine that the grandson of Moses, the man to whom God gave the law, would not pay any attention to God's law? Also, because Jonathan was the grandson of Moses, we know that this history happened soon after Joshua died, and before the judges ruled.

Read chapter 18:1-6

D. The Danites

1. The soldiers of Dan did not obey God and capture the land which God gave to their tribe. They were forced up into the mountains by the Canaanites and did not have enough room to settle. On your map, find the cities of Zorah and Eshtaol. These cities are in the tribe of Dan.

2. Instead of fighting as God had commanded, the disobedient Danites appointed five men to look for more land for part of their tribe to live. As they traveled, they came to Micah's house, and discovered that Micah had a priest. They asked the priest to ask God about their fortunes, and without even asking God, the Levite answered, "Go in peace."

3. The five scouts found Laish, a city at the northern tip of Canaan. Find it on your map. They went back home, took 600 soldiers with them, and set out again. They knew they could capture the city, because the people lived quietly and peaceably; and there was no king to stop them.

4. Once more they stopped at the house of Micah on their way to capture Laish. The 600 men stood at Micah's door, while the five scouts robbed Micah of all his images, verse 17.

5. When the priest asked what they were doing, they persuaded him to become a priest for the tribe of Dan instead of the household of Micah. The priest, who cared only about himself, gladly went.

6. Micah tried to fight the Danites, but he was badly outnumbered and gave up, and the Danites went on their way with Micah's idols.

7. The Danites were easily able to capture the quiet city of Laish, and they

270

settled there, and called the place Dan.

DO NOT FORGET that whenever men do what is right in their own eyes, it is never good nor pleasing to the Lord.

WORD STUDIES
1. anarchy — no government, lawless confusion
2. ephod — the garment, or robe, of a priest
3. terraphim — small household gods

LESSON 78
The Levite at Gibeah
Judges 19-20:7

BEFORE WE BEGIN, this lesson and the next one also belong to the time before Jehovah gave judges to Israel. It was still the time when everyone did that which was right in his own eyes. Chapter 20:28 tells us that Phinehas, the grandson of Aaron, was priest at this time. That is the reason we know that this history also took place soon after the death of Joshua.

Read Judges 19:1-10

LESSON OUTLINE

A. The Levite and His Concubine*

1. We meet another Levite in this lesson, who was supposed to live in one of the forty-eight cities for the Levites, but who disobeyed and lived in the area of Mount Ephraim.

2. This Levite was living with a concubine from Bethlehem in Judah. The concubine did not live as a faithful wife with the Levite, but wanted to live with other men, and finally she ran away and went to her home town of Bethlehem. Find it on your map.

3. The Levite did not see her for four months. He was lonesome for her and wanted her back again. Does that tell you something about the Levite? He was lonesome for a godless, unfaithful wife.

4. He came to her father's house:

    a. not to scold his concubine for running away;

    b. not to tell her she was sinning;

    c. but to be friendly and ask her to live with him again.

5. The concubine's father was glad to see the Levite. He was a man just like the Levite and his concubine. All three were interested in the pleasures and good things they could find in this world.

    a. For three days they spent their time eating and drinking and being merry.

    b. On the fourth day, when the Levite suggested going home, the father of his concubine persuaded him to "comfort thine heart with a morsel of bread." Their eating and drinking lasted all day.

272

    c. On the fifth day, once more the father persuaded the Levite to stay for food and a good time.

6. This time the Levite insisted on leaving in the afternoon, which was really too late to start on a long journey.

Read verses 11-21

B. At Gibeah

1. In the late afternoon they arrived at Jerusalem which was called Jebus in those days, because the Jebusites still lived in the city.

    a. The Levite's servant suggested that they stay overnight in Jerusalem.

    b. But the Levite did not want to stay in a city of strangers. He wanted to find a city where his fellow Israelites lived.

2. So they traveled over the border to the land of the tribe of Benjamin and came to the city of Gibeah. Find it on your map. These people were Israelites, but no one in the city showed them any hospitality. The people of Gibeah should have remembered God's words in Deuteronomy 10:19. Read it.

3. The Levite and his concubine decided to camp in the street — in the market place.

4. Just then an old man on his way home from work in the fields came past. This man did not live in Gibeah, but in Mount Ephraim, where the Levite had come from. He was staying in Gibeah for a time.

5. Very quickly the words of the Levite were filled with piety*, verse 18. But his piety was a lie. He said he was going to the house of the Lord. The truth was that he had no thought for the Lord. He wanted the old man to realize how bad the people of Gibeah were: that although God honored him by making him a priest in His house, God's people would not think of giving him hospitality.

6. The old man listened and took them in.

C. The Evil Deed

1. Remember that the people of Gibeah lived in the line of God's covenant people. They had seen His wonders in Jericho and Ai and in all the victories of Israel under Joshua's leadership.

2. But the men of Gibeah were not God's true covenant people. They had turned away from God and stubbornly turned to the works of the devil. Read verse 22. Notice that these were men of Belial, another name for the devil. Their sin was the same as the sin of the men of Sodom. You studied it in Lesson 18.

a. Long ago, the Sodomites wanted the two angels who were in Lot's house, so they could mistreat them and abuse their bodies.

The men from Gibeah wanted the Levite so they could mistreat his body.

b. In Sodom Lot offered his daughters to the evil men at his door.

In Gibeah the old man offered his daughter and the concubine to his evil neighbors. Read verse 24.

3. In the end, the old man pushed the Levite's concubine out to the men of Belial and they abused and mistreated her all night.

4. This awful deed was done by men who called themselves the children of Jehovah, who knew God's law and boldly disobeyed it.

Discuss in class why the sin of the men of Gibeah
was greater than that of Sodom.

Read verses 26-28

D. The Result

1. Early in the morning, the Levite found his concubine lying at the door of his house, and said, "Up, and let us be going." He had slept in safety all night, and he did not have any worry or concern about the suffering of his concubine through her night of torture.

2. When she did not awake, he discovered that she was dead. The Levite put her body on his ass and hurried home.

3. He had decided that all Israel must know of this horrible sin of the men of Gibeah, and he chose a shocking method of telling them. He cut his concubine into twelve pieces and sent a piece of her body to each tribe, and asked them to speak their minds, verses 29, 30.

Read chapter 20:1-7

4. When all Israel came together, the Levite told his story. In verse 5 he told the men of Israel that the men of Gibeah wanted to kill him. That was a lie. He did not tell the men of Israel that they pushed his concubine out to the evil men of Gibeah. He did not tell the men of Israel that his concubine was a runaway, and he was bringing her back. He did not tell the men of Israel that he had not cared what happened to his concubine. He put all the blame on the men of Gibeah. The truth was that all of them had sunk into the deepest pit of sin.

DO NOT FORGET that this is one of the low points in the history of Israel. The

274

prophet Hosea, in telling us about Israel's terrible sins, mentions the sins of Gibeah as the worst. Read Hosea 9:9 and 10:9.

WORD STUDIES
1. concubine — a woman who lives with a man without marrying him; or a second wife
2. piety — honor and reverence for God

LESSON 79
The War with Benjamin
Judges 20:7 - Judges 21

BEFORE WE BEGIN, civil war was about to begin in Israel. Civil war is war between two parts of the same nation. In this war most of Israel was trying to destroy one tribe: the whole tribe of Benjamin. Remember, the Israelites, although they were called God's covenant people, were evil. Only a few God-fearing children of God remained in the land.

Read Judges 20:8-14

LESSON OUTLINE

A. Preparation for War

1. The Israelites listened to the words of the Levite and believed them. Verse 8 says that they arose as one man. They were agreed: the men of Gibeah must be killed and the city must be destroyed.

2. No one thought of going home. They were ready to fight. Because it was necessary for the army to have food and supplies, they chose one man out of ten to take care of the needs of the rest of the soldiers.

3. Only the tribe of Benjamin was missing. The soldiers of the rest of the tribes sent messengers to the men of Benjamin asking them to bring out the evil men of Gibeah to be killed for their wickedness. The Benjamites refused. They sided with Gibeah and they prepared themselves for war against the rest of the tribes.

4. These were the uneven battle lines which were drawn:

    a. the eleven tribes of Israel — 400,000 soldiers;

    b. the Benjamites — 26,700 men, of whom 700 soldiers were left-handed and could sling stones within a hair-breadth of a target.

B. The First Two Battles

1. Before they fought, the Israelites went to the house of God in Shiloh (probably by sending messengers) to ask which tribe should lead in battle, and Jehovah answered, "Judah," verse 18.

2. In the first battle, the small army of the tribe of Benjamin won, and killed 22,000 of their brothers, the Israelites.

3. The amazed army of the eleven tribes had two reactions:

    a. They encouraged themselves. They still felt confident that they would win. They had the power and the larger army.

b. At the same time, they wept. It was hard for them to understand why God had made them suffer defeat. They asked Jehovah if they should fight another battle against their brother Benjamin, and He answered, "Go up against him."

4. In the second battle, the Benjamites won again and killed 18,000 Israelites. A total of 40,000 Israelites had been killed.

Read verses 26-35

C. Israel's Repentance

1. The sad and discouraged Israelites went to the house of God and wept before Him. They fasted a whole day and offered burnt offerings and peace offerings to Jehovah.

2. Why did they lose the two battles the Lord told them to fight?

a. Their hearts were not right before Jehovah. They were still trying to win in their own strength.

b. In a way, all of Israel was responsible for the sin of the men of the tribe of Benjamin, because they were all one nation, and the sin was in their nation. God wanted the whole nation of Israel to repent.

c. Besides, even though the rest of Israel had not done such a horrible sin as the men of Gibeah had, all of Israel worshipped idols and disobeyed God's laws. Israel did what was right in their own eyes. The Lord was teaching Israel to see their sins and to be sorry for them.

d. It took the death of 40,000 of their men before they repented with tears and fasting.

3. Phinehas, Aaron's grandson, who was the priest in God's house, asked the Lord whether the Israelites should go out and fight again or stop fighting. Read the Lord's answer in the last part of verse 28.

D. The Third Battle

1. This time Israel set up an ambush behind the city of Gibeah. The main part of the army "put themselves in array against Gibeah, as at other times," verse 30. The army of Israel turned back and ran when the men of Gibeah came out of their city. When they had drawn the soldiers out of Gibeah, the 10,000 chosen soldiers in the ambush set fire to the city, and the men of Gibeah were caught between two armies. Does it remind you of the strategy of the battle of Ai?

2. Then Israel killed all the people of Benjamin and destroyed all their cities, just as they had done to the Canaanites. Only six hundred men escaped into the desert and stayed at the rock Rimmon for four months.

E. Wives for the Men of Benjamin

1. After the Israelites had destroyed the people of Benjamin, they were sorry, for one of the tribes in Israel was missing. Only six hundred men survived. Without wives, they would not have children, and Benjamin would be destroyed forever.

2. The elders of Israel set about to solve this problem. They did not come to God and ask His will, but worked out their own plan.

a. They had sworn that if any city in Israel did not fight against Benjamin, its people would be killed. Now they discovered that Jabesh-Gilead had sent no soldiers.

b. Israel sent 12,000 soldiers to destroy Jabesh-Gilead and its people, except the young girls who could be wives for the Benjamites.

Discuss in class whether it was right of Israel
to destroy Jabesh-Gilead in this way.

Read Judges 21:12-15

c. The soldiers came back from the battle with four hundred girls, whom they had kidnapped. They went in peace to the rock Rimmon and gave the girls as wives for the Benjamites.

3. But they were two hundred wives short. How could they get them? There was a yearly feast to the Lord at Shiloh where young maidens danced. Find Shiloh on your map. The Israelites told the Benjamites to kidnap a wife from these maidens who danced before the Lord; and they asked the fathers of the girls to let them marry the Benjamites. Read chapter 21:21. In this way they saved the tribe of Benjamin.

DO NOT FORGET to read the last verse in the Book of Judges. Israel needed a king, who would be the type of Jesus the King. They were looking to Jesus to save them from the awful sins they had committed.

LESSON 80
Othniel and Ehud
Judges 3

BEFORE WE BEGIN the story of Othniel, the first judge, we should know that he ruled rather soon after the death of Joshua and Caleb. Othniel was still one of the men of the older generation in Israel, who had been born in the wilderness and had fought under Joshua. This means that all the wickedness of Israel which we studied in our last four lessons took place in a very short period of time, while Othniel still lived.

Read Judges 3:5-8

LESSON OUTLINE

A. Cushan-Rishathaim

  1. Once again, in verse 5, God tells us, "And the children of Israel dwelt among the Canaanites." It was exactly the opposite of what God had told them to do. This was a new generation of Israelites. The fathers and mothers who had seen God's wonders had died. The children had grown up and were now the men and women in Israel. What were they like?

    a. They were tired of war. They did not feel like obeying God's command to drive out the heathen from their land.

    b. They left the idols of the heathen in the land. This was their greatest sin, because they were saying no to the worship of Jehovah and yes to idol worship.

    c. They married the heathen people of the land. It seemed to them as if peace had come to their land. They had comfort and prosperity.

    d. They forgot that if they continued in these sins, it would be the end of the nation of Israel, and the end of the worship of Jehovah.

  2. Verse 8 tells us that Jehovah's anger was hot against Israel. He sold them into the hand of Cushan-Rishathaim, king of Mesopotamia.

    a. This king was not one of the Canaanite kings, but came from far away, most likely from the area of Haran, where Laban lived many years earlier.

    b. Jehovah sold Israel into the hand of this king. He put the idea into the mind of the king.

    c. The last part of the name Cushan-Rishathaim means double wickedness. The whole nation of Israel was conquered by Cushan-

Rishathaim's soldiers. They easily won the victory, because Israel did not feel like fighting their enemies.

3. This was the Lord's way of chastising His people. For eight years the king kept soldiers in the land of Israel.

Read verses 9-11

B. Othniel

1. Who was Othniel? It is most likely that verse 9 means that Othniel was Caleb's younger brother (not his nephew). His name means Lion of God, and he came from the tribe of Judah. Already in this early time of the judges, Judah was the leader of the tribes of Israel. God was already pointing to Judah as the tribe from which the kings of Israel would come.

2. The Spirit of Jehovah came upon Othniel. God gave a special measure of His Spirit to Othniel at this time, which made him able to judge Israel and be brave to fight God's enemies. Notice that Othniel had the Spirit of Jehovah, the Covenant-Friend of His people, Who will always save His people.

3. Before he fought, Othniel judged Israel. He told them to leave their idol-worship and repent of their sins and turn to Jehovah. They would win the victory only if they obeyed and loved the Lord.

4. Jehovah gave Israel the victory over Cushan-Rishathaim. He fought for His people. And they had rest from their enemies for forty years. Othniel probably did not live through all those forty years, but the Israelites remembered him as their leader and served Jehovah.

C. Eglon, King of Moab

1. Gradually the people began to turn away from serving Jehovah. During those forty years, another group of children became grown-ups; and it was easy for them to turn away from worshipping Jehovah. Verse 12 says that "Israel did evil again." Not everyone in Israel turned away, for God always had His own children in Israel.

2. Now a new king appeared: Eglon, king of Moab. God strengthened Eglon's army so that he wanted to fight Israel. Eglon wanted to fight because he hated Israel. God wanted Eglon to fight because He loved Israel and because He wanted to chastise His people by using Eglon's mighty army.

3. This time God chose one of Israel's neighbors to be their enemy. Moab asked Ammon to help them fight Israel. (Remember, Moab and Ammon were both sons of Lot, which made them relatives of Israel.) Moab also asked Amalek, the nation which descended from Esau, to help them. These three

280

nations invaded Israel, crossed the Jordan River, and the king of Moab made his headquarters in Jericho, called the city of palm trees. It was the city which Israel had destroyed. Now it must have been rebuilt. Find Moab, Ammon, Amalek, and Jericho on your maps.

4. Because Israel did not trust in the Lord, they were powerless. Eglon did as he pleased:

    a. He made them pay tribute — gold or silver, the fruits of the land, and servants.

    b. The Moabites served the idol Chemosh, to whom they sacrificed people, usually children. Eglon may have forced the Israelites to give up their children as sacrifices to Chemosh.

    c. This oppression lasted eighteen years. It took Israel eighteen years to learn their lesson.

5. When they could not bear their burdens any longer, Israel cried to Jehovah for help.

Read verses 13-30

D. Ehud

1. God gave Israel a deliverer: Ehud, a left-handed Benjamite. In our last lesson we learned about many left-handed men in Benjamin. Ehud was a man who not only fought skillfully with his left hand. He had faith, and Jehovah raised him up to be Israel's deliverer.

2. Ehud had made plans.

    a. He made himself a two-edged dagger and carried it under his garment on his right side, just opposite from the way soldiers usually carried their daggers.

    b. He had prepared an army in Israel to be ready to fight.

3. Ehud brought the tribute from Israel to King Eglon. He took along some men to carry the goods: gold, silver, fruit, crops. After they had delivered their tribute, Ehud went back with his men to Gilgal, in the middle of Canaan. There he left the men at the stone quarries, so they could get the soldiers from Mt. Ephraim to be ready to fight. (See verse 27.)

4. Ehud went back to Jericho alone. He found Eglon, who was a very fat man, in his summer parlor, a cooling room built on the roof, to catch the breeze.

5. He said to the king, "I have a secret errand unto thee." Because it was secret, Eglon sent all his servants away. That is just what Ehud wanted.

Alone with Eglon, he came near to the king, and Eglon stood when Ehud said, "I have a message from God unto thee." This was the moment Ehud had been waiting for: with his left hand, he plunged his dagger into the king's belly, killing him.

6. Then he went out, locked the door, and escaped. Finding the door locked, the servants waited for their king to call them, meanwhile giving Ehud the time he needed to escape. When at last they opened the door, the servants found Eglon dead on the floor.

Discuss whether Ehud committed murder or killed Eglon by faith.

7. Ehud blew the trumpet, a signal for war. The Israelite soldiers came to him, and they set a guard at the fords* of Jordan, where the enemy soldiers crossed the river, and they killed 10,000 of their enemies there.

DO NOT FORGET that Jehovah was teaching His people to fight not armies, but to fight the battles of the Lord in faith. Today He teaches us, in different ways, to fight in faith — not with swords, but with our words and our lives, to tell the world that we belong to Jesus, Who always has the victory.

WORD STUDIES

ford — a shallow place in a river that can be crossed by wading

LESSON 81
Deborah and Barak
Judges 4 and 5

BEFORE WE BEGIN, the Israelites lived in peace for eighty years after Ehud began to judge them. We do not know how long Ehud lived, to teach them the fear of the Lord. This does not mean, either, that all the people of Israel stopped worshipping idols. During the eighty years, when Israel turned to evil, God gave them Shamgar as judge (chapter 3:31). He lived near the land of the Philistines and he must have been a farmer, for he fought with an ox goad, an instrument about eight feet long, with sharp points to make the stubborn oxen move. By a wonder, God gave him the power to kill six hundred Philistines with his ox goad and to deliver his people from the oppression of the Philistines.

Read Judges 4:1-5

LESSON OUTLINE

A. Jabin Oppresses Israel

1. After Shamgar, when Israel refused to obey the Lord, but turned to worship Baal and Ashtaroth, the Lord sent Jabin, one of the Canaanite kings in the north, to invade their land and rule them with an iron hand for twenty years.

   a. We have met a Jabin in Joshua's time (Joshua 11:1) who was one of the kings of the north and whose kingdom Joshua destroyed.

   b. Jabin was the name of all their kings: and this King Jabin must have restored his tribe to its former strength, so that he and his soldiers were able to conquer Israel.

2. The conditions in Israel were terrible at this time:

   a. We learn from Deborah's song in chapter 5:6 that the people were so afraid of their enemies that they would not use the highways, but chose bypaths and fields.

   b. The soldiers in Israel had no weapons (chapter 5:8), while Jabin threatened them with nine hundred chariots of iron.

   c. Deborah's song tells us, too, that not many of the Israelites were willing to fight. Only Naphtali and Zebulon, and parts of Ephraim and Benjamin came to help deliver Israel. Find these places on your maps.

3. But some of God's people cried to Him, and He called Deborah, the wife

of Lapidoth, to be a prophetess and a judge. Usually God chose a man to lead His people. But this time there was no man with enough courage and fear of the Lord in his heart to become a leader in Israel. In all of Israel, Jehovah found no man able or willing to lead His people in battle.

a. So He chose a woman to be a prophetess, and He spoke to her and gave her messages for His people.

b. Jehovah also called Deborah to be a judge in Israel. She sat under a palm tree between Ramah and Bethel. Find these places on your maps. From her seat under a palm tree, she spoke God's words: she told her people why Jehovah was making them suffer through King Jabin and his army, and she told them to be sorry for their terrible sins.

c. It seemed as if Deborah stood almost alone, for there was only a little remnant* of God's people left in the land.

Read verses 6-10

B. God Calls Barak

1. God told Deborah to send a message to Barak, telling him to be captain of God's army. Barak lived far north in Kedesh in the tribe of Naphtali. Find it on your maps. The Lord also told Barak to gather 10,000 soldiers from Naphtali and Zebulon and travel south to Mt. Tabor. Follow their route on your maps.

2. Notice how the Lord was doing the organizing of this battle: He drew Sisera, the captain of Jabin's army, to the River Kishon, in order to give Israel the victory there.

3. Barak loved the Lord and believed His words. But he had to face such great danger for the cause of the Lord. Think about the two armies:

a. Sisera came with a mighty host of men.
Barak had 10,000 soldiers.

b. Sisera had 900 iron chariots.
Barak's soldiers had no weapons.

c. Sisera's army was well-trained.
Barak's men were not interested in war.

4. What was Barak's answer to the Lord? He did not say no, for he knew that in Jehovah's strength he would deliver Israel. But at the same time he was weak. He would not go to battle without Deborah. Deborah reproved* him and told him that the honor of the battle would not go to Barak, but to a woman, whom we shall soon meet.

Discuss in class what you think of Barak.

Read verses 14-17

C. The Battle

1. Deborah went with Barak and his army to the battlefield; and it was Deborah who decided when the right moment had come to attack their enemy, verse 14.

2. The Lord fought this battle for Israel. His weapons were His creation. He sent a terrible storm of wind and rain. In her song in chapter 5, Deborah says that the stars in their courses fought for them, and that the River Kishon swept away Sisera's army. Their chariots were of no help in the water and the mud, for they bogged down. The Angel of Jehovah helped His people in their danger, and Israel won a complete victory. Not an enemy soldier survived, verse 16.

Read verses 17-24

D. The Honor Goes to Jael

1. Where was Sisera? He left his army and fled on foot, and soon came to the house of Heber the Kenite.

    a. Do you remember that in Lesson 57 we met Hobab, Moses' brother-in-law? Moses begged Hobab to go through the desert to Canaan with Israel, and he did.

    b. Heber was a descendant of Hobab, and was called a Kenite.

2. Most of the Kenites lived in southern Canaan, but Heber and his wife Jael lived near Jabin. They hated Sisera, Jabin's captain, but Sisera did not know it. He did not know that they loved God's people and hated Israel's enemies.

3. Jael went out to meet Sisera and welcomed him into her tent. When the tired captain lay down, she covered him.

4. When he asked her for water, she brought him milk.

5. Sisera wanted to rest. He asked Jael to guard the tent door and to tell a lie: that no one was in her tent.

6. But when he slept, Jael took a hammer and a tent nail and drove it into his temples* so that he died. Did Jael commit cold-blooded murder? No:

    a. For Deborah, in her song (chapter 5:24), blessed her in the name of the Lord.

    b. Jael was fighting the Lord's battle, and it was His order that all His enemies would perish. See chapter 5:31.

7. Even though honor went to two women, Deborah and Jael, turn to Hebrews 11:32 and see whom God honors there. Barak was weak, but he was God's hero of faith.

DO NOT FORGET that in the battle which was fought at Megiddo (chapter 5:19) Jehovah delivered His people. Megiddo is a picture of another battle, still to come at the end of the world. (Notice that the names are similar.) It is the battle of Armageddon, the last battle in this world, when God will deliver all His people out of this world of their enemies and take them to heaven forever.

WORD STUDIES
1. remnant — a small remaining number of people
2. reprove — to express disapproval, to scold
3. temple — a place on each side of the head above the cheek bone

LESSON 82
God Calls Gideon
Judges 6

BEFORE WE BEGIN, the last verse of chapter 5 says that the land had rest for forty years. But in the first part of chapter 6, we learn that after the forty years the Israelites did evil again. This time the Lord sent Midian to trouble the Israelites, so they would cry to Him once more, and repent. We could say that Midian was a half-brother to Israel. Remember that Midian was the son of Abraham and his second wife, Keturah. Both Midian and Israel had Abraham for their father. Find Midian on your map for this lesson.

Read Judges 6:1-10

LESSON OUTLINE
A. The Midianites Oppress Israel

1. Midian made an alliance with Amalek and other tribes east of the Jordan River. Find Amalek on your map. Midian and Amalek oppressed Israel in an entirely new way. They did not station their armies in the land, but came with bands of soldiers to plunder*.

    a. These enemies let the Israelites plant their crops and take care of them until they were ready to harvest. Then the Midianites would sweep through the land, taking all the ripe crops, and destroying those they could not carry away with them.

    b. They left no food for the Israelites nor for their animals. The people were starving. They were poor. They were treated cruelly by their enemies, and they hid in dens and caves of the mountains to escape.

    c. The rule of Midian lasted only seven years, but the Midianites were so cruel and their oppression was so severe that the whole land of Israel was being destroyed.

2. When the Israelites could not stand it anymore, they cried to Jehovah. They asked God to defeat their miserable enemies. But they cried to Jehovah with hearts and lips which still worshipped Baal and Ashtaroth. At the same time, they thought that God should do whatever they asked Him.

3. To teach His people, God sent a prophet. The prophet told them how the Lord had always helped Israel in the past, because He loves His people; and he ended with, "But ye have not obeyed my voice." That was God speaking!

287

First Israel had to learn to cry to Jehovah with hearts that were sorry for their sins.

Read verses 11-18

B. God Calls Gideon

1. When Israel repented, the Lord sent them a deliverer. He called Gideon, from the tribe of Manasseh, not a very important tribe in Israel. Gideon came from a poor, unknown family, and he said he was the least in his father's house, verse 15.

2. This is the first time in the period of the judges that Jehovah Himself called a judge. Verse 12 tells us that the Angel of Jehovah came to Gideon. The Christ of the Old Testament called him! He came to this unknown and humble Gideon, and said, "The Lord is with thee, thou mighty man of valor*."

3. What was Gideon doing when Jehovah called him? He was threshing. Usually oxen threshed wheat by tramping on it on a threshing floor. Gideon was in a winepress, a shelter in a rock, beating the grain secretly, with a stick. The Midianites were not bothering him. Gideon's family must have lived in an out-of-the-way place, which the Midianites had not discovered.

4. Gideon wondered why God called him a mighty man of valor. If that were true, why were the Midianites oppressing them so that people had to hide in caves and thresh in winepresses? Didn't Jehovah save His people by taking them out of Egypt? Would He save Israel again? Gideon knew that only Jehovah could deliver them from the Midianites.

Read verses 19-23

C. The Sign

1. Gideon wanted to be sure that Jehovah Himself was speaking to him. He killed a kid and made unleavened cakes. The Angel of Jehovah told him to put the food on a rock and pour out the juice. The Angel did not eat the food, but touched it with His staff. Fire came out of the rock and burned it. The food was a sacrifice, a burnt offering to the Lord.

2. It showed Gideon that the Angel of Jehovah is God and that He accepted Gideon's offering.

Discuss in class how Gideon
must have felt after the wonder of the sign.

3. Gideon built an altar and called it Jehovah-Shalom, which means Jehovah-Peace.

4. But Gideon and his family were not strong in the faith of Jehovah. They believed that He was Israel's God, but they allowed idols in their home, too. They had an altar to Baal and an Asherah Pole (which the Bible calls a grove). It was a pillar of wood which looked like the goddess Ashtaroth.

5. Jehovah told Gideon to destroy the idols in his father's house.

   a. He must show to all the people around him that the idols are no gods.

   b. He built an altar to the Lord and sacrificed an ox on it, to show that Jehovah is God alone.

   c. He was challenging the people in the name of Jehovah.

6. Yet he was fearful. He and his ten servants destroyed the idols and altars of Baal in the darkness of the night.

7. In the morning, when the men of the city saw that their gods were gone, they wanted to kill Gideon; but Gideon's father said, "Let Baal plead for himself." He meant: if Baal is a god, he can defend himself.

Read verses 33-40

D. The Second Sign

1. The fact that Gideon was threshing grain tells us it was harvest time. The Midianites could be expected any time to take away Israel's crops. They had already crossed the Jordan and pitched at Jezreel. Find it on your map.

2. Gideon blew his trumpet, a sign for war, and sent messengers to the northern tribes, telling them to come to the battle. He was ready for war, and trusted in Jehovah.

3. Then Gideon asked for another sign:

   a. not because he did not believe God's words;

   b. but because he wanted to make sure that God would save Israel with Gideon as their leader.

4. This was the sign:

   a. He put a fleece on the threshing floor and asked that the next morning the fleece be wet with dew, and that the floor be dry. When he looked the next morning, the fleece was so wet he wrung out a bowl full of water. And the floor was dry.

   b. He asked God to turn the sign around the next day, so that the floor would be wet and the fleece dry the next morning, and it was.

5. This is the meaning of the sign:

   a. Because the dew is a sign of God's blessings, and the fleece was a sign of Israel, Gideon asked God to show him that He blessed Israel, but left

289

the heathen nations around Israel dry, with no blessings.

b. But what if the fleece was dry because Israel's faith was weak, and it seemed as if they had no blessings from God? And what if God gave the heathen nations power over Israel? Was God still blessing Israel? The answer was yes: even when enemies came, God was bringing His salvation to Israel.

DO NOT FORGET that Gideon's story is for us. When we sin and are not obedient to the Lord and do not feel that we love Him very much, He always makes us sorry and forgives us, because He always has blessings for us, His children.

WORD STUDIES
1. plunder — to rob someone of goods or property by violence
2. valor — bravery, courage

LESSON 83
Gideon's Victory by Faith
Judges 7

BEFORE WE BEGIN, notice that Gideon is called by his new name in verse 1: Jerubbaal, which means Let Baal fight. Gideon earned the name when he fought Baal by destroying Baal's altar; and he was ready to fight Baal's followers. Gideon was up early in the morning, ready for the battle.

Read Judges 7:1-8

LESSON OUTLINE
A. The Lord Sifts* Gideon's Army

   1. The Midianites were in northern Canaan. They had crossed the Jordan at Jezreel, and were in a valley there. Gideon and his army camped near the hill of Moreh, at the fountain of Harod, which was the water supply for his army. They could look down on the large host of their enemies. Find these places on your maps.

   2. Gideon was ready for battle. God was not. Jehovah said, "The people that are with thee are too many."

      a. Gideon had 32,000 men, a very small army.

      b. Midian's soldiers in the valley looked like grasshoppers, when they come in plagues and sweep the land, and Midian's camels were without number, verse 12.

      c. If we saw both armies, we would say the opposite was true: Gideon's army was far too small and unprepared. We would say, "There are not nearly enough soldiers, Gideon. Blow the trumpet again, and get more men to fight."

   3. What was the Lord's reason for wanting Gideon's army smaller?

      a. So that Israel could not be proud, and say, "My own hand hath saved me." verse 2.

      b. It had to be very clear to Israel and to Midian that the salvation of Israel was Jehovah's work: that He is their salvation, and that He saved them from their enemies, and that He will have all the glory.

      c. That is the reason God chose such a humble and unknown person as Gideon. All He needed was a small army. An army of 32,000 men was too big.

4. God told Gideon to tell his army, "Whosoever is fearful and afraid, let him return." Many years ago already, God had given that law to Moses in Deuteronomy 20:8.

    a. These soldiers of Gideon had found it easy to come when Gideon blew the trumpet. It was patriotic to fight! There was no enemy in sight, either.

    b. When they saw the soldiers of Midian in the valley, they lost the courage of their faith.

    c. 22,000 men left Gideon's army. Now his army numbered only 10,000 men. Two-thirds of his army was gone.

    d. Do you think Gideon was amazed when so many soldiers left him? God was giving him a hard test of his faith.

5. Next, God told Gideon that 10,000 soldiers were still too many. He instructed Gideon to tell them all to march to the waters formed by the fountain of Harod. The soldiers were thirsty after their march, and Gideon told them all to take a drink at the fountain. God told Gideon to watch how the men drank, and separate them into two groups. This was the test:

    a. Those who stayed on their feet and bent down, took a handful of water, and lapped it from their hands as a dog laps, were to be separated into one group.

    b. Those who got on their knees or lay flat and drank water from the pool, Gideon put in a second group.

6. This was the meaning of the test: the soldiers showed by their actions what lived inside their souls.

    a. The first group had only one thing in mind: the battle of Jehovah. They were ready to get on with the battle. There was no time to be lazy or pamper themselves.

    b. The second group was more interested in their own comfort. The battle was not urgent to them. They were not eager, with their hearts and minds, for God's cause.

7. Gideon counted the soldiers in each group.

    a. In the first group were 300 soldiers.

    b. In the second group were 9,700 soldiers.

8. Jehovah told Gideon to send the 9,700 soldiers home. He did not want an army. He wanted only a band of 300 men, so that everyone could plainly see that the victory was Jehovah's work.

B. God Prepares Gideon for the Battle

1. Jehovah told Gideon: "Arise, get thee down unto the host; for I have delivered it into thine hand," verse 9. In God's counsel (His plan), the battle was already finished and won; and God wanted Gideon to know it.

2. Gideon trusted Jehovah. God had given him faith in his heart. But God saw fear in Gideon's heart, too. Suddenly most of his army was gone. His faith was shaky.

3. Knowing Gideon's heart, Jehovah said, "But if thou fear to go down, go with Phurah thy servant down to the host," verse 10. God asked Gideon to go alone, with only one servant. What if he were caught by the enemy?

> Discuss in class how we usually trust Jehovah,
> but when He puts us in great danger, we fear.

4. In the darkness of the night Gideon and Phurah went to the edge of the camp of Midian. There they heard two guards talking about a dream one of them had. Read it in verse 13.

a. The cake of barley bread was the kind of bread the very poor people ate. It was a picture of the Israelites, who were poor and miserable because Midian had oppressed them so badly.

b. The tent in the dream was a symbol of all the army tents of Midian. When all the tents of Midian were turned upside-down, Midian would be defeated.

c. The other guard knew what the dream meant: "This is nothing else save the sword of Gideon."

5. Gideon bowed down and worshipped Jehovah and went back to his little band of men. Why did God want Gideon to hear this dream? God wanted Gideon to know that the Midianites understood that God had called Gideon to win a great victory over them. Their nerves were on edge. They knew they were doomed. The littlest thing would make them flee; and Gideon now understood their fear.

C. The Battle

1. These were Gideon's instructions to his soldiers:

a. Carry a trumpet in your right hand, and a candle with a pitcher over it in your left.

b. The light of the candle was hidden until Gideon gave his men a signal.

c. Not one of the soldiers carried a sword. They had no intention of using swords.

d. Gideon divided them into three companies of one hundred soldiers each.

2. Gideon, with one of the companies of soldiers, gave the signal at the middle watch (midnight). Then all the soldiers blew their trumpets, smashed their pitchers, and shouted, "The sword of the Lord, and of Gideon!"

3. The sudden noises and the eerie lights of the candles woke the Midianites out of a sound sleep; and the Lord made them confused. They fought one another and they fled.

4. Gideon and his men fought by faith, without swords. For the sword which won the victory that night was the sword of the Word of Jehovah.

DO NOT FORGET that we in our churches are often like Gideon's army: small and not important in the world. Only Jehovah can save His people, His church; and He calls us to be humble Gideons, to work and to fight by faith.

WORD STUDIES

sift — to separate one part from another

LESSON 84
Gideon Finishes His Work
Judges 8

BEFORE WE BEGIN, we must not think that the battle was finished when the Midianites fled. If Israel allowed them to flee to their own land, they could rest, find their courage, and come back and oppress Israel again. God told Gideon that Midian must be pursued, and that the leaders must be caught and slain, and the tribe of Midian destroyed.

Read Judges 7:24, 25

LESSON OUTLINE

A. The Pursuit

1. Gideon needed more men to pursue and capture the Midianites. He put out a call once more to Manasseh, Naphtali, and Asher, this time to help him finish the war. He called the men from Ephraim, too, and they came to help.

2. Gideon instructed the Ephraimites to cut off the Midianites' retreat just before the Jordan River, near to Ephraim, where little streams and brooks join the Jordan, at Beth-barah. Find it on your map.

3. The Midianites had separated. The main army was near Beth-barah, and when Ephraim pursued them, they destroyed the army and caught and killed two princes of Midian: Oreb (whose name means Raven) and Zeeb (whose name means Wolf).

4. Meanwhile, Gideon and his 300 men went across the Jordan River to pursue two other princes of Midian: Zeba and Zalmunna, and their 15,000 soldiers.

5. After the men of Ephraim killed Oreb and Zeeb, they took the heads of these men across the Jordan to Gideon.

Read Judges 8:1-3

B. Trouble With Ephraim

1. You would think that this would be one of the happiest days in the lives of these soldiers. God was giving them the victory over their cruel enemies. It called for a celebration!

2. But the Ephraimites came with quarrelsome tongues to Gideon, with the words of verse 1. Read it once more. They came to a humble Gideon, whom God had made a hero of faith. Weren't they happy that Jehovah gave Israel

such a great victory through Gideon? Weren't all the Israelites working for the same cause?

3.   The men of Ephraim were not interested in God's cause. They were jealous and angry that their small brother-tribe, Manasseh, had the victory. Ephraim wanted the honor. They thought they should be the leaders. But Jehovah did not need proud men who fought in their own strength. He needed a humble Gideon.

4.   Gideon and the men of Ephraim argued sharply, verse 1; but in verse 2 Gideon gave them a soft answer. Verse 2 asks: did not Ephraim do better in pursuing the Midianites than Gideon did with his trumpets and pitchers and candles in the battle? Ephraim had already killed two princes!

Discuss in class what Gideon's soft answer
did to the men of Ephraim.

C. The End of the Pursuit

1.   Gideon and his 300 chosen soldiers crossed the Jordan and chased the two princes, Zeba and Zalmunna, who were fleeing far ahead of them in the wilderness.

2.   Gideon's army were faint — tired and hungry — but still pursuing. Their work was not finished. They must have felt like taking a day to rest, but the Lord's work spurred them on, and filled them with the enthusiasm to keep up the chase.

3.   Running through the tribe of Gad, Gideon and his men came to the town of Succoth. (Do you remember from Lesson 31 that Jacob built booths at Succoth many years earlier?) At Succoth they asked for bread because they were so faint. The men of Succoth should have been eager to offer them food. They were Israelites, working for the same cause: to destroy God's enemies. But the men of Succoth answered: first defeat Zeba and Zalmunna, and then we will help you. They were cowards, and not interested in God's cause. Gideon told them he would punish them by tearing their flesh with the thorns of the desert on his way back, verse 7.

4.   At Penuel, the people also refused to give their leader and his soldiers food. This time Gideon vowed to break down the tower of their city on his way back home.

5.   When he came to Karkor, Gideon and his army destroyed the army of Midian and took Zeba and Zalmunna as prisoners. Find Succoth, Penuel, and Karkor on your maps.

6. On their way home, Gideon and his men

    a. taught the elders of Succoth with thorns and briars from the desert;

    b. beat down the tower of Penuel, where the people had run for safety, and killed all the men of the city;

    c. killed Zeba and Zalmunna, after Gideon found out that they had killed all his brothers.

7. Read verse 28. Not one bit of Midian's power was left. They were humbled and weak, and never again attacked Israel.

Read verses 22 and 23

D. Israel Wants Gideon To Be Their King

1. When the people of Israel said to Gideon, "Rule thou over us," they wanted him to be more than a judge. They wanted a king whose sons and grandsons would rule after him.

    a. The Israelites wanted to honor Gideon and show their thankfulness for saving them from the cruel oppression of the Midianites.

    b. Their reason for honoring Gideon was: "For thou hast delivered us out of the hand of Midian." That was not true. Jehovah had delivered them. They forgot what Jehovah had done for them, and they wanted to honor a man.

2. What was Gideon's answer?

    a. "The Lord shall rule over you." Israel was not like the heathen nations around them, who were ruled by the will of a man.

    b. Israel was God's people, who were ruled directly by God; for Israel was a type of the heavenly kingdom of God, where all God's children will live forever, with Jehovah as their King.

Read verses 24-27

E. Gideon's Last Days

1. After all the tribes of Israel had showed him such great honor, Gideon lost some of his humility. He asked the people for some of the spoils they had taken from the Midianites: the golden earrings and ornaments and beautiful garments. The people gave willingly, and Gideon became a wealthy man.

2. Gideon made an ephod, a priest's garment, set with precious stones, with which the priests asked God's will. Maybe Gideon's motive was right: he did not want Israel to turn to idols again, but to worship Jehovah. However, Gideon did wrong by acting as a priest when God had not called him to be a priest. The result was that the people made an idol out of the ephod.

3. When Gideon was rich, he took many wives, and he had seventy sons. Gideon's riches in the latter part of his life were his downfall. He was not God's humble and obedient servant anymore.

DO NOT FORGET that being poor and humble is good for us, for then we lean on the strength of Jehovah. Riches and power are not wrong, but they are temptations for God's children to turn from Him and lean on themselves. Pray that you will always have grace to lean on Jehovah.

LESSON 85
The Evil Rule of Abimelech
Judges 9

BEFORE WE BEGIN, we should know that the results of Gideon's sins in the last
part of his life brought serious trouble to Israel. The jealousy of the men of
Ephraim flared up again, because all Israel went to worship the ephod Gideon
had made. But the tabernacle of Jehovah was in Shiloh, in the territory of
Ephraim, and the men of Ephraim wanted Israel to worship there, not because
they loved Jehovah, but because they wanted to be important.

Read Judges 9:1-6

LESSON OUTLINE

A. Abimelech's Evil Deed

1. Abimelech was the son of Gideon and his concubine, a godless Hivite slave
girl descended from Shechem, the son of Hamor, whom we met in Jacob's
time. His name Abimelech means "my father is king." This name tells us
that after all Gideon did like the idea of being a king.

2. When he was grown, Abimelech left Ophrah, where his family lived, and
went to live in Shechem, where his heathen mother's family lived. He gave
the men of Shechem a choice: which is better — that seventy men rule over
you, or that one rules? He quickly added, "Remember, I am your flesh and
blood." Abimelech asked a crafty question, with his selfish goals in mind.

   a. Shechem did not need a king to rule over them, and God forbade it.

   b. It was a lie that all seventy sons of Gideon planned to descend on
   Shechem and rule the city.

   c. Only Abimelech had the idea and ambition to become their king.

3. The people of Shechem listened to Abimelech, and said, "He is our
brother." They wanted to make him their king. It did not matter to them
that Jehovah is King in Israel.

4. They gave Abimelech seventy pieces of silver from the house of Baal,
which he used to hire evil men to help him murder his brothers. They went to
Ophrah and killed all seventy brothers, except one, on one stone. Only
Jotham, the youngest, escaped.

5. What a horrible crime in the nation that was supposed to be God's people!
Why did Jehovah allow such a bloody slaughter of the sons of Gideon?

a. When Gideon made his ephod and worshipped it, he taught his children idol-worship, too. Chapter 8:27 tells us that the ephod became a snare (a trap) for Gideon and his house. It means that his sons also turned from the fear of Jehovah.

b. Now God was using one evil man (Abimelech) to bring judgment on his idolatrous brothers.

6. Only Jotham, the youngest, escaped; for it is likely that the Lord found some good in him.

B. Jotham's Fable*

1. All the men of Shechem, also of Millo, which was the castle or fortress, came together to crown Abimelech king.

2. Jotham was there, too, but at first no one knew it. He stood on Mt. Gerizim, which rose high above Shechem on the south side. With a loud voice, he called out to them and told them a fable.

3. Read the fable in verses 8 to 15 this way: the teacher reads the story part; half the class reads what all the trees say; and the other half reads the answers of the olive and fig trees, the vine and the bramble*.

4. The meaning of Jotham's fable is as follows:

a. The olive and fig trees and the vine are good trees. They give people their delicious fruits. These trees are types of the God-fearing judges, such as Othniel, Ehud, and Gideon, who brought fruits of blessings to Israel.

b. The bramble is a worthless weed. The best thing to do with it is to burn it. It was a picture of Abimelech and of Ephraim, who were proud and evil murderers.

5. Read verse 16. Did you notice that Jotham chose his words very carefully? He did not accuse them of wrong-doing. He said, "If you have done well...." Otherwise, let fire burn you. That is what a bramble deserves. Then Jotham fled for his life.

Read verses 22-25

C. Treachery* in Shechem

1. On the surface, there seemed to be friendship between Abimelech and the men of Shechem. Their wickedness bonded them together.

2. But the Lord looked down on them and sent an evil spirit, not just a spirit of meanness or a nasty tongue. This was a spirit which came upon them suddenly, and was a very real devil, one of the evil spirits straight from hell.

This spirit whispered evil things and planted suspicions in their hearts.

Discuss how we can see the results of the work of very real devils
in men's hearts today.

3.   The result was that Abimelech and the people of Shechem plotted against one another, for the evil spirit put hatred and envy into their hearts.

a.   The men of Shechem decided to get rid of Abimelech.

b.   They set men to lie in wait for him, to try to catch and kill him.

c.   Abimelech had already left the city. He was careful, and stayed away. Meanwhile, the sneaky men who waited for him became bandits, and robbed anyone who came along.

4.   According to the law, every fourth year the Israelites were supposed to offer fruits to Jehovah. Read verse 27. The Shechemites offered their fruits to Baal; and they ate, drank, and were merry. That is when Gaal came on the scene. We do not know who he was, but he told the people, "Why should we serve Abimelech?" verse 28. Gaal wanted to be asked to become their leader.

5.   Zebul, a friend of Abimelech and also a ruler under him, heard Gaal's words and was angry. He sent messengers to Abimelech. Read verse 31. He told Abimelech:

a.   that the men of Shechem were fortifying their city;

b.   to wait in the mountains near the city.

6.   In the morning, Abimelech's army started to march. Gaal and Zebul stood at the gate of the city and watched. Gaal thought Zebul was his friend. When he said he saw people coming down the mountains, Zebul told him they weren't people, but only shadows. He did not want Gaal to know yet.

7.   When it was too late, Gaal realized it was Abimelech and his men. Abimelech came down and defeated Gaal and left the city. The next morning the people, thinking they were safe, went to work in their fields; and Abimelech came with three companies of soldiers and killed them all and covered the city with salt.

8.   Then he went to the neighboring city of Thebez and captured it. But many men and women took refuge in the tower of the city. When Abimelech tried to break down the tower, a woman threw down a millstone and injured him badly, and he told his armor-bearer to kill him. Read what God says about it in verses 56 and 57.

DO NOT FORGET that devils are very real; and although they, too, are in God's power, God uses them in this world for His good purposes. Do you ask God not to let the devils tempt you?

WORD STUDIES
1. fable — a short tale, with a special meaning in it
2. bramble — a prickly plant or shrub
3. treachery — deceiving, "double-crossing"

Jehovah Calls Jephthah
Judges 10-11:28

BEFORE WE BEGIN, we are ready to study the last period of the history of the judges. It marked the end of the worship of Gideon's ephod as an idol; for Gideon's sons, who kept up the idol worship, had been murdered; and there was no one to promote the worship of the ephod anymore. The Israelites went back to Shiloh and worshipped Jehovah there.

Read Judges 10:1-5

LESSON OUTLINE
A. Tola and Jair

1. These two men judged Israel after the death of Gideon. God tells us very little about them. Tola was the son of Puah, from the tribe of Issachar. He judged in Mt. Ephraim twenty-three years. We do not even know what enemy he fought.

2. Jair judged in the region of Gilead in the land of the tribe of Manasseh on the east side of the Jordan. His thirty sons, who rode on ass colts, helped him. Jair must have been a wealthy man, of high position. He ruled thirty cities, called "Cities of Jair."

Read verses 6-9

B. Israel's Terrible Sins

1. Verse 7 tells us that when Israel did evil again, the Lord sold them into the hands of the Philistines and the Ammonites. From matching other parts of the Bible with this verse, we learn that these two nations bothered Israel at the same time.

    a. Jephthah was the judge who saved Israel from the Ammonites, who bothered them on the east side of the Jordan River.

    b. At the same time Samson fought the Philistines in the southwest part of Israel.

    c. This period lasted about forty years.

2. This time, Israel's sin was that they served not only Baal and Ashtaroth, but the gods of all the heathen nations around them. Each heathen nation had its own special god, but Israel, who were supposed to be God's people, wanted to worship them all.

a. Notice that when God's people sinned, they fell lower and deeper into sin than the heathen did.

b. In verse six, count the number of gods they served. They did not stand still in their sins. They became worse and worse.

c. Formerly they had served Jehovah, too. Now they "forsook the Lord," verse 6.

3. To chastise His people, and bring them to repentance, Jehovah sent the Philistines and the Ammonites. The people suffered hard oppression, especially from the Ammonites. The soldiers of Ammon bothered the tribes east of the Jordan, and Benjamin and Ephraim on the west side. Verse 7 says that the Lord sold them to Ammon; and Ammon acted as if the Israelites were their property. They did what they wished with Israel. For eighteen years they crushed them.

Read verses 10-16

C. Israel Cries to Jehovah

1. The Israelites could not stand the cruelty any longer. They cried to Jehovah, probably through a priest: "We have sinned." It sounded as if they had repented, but Israel had not really turned from their idols. Now they wanted their idols and Jehovah. To them, God came in handy as a mighty power to help them when they were in trouble, but they were not sorry for their idolatry.

2. We know that this is true from the Lord's answer. He reminded the Israelites that He had always saved them when they cried to Him. Then He said the words of verse 13. Read it again.

Discuss in class whether the Lord's answer
surprises you.

3. Did God mean that He would not save His people? That cannot be. God meant that He would not save them under these conditions — that they bargain with the almighty God. He will save them only when they truly repent and put away their idols.

4. Once more the people came to God, verse 15. This time they were humble and sorry. They put away their idols. And Jehovah, Who is full of mercy and grace, forgave them, because He always loves His people.

5. Now Israel was ready to do the right thing: to fight their enemies. They chose soldiers and prepared for the battle, and camped at Mizpeh. Find it on your map for last week.

304

D. The People Choose Jephthah

1. The Israelites needed a leader, and the Lord directed them to Jephthah. He was a son of Gilead and a woman who was not his wife. Probably Jephthah was born before his father married his wife, the mother of his other sons.

2. Jephthah's brothers hated him and threw him out of the house because he was only a half-brother. He was in danger of his life and fled from the land.

3. In the land of Tob (we don't know where it was) he attracted other lonely or adventurous wanderers, and organized a sort of army. They may have fought some of Israel's enemies.

4. Soon Jephthah became known as a mighty man of valor, and a man who loved God and His people.

5. The elders of Gilead came to Jephthah in their time of trouble, and asked him to be their captain. We do not read that his brothers asked him to come back, nor confessed their sins of sending him away.

6. A surprised Jephthah asked: "Didn't you hate me and send me away?" When the elders urged him, he asked whether he would be their leader after the war was over. Jephthah wanted a place to live among God's people. And the answer of the elders was yes.

7. Jephthah went to the army at Mizpeh, and became captain. At Mizpeh he told the Lord all that had happened. He was a man who lived close to the Lord. He also wanted God to witness the agreement between the elders and himself, and to judge the elders if they did not keep their word.

E. Jephthah Tries to Negotiate*

1. Jephthah is the only judge who tried to settle the troubles peaceably before the war was fought. Jephthah sent a message to the king of Ammon:
    a. not to fight, for there was no cause for war;
    b. that Ammon must be sorry for oppressing Israel;
    c. and agree that the land of Canaan belonged to Israel.

2. The king of Ammon insisted that the people of Israel stole the land from his forefathers when they came to Canaan from the desert.

3. Once more Jephthah sent messengers to the king of Ammon. He denied that Israel took any land away from the heathen nations.
    a. He reminded the king that they even asked permission to walk through Edom and Moab.

    b.   He told the king that they walked around these countries.

    c.   He went on to show that Sihon and Og had started war with Israel, and that God had defeated them and that God had given His people the land. Jephthah knew his Bible history!

4.   He asked the Ammonites to be satisfied with the land which Chemosh their god had given them; for Israel possessed the land the Lord had prepared for them in Canaan, verse 24. Do you think Jephthah believed that the idol Chemosh gave the Ammonites their land? No, he was just speaking their language.

5.   But the king of Ammon would not listen to Jephthah.

DO NOT FORGET that although Jephthah lived alone in another country for a time, he always had God in his thoughts. He took God into His confidence and told Him his secrets and his troubles. It is a wonderful way for God's child to live.

WORD STUDIES

negotiate — to bargain with or persuade someone to reach an agreement

LESSON 87
Jephthah as Judge
Judges 11:29 - Judges 12

BEFORE WE BEGIN, we should know that often in the Bible the whole area east of the Jordan River, the territories of Reuben, Gad, and Manasseh, was called Gilead. When the spirit of the Lord came upon Jephthah, he went through all the land of Gilead, gathering an army. He came back to Mizpeh, ready to attack the Ammonites.

Read Judges 11:30, 31

LESSON OUTLINE

A. Jephthah's Vow

1. Before he led the battle against Ammon, Jephthah made a vow — a promise — to Jehovah. God's people in Bible times, and ever since, have made vows to the Lord. God's people do not have to make promises to Jehovah, but they may. If they do make a vow, they must keep it.

    a. You remember the vow Jacob made at Bethel on his way to Laban's house. He promised to come back to Bethel when Jehovah brought him back safely. And the Lord had to make him keep his promise, Genesis 35:1.

    b. The Lord does not want His people to make foolish or sinful vows, nor to make a vow to bargain with God.

    c. Jephthah's vow came from a heart filled with love for God and His people. We know he made his promise by faith, for in Hebrews 11:32 God names him with the heroes of faith.

Discuss in class in what kinds of situations
you could make a vow to the Lord.

2. Remember that Jephthah had been thrown out of his father's house and out of Israel. There was no place in God's land for him. When he was called back, he became their leader, the one to save Israel. He knew, because God had done all these things for him, that he could not win a victory except by God's power.

3. Before the battle, he promised Jehovah that when he came home in peace, he would give to the Lord whatever came to meet him. Some people think he expected an animal to meet him and that he would sacrifice that animal to Jehovah.

307

4. But notice closely Jephthah's words in verse 31: "whatsoever cometh forth from the doors of my house to meet me."

   a. Animals usually do not come from the house. People do.

   b. Animals, cattle and sheep, do not greet people either.

5. No, Jephthah very likely expected a person to come running out of the house to meet him. That person "shall surely be the Lord's." It means that the person's life would be given to serve Jehovah. Animals cannot do that.

6. The problem in verse 31 comes when we read, "And I will offer it up for a burnt offering." Could Jephthah offer a person as a burnt offering? No, for God's law forbade it. The answer to the problem is that it is better to translate this verse, "and I will offer it up for a whole offering." The whole life of the person who met Jephthah would be offered to serve Jehovah.

Read verses 32, 33

B. The Battle

1. Now Jephthah was ready to fight Ammon, the powerful and cruel enemy who had oppressed Israel for eighteen years. The Lord gave him a complete victory. Jephthah cleared the land of Ammonites.

Read verses 34-40

2. When Jephthah came back to his home in Mizpeh, his happy daughter, his only child, met him with timbrels and dances, probably with her friends at her side. It was a celebration!

3. Although Jephthah knew this might happen when he made his vow, he was sad; for his only daughter must dedicate her whole life to Jehovah. She would have no room in her life to get married and have children. This meant that Jephthah's name and family would die out in Israel.

4. His daughter was calm, and said, "Do with me according to that which hath proceeded out of thy mouth." She asked only that she and her friends go to the mountains for two months to be sad because she could not have a husband and family.

5. Every year after that, the women of Israel spent four days a year to praise (not lament) the daughter of Jephthah.

Read chapter 12:1-7

C. Ephraim's Shibboleth

1. Jephthah was not finished with his problems, for now there was trouble inside Israel. All Israel should have been happy and relieved that the cruel Ammonites were gone forever. They could all worship Jehovah in unity again.

2. One tribe, Ephraim, could not join the rest of Israel in gladness and thanksgiving to God.

   a. The men of Ephraim came to Jephthah in anger, bitterness, and jealousy. They threatened to burn Jephthah's house over him.

   b. Their question, "Why did you not call us?" was a lie. Jephthah had called them, but they had not come, verse 2.

   c. Remember that the tribe of Ephraim was not happy unless they were the leaders. They wanted all the honor.

   d. The people of Ephraim were selfish, always looking out for themselves.

   e. Most of the Ephraimites were not interested in God's glory.

3. All this bitterness had happened once before, when Gideon was judge. Gideon spoke softly to them and humored them.

4. But Jephthah made plans to meet them and fight (verse 4), not because he was a fierce man, for not long ago he had tried to avoid war with the Ammonites by talking with their king. This time, however, things were different.

   a. Ephraim had come with a threat: we will burn your house!

   b. Jephthah was not able to reason with the men anymore, for Ephraim wanted to destroy the men of Gilead.

5. Their armies came together for war on the east side of the Jordan, and Jephthah's army won.

6. The defeated army of Ephraim fled. To reach their homes, they had to cross the Jordan River. But all the fords of the Jordan were taken by Jephthah's soldiers, who guarded the fords, and had orders to kill the Ephraimites. How would they know who were Ephraimites and who were Israelites from other tribes? They were from the same nation and they looked alike.

   a. They could ask, "Are you from Ephraim?" but the Ephraimites could lie, and say no. For them, the answer was a matter of life and death.

   b. Jephthah's soldiers thought of a way. The Ephraimites spoke a dialect, and they could not pronounce the sh sound. So the men of Jephthah's army said, "Say Shibboleth" (which means stream) and they said, "Sibboleth."

   c. It was a simple test, a matter of only one letter. But saying "sibboleth" meant death. The men of Gilead killed 42,000 men of Ephraim.

7. Jephthah judged Israel six years. After that three more judges ruled. All we know about them is that:
   a. Ibzan, from Bethlehem, judged Israel seven years;
   b. Elon, from Zebulon, judged Israel ten years;
   c. Abdon, from Ephraim, judged Israel eight years.
8. Are you learning the names of the judges in order?

DO NOT FORGET that pride is one of the worst sins. God's children often fall into the sin of the Ephraimities, the "me first" and the "I deserve the credit" attitude. If that sin bothers you, think of the words of Jesus in Matthew 5:5: "Blessed are the meek; for they shall inherit the earth."

LESSON 88
The Birth of Samson
Judges 13

BEFORE WE BEGIN, remember that while Jephthah was busy fighting wars with the Ammonites, who were bothering Israel in the northeast part of their land, the Philistines were bothering the Israelites in the southwest. Find the land of the Philistines on your map for Lessons 88 to 90. Samson was the judge whom Jehovah called to deliver Israel from the Philistines. He and Jephthah judged at the same time.

Read Judges 13:1-5

LESSON OUTLINE

A. The Angel Visits Manoah's Wife

1. Israel did evil again, and the Lord made them slaves of the Philistines, who oppressed them forty years. The Israelites had to suffer all the hardships the Philistines put on them, but we do not read that they repented from their sins.

    a. Samson was born about the time of the beginning of the oppression of the Philistines.

    b. He was judge the last twenty years of the oppression.

2. Manoah and his wife were Danites, from Zorah. Find it on your map. They were obedient Danites, who had stayed in their territory and did not move north with the rebels at the time of Micah. Manoah and his wife had no children.

3. The Angel of Jehovah came to Manoah's wife. Once more the Christ of the Old Testament, Who appeared as a messenger at special times, came to tell good news. He told her: "You are a woman who cannot have children;" and in the same sentence the Angel promised her a son, a wonder-child, who would begin to deliver Israel. This was a special message because:

    a. We usually read that before Jehovah came to help them, Israel repented. This time they kept living in their evil ways.

    b. Other judges were called after they grew up. Samson was called before he was born.

    c. Samson delivered Israel alone, not with large armies or great victories. Samson would only begin to deliver Israel.

4. The most important part of the Angel's message was that this son would be a Nazarite, even before his birth. A Nazarite was known by three signs:

    a. He might not cut his hair.

    b. He might not eat grapes nor the wine made from grapes.

    c. He might not touch a dead body, for it was unclean.

5. What did these signs of a Nazarite mean? That he was consecrated to the Lord, a man who lived separate from the sinful world. Some of God's people made temporary Nazarite vows, at certain special times in their lives. Some, like Samuel and John the Baptist, were called by God to be Nazarites for their whole lives. Only Samson was born a Nazarite.

    a. The long hair of Samson was a sign of strength. It showed that all his strength was devoted to Jehovah.

    b. Grapes, and especially the wine from grapes, were signs of the sinful pleasures in this world. By not drinking wine, the Nazarite showed that he would not live with worldly pleasures, but was free to spend his life serving Jehovah.

    c. A dead body was a sign of the end of sin: death. The Nazarite kept his body clean, separate from death.

6. Before he was born, Samson's mother might not drink any strong drink nor touch anything unclean; for God called Samson to be special even before he was born, verse 4.

7. The whole nation of Israel was supposed to live separate from the wickedness of the heathen around them, but they disobeyed. God called Samson to show these disobedient children of God that he was a Nazarite — that he was a sign of being separate.

Read verses 6-22

B. The Birth of Samson

1. The excited wife of Manoah told her husband the news. She called the Angel "a man of God." This tells us that He appeared in the form of a man, a human being, but different from an ordinary man: His face was "very terrible." She saw holiness in His face.

2. Manoah prayed Jehovah that the Angel would come again, and God answered his prayer. Once more the Angel came to Manoah's wife, alone in the field, and she ran from the field to get her husband.

    a. The Angel of Jehovah did not give them any new instructions.

    b. But He repeated the rules of the Nazarite, which they must follow.

3. This was a wonderful day for Manoah and his wife. Manoah wanted this special time to last longer. He asked permission to get some food ready, to kill a kid, and prepare it.

4. The Angel refused to eat, but suggested that Manoah offer the meat as a sacrifice, a burnt offering to Jehovah.

5. Manoah still did not realize that he was talking with the Angel of Jehovah, God Himself! He asked the visitor His name; but the Angel did not tell, because His name is wonderful (not secret, as verse 18 is translated). It is too wonderful for sinful people to hear.

6. Then Manoah took the young animal, laid it on a rock as an offering to Jehovah, and a miracle happened. The Angel of Jehovah gave fire for the offering, and went back to heaven in the flame. This miracle told Manoah and his wife two things:

  a. that God had accepted their sacrifice.

  b. they knew His promise would come true, for it was God, Whose name was Wonderful, Who had made the promise.

7. Manoah, who was weaker and not as sensible as his wife, said, "We shall surely die, because we have seen God." His wife, using her common sense, told her husband that Jehovah would not have accepted their offering nor promised them a son if they were going to die.

Read verses 24, 25

8. Some students of the Bible think that the Spirit of Jehovah (verse 25) gave Samson his physical strength only, but not the Spirit of God in his heart. They say that Samson played cruel tricks, he had a frightening sense of humor, and he was moved by hatred, not the love of God. Is this true? No.

9. Verse 24 tells us that the Lord blessed him. And the Lord never blesses the wicked. Besides, Samson loved God and His people. With grace in his heart, he fought for Israel. And God includes Samson in the heroes of faith in Hebrews 11. A hero of faith always looks to Jehovah for his strength. But Samson's character was not always so nice, and he fell into serious sins. We will hear more about this in our next lessons.

Discuss in class other Bible characters
who were heroes of faith and who had many faults and sins.

DO NOT FORGET that Samson was strong when he stood alone before Jehovah as a Nazarite. But when he wanted the evil pleasures around him, he sinned badly. Verse 5 tells us that Samson only began to deliver Israel. He looked to Jesus, Who was not a Nazarite, but a Nazarene, (from Nazareth). Samson failed to save Israel from their sins. He looked forward to his Savior, Who did not have to live separate from the world, but Who overcame* the world and saved His people.

WORD STUDIES
overcome — to conquer, to defeat

LESSON 89
Samson Troubles the Philistines
Judges 14-15:8

BEFORE WE BEGIN, we already learned in our last lesson that the Spirit of Jehovah began to move Samson in the area where he lived: in the camp of Dan, between Zorah and Eshtaol. When the Spirit moved Samson, God made him feel as if he must fight God's enemies. In this lesson, Samson visited Timnath, another city in Dan. Find these three cities on your maps. In Timnath, on the border of Israel and Philistia, the Israelites and the Philistines lived in peace together.

Read Judges 14:1-9

LESSON OUTLINE

A. Samson's First Trip to Timnath

   1. Why did Samson go to the Philistines at Timnath?

      a. Because he was a Nazarite, chosen by God to serve Him in a special way. When God's Spirit came upon him, he wanted more than anything else to make trouble for Jehovah's enemies. He went to Timnath to make trouble!

      b. At the same time, Samson was not a perfect Nazarite. He had one glaring weakness: he fell in love with heathen women. He could not stay away from them.

      c. He found a young woman who pleased him well, verse 3. If he married her, he would be living among the Philistines, and he would be able to start arguments and make trouble for them and fight them, for God's sake.

   2. Is it hard for you to understand Samson? He was a man of opposites: a man with special gifts from Jehovah, and a man with distasteful sins.

   3. When Samson told his parents that he wanted a Philistine wife, they were dismayed. Samson, a Nazarite before the Lord, must have a wife from his own covenant people. God's law, in Exodus 34:15 and 16, did not allow God's people to marry heathen wives. If he married this Philistine girl, he would be a picture of wicked Israel who left Jehovah and worshipped idols.

   4. Samson did not listen to his parents' words. Twice he demanded, "Get her for me." He was not a very nice character and he was not obedient. He demanded his own way.

315

5. But do not forget that deep inside Samson there was a reason for marrying this girl, for Jehovah was stirring him. His parents did not know why he chose this Philistine girl, but Samson knew he needed a cause to fight the Philistines.

a. The Philistines and the Israelites lived in outward peace and friendship, and worshipped the same idols. The Israelites were not interested in being roused to battle with their enemies.

b. Samson could not suddenly start killing the Philistines on the street. He needed a cause, an argument which would start a fight. That is the reason Samson chose the way of marrying one of his enemies:

1) He wanted her. She pleased him well.

2) At the wedding feast he would find an occasion for a fight.

6. On the way to Timnath, he wandered away from his parents. He seemed to be a lone warrior*. Suddenly, God put a young lion in his way. We must not picture Samson as a giant, with huge muscles. He was an average young man, who until this moment did not know he was exceedingly strong. Now the Lord showed him by a wonder that he could easily kill the lion. It was a special gift of the Spirit of the Lord; and Samson kept this wonder to himself, not even telling his parents.

7. In Timnath, he talked with the Philistine girl, she pleased him, and he and his parents went home.

Read verses 10-20

B. Samson's Marriage

1. Samson wanted to go back and marry the young woman, for she still pleased him. We must understand:

a. that his marriage was a sin;

b. at the same time, that God in His plan willed that Samson would marry her, for the purpose of saving His people.

2. How can we fit this together? By understanding that this sin of Samson served God's plan for Israel's good.

> Discuss in class how God has used the sins of other saints
> for His purpose. Start with Jacob's lie to his father Isaac.

3. On the way back to Timnath, without telling his parents why, Samson wandered off to the place where he had killed the lion. In the carcass of the lion he found bees and honey. Samson ate some of the honey and gave some to his parents. They did not know where it came from, of course, but Samson kept the lion and the honey in his mind. He had a plan.

316

4. Wedding feasts usually lasted seven days, and Samson did not seem to enjoy the feast. He was given thirty Philistine companions, who were really his enemies. He was thinking more of the conflict* he would cause than of the feasting; for already on the first day he told his riddle. Read it in verse 14. The terms of the riddle were:

    a. thirty tunics (undergarments) and thirty robes for the Philistines if they could guess the answer;

    b. thirty tunics and thirty robes for Samson if they could not guess it.

5. During all the seven days of the feast, Samson's wife pestered him. She wept and she accused him of hating her. Samson argued that he had not even told his parents. Why should he tell her?

6. On the seventh day, Samson told his wife the answer. She was not a loving, loyal wife. Immediately she told the thirty friends who had been given to Samson. She had a good reason for telling them: they had threatened to burn down her house upon her and her family if she did not get the answer, verse 15.

7. On the seventh day, the men gave the answer: "What is sweeter than honey? and what is stronger than a lion?" Samson said, "if ye had not plowed with my heifer. . ." which means, "If you had not conspired with my wife. . . you would not have found out."

8. Samson went out to get thirty changes of clothes. He did not harm the thirty men at the wedding. He would not fight for personal reasons, just because they cheated in getting the answer. He went to Ashkelon (find it on your map) and the Spirit of Jehovah came over him and he killed thirty Philistines. Samson gave the garments of the men of Ashkelon to the thirty wedding guests. His wife was given to another man. It was a strange ending for a wedding.

Read Judges 15:1-8

C. Samson's War With the Philistines

1. After a time, Samson announced that he was going to visit his wife. Most likely he had heard that she now was another man's wife, but he wanted people to know that he went to make trouble for the Philistines.

2. The girl's father was frightened, and offered to give Samson her younger sister as his wife. Samson refused.

3. Because his own people of Israel would not help him fight their enemies, Samson turned to the animals of the forest. He caught 300 foxes (or jackals)

and tied their tails together in pairs of two, with a firebrand between their tails. This was a wonder. No ordinary man, all alone, could handle 300 wild animals and tie them together in pairs. God made the forest animals help to fight His enemies.

4. Yet it was a cruel kind of joke which Samson played on his enemies. When he lit the firebrands, the foxes ran in panic. God saw to it that the animals scattered through the grain fields of the Philistines. God used Samson's clever plan to destroy a huge area of the Philistines' crops.

5. The Philistines thought that Samson's battle was with his wife's family. So they went and burned his wife and her father.

6. But Samson's battle was with all the Philistines. He went after the men, and all alone, smote them "hip and thigh," verse 8. He disabled their legs, leaving them helpless. He did it by the Spirit of Jehovah.

DO NOT FORGET that Samson, a man hard for us to understand, a man who loved idolatrous women and who had a cruel sense of humor, was a hero of faith, a Nazarite who was moved by the Spirit of the Lord. He fought God's enemies, and looked to Jesus to take away his ugly sins.

WORD STUDIES
1. warrior — a man experienced in warfare
2. conflict — a clash, a struggle, a battle

LESSON 90
Samson's Last Days
Judges 15:9-16:31

BEFORE WE BEGIN, have you noticed that Samson often went away alone? He seemed to like to be by himself. Part of the reason was his character. He was not a sociable man. The main reason was that his own people, the tribe of the Danites, did not like him because he made war with the Philistines. In verse 8 we read that he went to the top of the rock Etam, in Judah, just over the border. Find it on your map.

Read Judges 15:9-17

LESSON OUTLINE
A. Ramath-Lehi

1. What was the attitude of the men of Judah toward Samson? The Philistines had ruled over Judah so long that the people had no more fight left in them; and they did not want Samson to stir up trouble.

2. What was the attitude of the Philistines toward Samson? They knew Samson fought through the wonder of God's power, and they were frightened. Yet they wanted revenge: not to kill him, but to bind him and torture him, verse 10.

3. They heard that Samson was at Etam, but they did not dare go there to bind him themselves, even though they came with more than 1,000 men. They had a different strategy*.

    a. They went to Lehi to fight the men of Judah. Find Lehi on your map.

    b. When they threatened the men of Judah with death if they did not bind Samson, they would force Judah to bind Samson.

4. Judah agreed. Samson's fellow Israelites had fallen very low:

    a. they disowned Samson;

    b. they joined God's enemies;

    c. the name for them is traitors.

5. Judah came to Samson with an army of 3,000 men! They asked a hopeless question: "Don't you know the Philistines rule over us?" They did not even seem to realize that this was not an ordinary fight, but that it was God's cause **against the** devil's cause.

    a. Samson could easily have fought them, but they were his own people.

    b. He let them bind him with two new cords, and take him from Etam to Lehi, where the Philistines were stationed.

Discuss in class how you think
the Philistines felt when they saw
Samson coming, bound hand and foot.

6. When the Philistines shouted, the Spirit of the Lord came upon Samson, and he broke the ropes as if they were burned flax.

7. Now he needed a weapon. The only thing he saw was the jawbone of an ass. With it he killed 1,000 Philistines: one man against a thousand! We do not know how many Philistines escaped.

8. What about the men of Judah? They just looked on. The Bible does not tell us about any words of repentance. And Samson, the lone warrior, made a victory song. Read it in verse 16. He called the place Ramath-lehi, which means the lifting up of the jawbone.

Read verses 18-20

9. When the battle was over, Samson was so thirsty that he thought he would die. Besides needing water so badly, after the excitement of the battle, he was down in the dumps.

10. But Samson was God's child. He prayed for water, so that the Philistines could not capture him. God heard his prayer and made a hollow in the rock (not the jawbone), and Samson drank. The name En-hakkore means well of him that called, verse 19.

Read Judges 16:1-5

B. Samson and Delilah

    1. Some years must have passed. In verse 1, we find Samson in Gaza. Find it on your map. At Gaza he visited a harlot, an evil woman.

    2. The men of the city did not really know what to do with Samson. They waited all night but did not dare touch him. They boasted that in the morning they would kill him. Instead, they watched him take down the gates of the city, with the two huge posts, and carry them up a hill!

    3. Why did Samson do it? Because to take an enemy's gates was to have victory over him. Read what God told Abraham in Genesis 22:17. But Samson must have seen the humor and the surprise of his enemies. Now, more than ever, they wanted to know the secret of his great strength.

    4. Find Sorek on your map. In Sorek Samson saw Delilah, and he loved her.

320

The five lords of the Philistines, each a ruler of a city, were glad that Samson came to Delilah.

    a.   They could not conquer him in battle.

    b.   They could not keep him in a city with gates.

    c.   Possibly they could steal the secret of his strength through Delilah, if she would betray him.

Read verses 6-14

5.   They came to Delilah with bribes. Each lord offered her 1,100 pieces of silver (how many would that be altogether?) if she could make Samson tell her the secret of his strength.

    a.   The first time Delilah asked what made him so strong, he told her to bind him with seven green withs (catgut). What should Samson have done? He should have told her the truth: that Jehovah was his strength, that he was a Nazarite, separate to the Lord. Then he should have left. But he did not want to leave the pleasures of sin in Delilah's house. Notice, too, that Samson came close to telling her the truth when he used the number seven, for it is the covenant number, the number of Jehovah, Who gave Samson his strength to be a Nazarite.

    b.   The second time Delilah asked, he told her to bind him with new ropes which no one had used. Again, he came close to the truth: the ropes had to be separate from everyone, just as Samson was separate to Jehovah.

    c.   The third time Delilah asked, he told her to weave the seven locks of his hair, the long hair which was the part of Samson's Nazarite vow, and which everyone could see.

    d.   Each time that Delilah said, "The Philistines be upon thee," Samson easily broke loose.

Read verses 15-31

6.   Delilah did not give up. She pestered him and he was sick to death of it. He finally told her the truth about his Nazarite vow to Jehovah. Samson should have left this godless woman. His life was in danger. Yet, he would not believe that she would betray him. He enjoyed living with this evil woman.

7.   Delilah called a barber, and she made Samson sleep. Then they cut his hair. The last time she said, "The Philistines be upon thee," Samson was helpless, for Jehovah had left him. The cruel Philistines took out his eyes and made him grind in prison.

321

8. Slowly Samson's hair began to grow again. When the day came for the Philistines to make a great celebration to their god Dagon for letting them capture Samson, he prayed to Jehovah for strength just once more. He was led to the two main pillars of the house, and the Lord gave him the biggest victory of his life. He pulled down the building, killing more Philistines than he did in all his lifetime. Samson died, too, fighting the battle of faith against God's enemies.

DO NOT FORGET that Samson is a hard man to understand. He had so many sins and faults in his character. He also had great faith and love for Jehovah; and he looked forward to Jesus, to make him clean from his faults and to finish the battle against sin.

WORD STUDIES
strategy — a plan, especially in battle, for a special purpose

LESSON 91
Elimelech and Naomi Go to Moab
Ruth 1, 2

BEFORE WE BEGIN, although we have finished studying the Book of Judges, the Lord has told us one more story which happened during that period: the story of the Book of Ruth. God does not tell us just when it happened, but it probably took place in the early period of the rule of the judges, possibly in Gideon's time.

Read Ruth 1:1, 2

LESSON OUTLINE

A. Elimelech and Naomi Leave Israel

1. This book of the Bible is not a history of one of the judges, but the story of a small family from the tribe of Judah, a humble and unknown family. The Lord has given us a glimpse of about twelve years in the life of this family, for a very special purpose, which we will discover later in our lessons.

2. It was a family with beautiful names. The father Elimelech (my God is King) and mother Naomi (pleasant one) lived in Ephrath (fruitful) near Bethlehem (house of bread). Find Ephrath and Bethlehem on your map for next week's lessons. They had two sons, Mahlon and Chilion. We do not know the meanings of their names.

3. This family lived in Canaan, the promised land, a land of blessing, a type of the perfect promised land in heaven. Elimelech and Naomi knew that the Lord had gathered His people on Mt. Gerizim and Mt. Ebal in Joshua's time, and had told them to serve Him faithfully and obey His commandments. They they would be blessed. Read Deuteronomy 28:3, 4.

4. If they disobeyed and served idols, they would be cursed. Read Deuteronomy 28:16, 17.

5. Elimelech and Naomi knew that riches on this earth — plenty of food and clothes and money and crops — were pictures of God's love and blessing.

6. But this was the time of the judges, when everyone did what was right in his own eyes. Most of the people of Israel had turned from Jehovah to idols. To bring His own children back to Himself, and to punish the wicked Israelites, Jehovah sent enemies who robbed the land, or He kept back rain from the land. We do not know what caused this famine at the time of Elimelech and Naomi, but we know that it was severe.

7. Because the Book of Ruth tells us that Elimelech's family was faithful to the Lord, we know they suffered, not because they were evil, but because of the wicked idolaters in the land. They were so tired of the famine, they decided to move to Moab.

a. It was not the same as if we move to Canada or France or Singapore. We can worship the Lord anywhere.

b. But in Old Testament times, Canaan was the only land where God's people could worship Jehovah. Only when they worshipped at the tabernacle and saw all the pictures and types, did they know of their salvation in Jesus Christ. Nowadays, the country in which we live is not important, for God has given salvation to people of all nations.

8. Elimelech and Naomi asked the wrong question: "Where do we go to get our daily bread?" instead of, "What have God's people in Israel done wrong?" They decided to leave Canaan, where God fed them with the Bread of Life, and live in Moab, where they would have bread in their stomachs. Their plan was to sojourn there, to stay only a short time. Trace their trip from Ephrath to Moab on your map.

Read verses 3-5

B. Their Life in Moab

1. The family had plenty to eat in Moab, and they stayed on. Then God spoke to them by taking away Elimelech's life. He told them by his death that they must go to the only land where God showed them everlasting life. But Naomi did not listen to God.

2. She stayed in Moab with her two sons. As they grew older, she taught them the fear of the Lord; but she taught them in disobedience — in the wrong country. Both boys married heathen girls.

3. Naomi had heard that the famine in Israel was over, verse 6, but she liked the good life in Moab, and stayed for ten years.

4. Then God spoke to her once more, and took away her two sons. Naomi had to learn the hard way from Jehovah.

Read verses 6-22

C. Naomi's Repentance and Return

1. Now Naomi saw her sin, was sorry, and started out for Canaan. She had turned from sin to God, and from Moab to Canaan. She planned to go back alone, and urged Ruth and Orpah, her daughters-in-law, to stay in Moab. Why?

a.   They must not go to the promised land because they loved Naomi, or wanted an adventure.

b.   They must go to Canaan only because they loved the Lord and His people more than anything else.

2.   Orpah was not interested in Jehovah and His love, but Ruth clung to Naomi and said the words of verse 16. Read it once more. Ruth wanted to go to God's people, live with them, belong to them, die there, and be buried in the land of promise.

Discuss in class why Ruth went back, but Orpah did not.

3.   When the people of Bethlehem saw Naomi coming back with her daughter-in-law, they said, "Is this Naomi?" Why did they ask?

a.   Because, with all her trouble and sadness, she had changed. She looked old and sad.

b.   She told them it was the Lord Who sent this bitterness to her, verse 20. But Naomi was not bitter. She had repented, and was happy to live in the promised land again.

Read Ruth 2:1-3

D.   Naomi and Ruth in Canaan

1.   Naomi and Ruth were very poor. How would they get food? The Lord had taken care of that. Read Leviticus 23:22. It was the beginning of the barley harvest, and Naomi told Ruth to glean* in the fields of Boaz, a relative of Elimelech.

a.   Boaz was a godly man. Read in verse 4 how he greeted his workers.

b.   He was kind to Ruth and told her not to go to any other field to glean, verse 8.

c.   He knew that Ruth, a heathen girl, chose to live in Israel with God's people, verse 11.

d.   Boaz told his servants to let some handfuls for her drop on purpose, verse 16. Boaz seemed to be attracted by Ruth's humble ways, her love for Naomi, and her willingness to work.

2.   Ruth gleaned in Boaz' field until the end of the barley harvest.

DO NOT FORGET that Naomi's life was a picture of our lives. She fell into sin. So do we. She was sorry. So are we. She went to Canaan, the land of salvation, for she knew she was saved. God tells us in our hearts that we are saved, too. Then she lived a life of holiness and obedience to Jehovah. So do we — not

325

perfectly, but with hearts which love to obey. In other words, we live a life of sin, salvation, and sanctification*, just as Naomi did.

WORD STUDIES
1. glean — to gather the leavings from a field after the crop has been gathered
2. sanctification — to live a separate, holy life before God.

LESSON 92
Ruth Becomes a Mother of Jesus
Ruth 3, 4

BEFORE WE BEGIN, in chapter 3:1, Naomi told Ruth she would look for rest for her. Naomi was not looking only for a peaceful, happy life for Ruth, but a life with a husband. Naomi was looking for a place in Canaan for Ruth, for Canaan was the church. Only by marrying an Israelite could Ruth become an Israelite, and find rest and salvation in Jesus. Both Naomi and Ruth were interested in her salvation and her place in the church.

Read Ruth 3:1-9

LESSON OUTLINE

A. Ruth Visits Boaz

1. During harvest time, the barley which was harvested each day was brought to a large threshing floor. In the evening Boaz and his men went to the threshing floor. Why in the evening? Because that is the time a cool breeze came up, and as the oxen trampled the grain, the stems and leaves blew away, and the kernels of barley could be gathered and stored.

2. Naomi instructed Ruth to go to Boaz' threshing floor, for Naomi was looking for a husband for Ruth, a God-fearing husband. She told Ruth to do two things:

    a. to change her clothes. Ruth had been wearing the clothes of a widow. Naomi wanted her dressed in the clothes of an Israelite girl who was ready for marriage.

    b. to lie down at Boaz' feet. It was a sign that Ruth wanted to be protected.

3. Reaping was a happy time. It was a time of work, and then of eating, drinking, and festivity. It was also the custom for the reapers to sleep right on the threshing floor.

4. When all was quiet, Ruth came softly and lay down at Boaz' feet. He awoke at midnight, frightened, because a woman lay at his feet. Verse 9 tells us that he spread his skirt (or cover) over Ruth; and Ezekiel 16:8 tells us it was a picture of Jehovah spreading the skirt of His covenant of friendship over Israel. That was what Ruth was saying by lying there: she did not want to be a heathen Moabitess anymore, but one of God's covenant children.

B. Boaz Makes a Promise to Ruth

1. Boaz was kind to Ruth. He called her "my daughter." It is likely that Boaz was older than Ruth, and probably a widower.

2. He promised that he would help her: he would do the part of a kinsman (a relative) and take care of her.

    a. But there was a nearer relative. He must first be asked to help Ruth.

    b. This relative was not likely to help her, for he had not even shown himself, nor helped her with food or shelter.

3. Ruth stayed at Boaz' feet until morning and left before it was light. Boaz filled her long veil with barley to take home to Naomi.

C. Boaz at the Gate

1. God really owned the land of Canaan, of course; and He told His people to use it. They might buy and sell the land to one another. When an Israelite bought a piece of land, he kept it, and his children and grandchildren inherited it. It was a type of buying a place in heaven for himself and for his descendants.

2. When an Israelite sold his land for some reason, he was allowed to buy it back again. When Elimelech sold his land because he went to Moab, he died, and could not buy it back. But his widow Naomi could. How? Naomi had come back to Bethlehem empty. She had no money.

    a. God had made a law about this. Read Leviticus 25:25.

    b. A relative could redeem (buy back) the land for the poor.

    c. In that way, Naomi could get her place back in Israel.

    d. The nearest relative took care of this, for it was important that God's people, with their families, kept their places in the covenant line of God's children.

Read Ruth 4:1-8

3. The next morning Boaz made work of getting the closest relative to redeem Naomi's property. He went to the gate of the city, the place where all business and the affairs of law were conducted. Do you remember that Lot did business there, too? Ten elders listened to Boaz, as witnesses.

4. Boaz called out to the relative.

    a. He asked whether the relative was willing to redeem, to buy back, the land for Naomi. The relative, whose name we do not know, agreed, verse 4. He could probably farm the land for Naomi and make some money, too.

b. There was one more detail: through the years it had been a custom in Israel to marry the widow, to have children, in order to keep the name of the man who had died in the line of his family. It meant that the relative would not buy the land from Naomi, and marry her. She was too old. He must buy the land from Ruth, marry her, and have a child who would carry on Elimelech's name.

c. Now the answer of the relative was no. Why? Ruth had no children. It probably meant she never would have any. If she did have a child, it would have Elimelech's name. Then the name of the relative might die.

d. The relative was a selfish man.

    1) He wanted property and money.

    2) He would not be obedient to God's laws.

    3) He was not interested in Jehovah's covenant.

e. Therefore he never had a name in Israel. God did not tell us his name, and He took it out of the land of promise.

5. Boaz finished the ceremony at the gate. Read Deuteronomy 25:9. The closer relative took off his shoe and transferred — gave away — the right of a redeemer. When God commanded that they spit in his face, it showed contempt* for the man who thought of himself instead of God's covenant promises.

Read verses 9-17

D. Boaz Marries Ruth

1. Boaz called the elders to witness that he bought the possessions of Elimelech and would take Ruth to be his wife. And the witnesses at the gate asked the blessing of Jehovah for Ruth: that she would be like Rachel and Leah, and build the house of Israel, which would be finished when Jesus was born.

Discuss in class what it meant in Old Testament times
to build the house of Israel.

2. Boaz married Ruth, and the Lord gave them a son; and the godly women of Bethlehem congratulated Naomi, who now had a grandson.

a. A joyful wonder had happened. Ruth, a heathen Moabitess, and also a child of God's covenant of friendship, now had a place in the promised land, by a wonder of God's grace. Ruth named her child Obed: the serving one.

b. Another joyful wonder was that Obed's father Boaz, who had redeemed Ruth's place in Israel, was also a type of Jesus, Who redeems all His people. He redeemed Boaz and Ruth and He redeems us with His blood; and He has a place for all of us in the heavenly Canaan.

    c.   The third joyful wonder is that Boaz was in the line of the ancestors of Jesus. If Boaz had not married, Jesus could not have been born. God brought Ruth from Moab to Canaan to be Boaz' wife and one of the grandmothers of Christ.

3.   In the Book of Ruth, God taught the Israelites and us, not only that the Savior would be born, but that the Gentiles (Ruth and us) would have salvation in Him.

4.   The Book of Ruth ends with the name David: from King David the line of kings will go on through Old Testament times until it ends with The King, Jesus, born in Bethlehem.

5.   For all these reasons, God gave us the Book of Ruth: to teach us about the line of Christ in the Old Testament.

DO NOT FORGET that just as Boaz, Ruth's redeemer, gladly took her as his bride, so Jesus, our Redeemer, promises to take us as His bride. Revelation 21:2 calls us the bride, the Lamb's wife. We will live in heaven with Him forever.

WORD STUDIES

contempt — to despise something or someone; to consider it worthless

LESSON 93
The Birth of Samuel
I Samuel 1

BEFORE WE BEGIN, remember that we are studying the third period of Old Testament history.

The first period starts with God's promise to Adam and Eve in Genesis 15 and ends with the flood.

The second period covers the flood to Israel's conquest of Canaan.

The third period includes the conquest of Canaan, the period of the judges, the history of the kings, and the captivity of Israel. The two books of Samuel tell the story of the end of the judges and the beginning of the rule of Israel's kings.

Read I Samuel 1:1-3

LESSON OUTLINE

A. The Setting

1. In verse one we meet Elkanah, a Levite who lived in the mountains of Ephraim. These mountains extended south into the territory of the tribe of Benjamin. The city mentioned in verse 1 is also known in its short form: Ramah. Find it on your map for next week's lessons.

2. Eli was judge at this time. He was judge at about the same time as Jephthah and Samson, toward the end of the period of the judges. Eli was already very old, and his two sons, Hophni and Phinehas, were wicked priests.

3. We learned that in the Book of Judges no mention is made of anyone worshipping at the tabernacle at Shiloh. But God saw to it that His tabernacle survived the lawless years of the judges. A few of God's children were still faithful worshippers of Jehovah. Elkanah was one of them. He sacrificed each year at Shiloh.

Read verses 4-10

B. Trouble in Elkanah's Family

1. Elkanah was disobedient to one of God's commands. He had two wives. Most likely he had married Hannah first; and when she had no children, he married a second wife, Peninnah. Elkanah loved Hannah, not Peninnah.

2. God gave Peninnah children, but Hannah still had none.

a. Just as Sarah and Rebekah and Ruth wanted children so they could have a place in Israel, so Hannah longed to have a child.

331

b.   There was nothing worse in Israel than to be a married woman without children. Hannah was puzzled about it. She loved Jehovah and she knew Jehovah loved her. Yet He did not show His favor to her and give her a child. It seemed as if the Lord was against her.

3.   Peninnah knew that Elkanah did not love her, and because she was a godless woman, she tormented Hannah. The worst times of Hannah's life were their trips to Shiloh, when Peninnah sat with all her children as they ate, and "provoked" her, verse 6.

4.   Elkanah was not very wise to give Hannah a double portion of food, to show how much more he loved her, for it made Peninnah jealous. And when Peninnah was cruel and Hannah cried, he asked a foolish question. Read it in verse 8. Hannah knew that her husband had his children by disobeying God and marrying Peninnah. Hannah wanted a child by asking God for it.

Read verses 11-13

C. Hannah's Prayer

1.   Although Hannah had often prayed for a child, she had never before prayed for a child at the tabernacle. Now she did.

2.   Her prayer was much more than just a prayer for a child.

a.   Her prayer was not for a daughter, but for a son.

b.   She asked God for a son, because she was praying in a very dark time in Israel's history, a time of disorder, of anarchy, and idolatry. Israel needed a deliverer!

c.   She wanted not just a child, but a child of God.

d.   It was time for a Nazarite, and she promised Jehovah that her son would be a Nazarite. Verse 11 mentions one sign of a Nazarite. Find it.

e.   She promised to give this son to Jehovah all the days of his life. If God gave her a son, he would be a Levite, as his father Elkanah was. Usually the Levites served part-time at the tabernacle, taking turns. This child would spend his whole life serving Jehovah. He would be a Nazarite-Levite.

3.   Hannah prayed this prayer silently. Only her lips moved.

Read verses 14-18

D. Eli's Reaction

1.   Eli, the high priest, saw her praying her fervent prayer. He thought she was muttering in a drunken stupor, and he gave her a gruff scolding. He did not even give her the opportunity to explain that she was praying from the depths of her heart because she was so sad and troubled.

2. Why did old Eli scold?

    a. Because in those evil times, he never saw women pouring out their souls to Jehovah.

    b. It was very common for drunken women to come to the tabernacle, because hardly anyone knew its holiness anymore.

    c. Eli's sons were very evil men, who were friends of the drunken women.

3. The worst part of all this evil was that Eli, as high priest, did nothing. He did not raise his hands in horror. He did not scold them or chase them away. Eli was a very easy-going man, and he tolerated the evil at Shiloh. Wickedness was a way of life at the tabernacle. The most Eli did was to give a mild scolding.

Discuss in class what you think of Eli.

4. Hannah spoke up to Eli. Read her words in verses 15 and 16 once more. Then Eli changed his attitude toward her and gave her his blessing.

5. Hannah felt better, verse 18. If Jehovah answered her prayer, she was willing to give up her son to the service of the tabernacle in Shiloh. She wanted God to use her son to bring Israel to repentance, so that Jehovah would preserve His people until Jesus came.

Read verses 19-28

E. Hannah's Prayer Is Heard

1. Soon Elkanah and Hannah had a son from the Lord, whom they named Samuel: heard of the Lord. For about three years, until he was weaned, Hannah kept her son at home, and did not go to the tabernacle.

2. When Samuel was old enough, she brought him, with a gift for the Lord, to the tabernacle.

3. She reminded Eli who she was, and Eli remembered her. She left Samuel at the tabernacle because he was "asked of the Lord." Then Hannah prayed a prayer that was a song. You will learn more about it on your worksheet.

DO NOT FORGET that Samuel was very young to leave his parents. How was he trained and taught? God does not tell us all these details. Perhaps the women who worked at the tabernacle helped Eli; and Eli saw in Samuel the godliness that was missing in his own two sons. The Lord took care that Samuel was trained in His fear.

LESSON 94
The Lord Calls Samuel
I Samuel 2:11-3:21

BEFORE WE BEGIN, I Samuel 2:11 tells us that Samuel stayed at the tabernacle and ministered to the Lord before Eli the priest. Ministered means served. Samuel was the Lord's servant in His house.

Read I Samuel 2:12-17

LESSON OUTLINE
A. Eli's Evil Sons

1. Eli's sons were sons of Belial (which probably means worthless). Belial is another name for Satan. Read verse 12. They knew Who the Lord is, but did not talk with Him, nor love Him, nor live with Him in love.

2. This is what Hophni and Phinehas did: they profaned* the tabernacle, especially the sacrifices.

    a. When God's people brought thank-offerings to the tabernacle, the people often sacrificed an animal and boiled some of it and ate it, as Elkanah and his family had done.

    b. God's law, in Leviticus 8:31, allowed the priests to spear some of the boiled meat for themselves. It was God's way of taking care of the Levites.

    c. God's law did not allow the Levites to take raw meat with their forks, nor meat with the fat on it; for God's rule was that the priests must first burn off the fat. The smoke of the burning fat must go up to Jehovah as a sweet smell. See Leviticus 3:3-5.

    d. The sacrifices were types of Christ's sacrifice of His flesh and blood on the cross, for His people. Sacrificing an animal was a solemn, holy occasion.

    e. Eli's sons did not obey God's law. They wanted raw meat, and meat with fat. If the people would not give it to them, they took it by force. Hophni and Phinehas robbed Jehovah of His sacrifices and did not care for salvation in Jesus Christ. It was one of the worst sins they could commit.

3. Father Eli scolded them very mildly, not nearly as sharply as he had rebuked God-fearing Hannah. Read verses 23 and 24. Eli's sons did not listen to their father, because it was God's purpose to kill them.

    Discuss in class whether you would like a father like Eli.

B. Samuel at the Tabernacle

1. During these evil times, Samuel lived at the tabernacle and served the Lord there, side by side with Eli and his two wicked sons. He wore the white linen ephod of a priest, a shoulder robe, tied at the waist with a wide belt (called a girdle in Scripture).

2. Each year his mother took him a coat, a bigger one each time she came.

3. Now Eli blessed Hannah, especially because she and Elkanah had given their son to serve Jehovah; and he asked Jehovah for more covenant children for them. The Lord heard Eli's prayer and gave Elkanah and Hannah three more sons and two daughters. God tells us in verse 26 that Samuel grew in favor with God and with men.

C. The Unknown Prophet

1. God sent a prophet to Eli. Who he was and where he came from we do not know. These are the words God put in his mouth:

a. that God had chosen Eli, a descendant from Aaron, to wear the ephod of a priest, to serve Jehovah, and to offer sacrifices. He had the highest task and greatest honor in all Israel.

b. The prophet scolded him for kicking at the sacrifices to Jehovah, and for honoring his sons more than the Lord.

2. The prophet went on to say that God would take away the priesthood from Eli's family. His descendants would be beggars, verse 36, and would die young, verse 32.

3. In verse 35, God promised that He would choose faithful priests from another family from Aaron (the house of Eleazar). Eleazar would be a type of the true high priest, Jesus Christ, the only Priest Whose sacrifice can pay for our sins.

D. God Comes to Samuel

1. God's Word was precious — scarce — in these last days of the judges. There was no prophet to speak God's Word, because God was silent, and gave no messages. Of course, Israel had the five Books of Moses, and they still worshipped at the tabernacle, but Jehovah did not come to them with new revelations of His will.

2. The child Samuel was already growing up to be a young man, but he had not yet had a direct revelation from God. He had never heard God speaking

to him. That is why verse 7 says that Samuel did not yet know the Lord. Samuel had not yet seen His appearance nor heard His voice.

3. Before the light which burned all night in the tabernacle went out, probably early in the morning, Jehovah came to him.

    a. Three times Jehovah came and stood beside Samuel and called him by name (see verse 10).

    b. Samuel heard and saw the Lord, but did not know it was the Lord. He thought it was Eli.

4. The third time, Eli finally realized it was the Lord speaking to Samuel. He told him to say the words of verse 9.

5. Once more the Lord came to him as at the other times, and this time He gave Samuel a message. It was Samuel's first revelation from God. Read verses 11-14.

    a. God's message to Samuel was very much like the message of the unknown prophet. Why? Because Eli and his sons did not listen to the first prophet.

    b. Samuel was afraid, verse 15. This was his first experience as a prophet of Jehovah, and he must have been uneasy, because he had to tell the old priest Eli the words of Jehovah's judgment. Eli told him, with an oath* (in verse 17), not to hide God's words from him.

6. Eli had heard the words of the unknown prophet, but he had not changed his ways. He did not demand obedience from his sons. Now he heard the same message from Samuel's mouth. This time it sounded worse, for the Lord had said that when Israel heard what will happen, their ears will tingle, verse 11.

7. Eli knew he would soon see God's judgment, but he was God's child (although a weak one) who said, "Let him do what seemeth good," verse 18.

DO NOT FORGET that Samuel lived in troubled times of disobedience and lawlessness. But Jehovah was with him and did not let any of his words fall to the ground, verse 19. Samuel's words were not useless nor broken words, which dropped to the ground, but were words of Jehovah, which spoke the truth to His people. From now on, God came again to the tabernacle at Shiloh and gave Samuel words to speak.

WORD STUDIES

1. profane — to show disrespect and to dishonor holy things
2. oath — a call to God to hear one' words or promise

LESSON 95
The Philistines Capture the Ark
I Samuel 4, 5

BEFORE WE BEGIN, we will see a change in the attitude of the Israelites in this lesson. The Lord appeared again at Shiloh and spoke to Samuel. The few faithful people of God in Israel were encouraged. The rest of the Israelites felt better, too; for they expected that now God would be with them, even though they still worshipped idols, and even though they did not repent of their sins.

Read I Samuel 4:1-2

LESSON OUTLINE

A. Israel Goes to Battle

   1. The change in Israel was mostly an outward change. Most of the Israelites were no different in their hearts. But they united to go to war with the Philistines, expecting that the Lord would fight for them.

     a. During the time of the judges, they had never come together as a nation to fight their enemies. Each judge ruled in a little part of the land.

     b. When the words of Samuel came to all Israel, they all prepared for battle at Ebenezer, while the Philistines were at Aphek. Find these places on your map for this lesson.

   2. The army of Israel was smitten* before the Philistines, and 4,000 soldiers were killed.

   3. Now we will discover another change in the Israelites: they asked why Jehovah had smitten them, and had not given them victory over the Philistines.

     a. They had listened to Samuel when he reminded them that they would have the victory only when Jehovah was on their side, and they thought that now Jehovah was on their side.

     b. For Samuel had called them to repent and turn to the Lord. They did, but only outwardly. They did not want to be sorry for their sins. They wanted victory over the Philistines.

     c. They were not ready to give up their idols, to trust in Jehovah, and love Him. They did not want to turn to Jehovah with all their hearts.

Read verses 3-11

B. Israel Fetches the Ark

337

1. The godless rulers of Israel suggested bringing the ark of Jehovah to the battlefield, that "it" may save us, verse 3. The little word it should be translated he; for the Israelites knew that the ark was God's dwelling place. Jehovah lived there.

   a. They remembered that when their fathers had taken the ark when they marched around Jericho, the walls fell down.

   b. They thought that if they brought the ark to the battlefield, Jehovah would give them another victory.

2. It did not bother the rulers that this time they were getting the ark in disobedience to Jehovah. They sent some men to get the ark.

   a. We do not know what happened at Shiloh, when they came to take God's holy ark. Was Eli there?

   b. We do know that God did not kill them for stealing His ark from the most holy place, and He came along with them to the battlefield — in His anger.

3. The great shouting of the Israelites when they saw the ark disturbed the Philistines. They knew all about the wonders God had done for Israel, for they said in their heathen way in verse 8: "these are the 'Gods' that smote the Egyptians."

4. Although the Philistines were afraid of God, they told one another to be strong and to fight.

5. Jehovah gave the Philistines the victory in the battle.

   a. They killed 30,000 Israelite soldiers. The rest of the soldiers fled.

   b. The Philistines took the ark, because God allowed them to capture it.

   c. Hophni and Phinehas were killed in the battle.

Read verses 12-22

C. Eli Dies

1. A runner (messenger) from the tribe of Benjamin came to Shiloh with news of the battle. Eli was sitting at the side of the road, trembling because the ark was gone from the tabernacle.

2. He heard the loud shouts from the city, for all the people in Shiloh were crying out. Eli could not go into the city because he was blind, verse 15.

3. The messenger came to Eli to tell him why the city was crying out.

   a. Israel was defeated.

   b. Hophni and Phinehas were dead.

   c. The ark of God was taken by the Philistines.

338

4. When Eli heard the news about the ark, he fell backward, for he was old and heavy, and his neck broke.

5. The wife of Phinehas was ready to have a baby. When she heard that her husband and father-in-law were dead, and that the ark was gone, her baby was born. She named him Ichabod, which means "no glory." Read verse 22. Then the God-fearing wife of Phinehas died.

Read chapter 5:1-5

D. The Ark in the Land of the Philistines

1. The ark was in the land of the Philistines, not because Jehovah was blessing them, for He was very angry with them. But God was using the Philistines and allowing them to capture the ark to teach His people Israel a lesson and to bring them to repentance. Remember that it was not the Philistines' purpose to do God's will. In their wickedness they thought they had captured God.

Discuss in class other wicked men in the Bible
whom God used to do His will.

2. When the Philistines brought the ark into the house of their god Dagon, they were saying that now Jehovah was in the power of Dagon.

3. God answered the wicked Philistines by showing them that Jehovah is God and Dagon is an idol. He did it by:

    a. performing great wonders;

    b. hardening the hearts of the Philistines.

4. They must have been fearful that something might happen to Dagon, for they came early the next morning to see their god. He was fallen on his face before the ark. Dagon was bowing down to the ark. He was subject to Jehovah. The Philistines understood, but with hard hearts they picked up their god and put him in place again.

5. Early the next morning when they went to Dagon's house, they saw plainly that Jehovah is God; for Dagon's head and hands were cut off on the threshold. Their god had no brains nor power. Instead of saying that Dagon was no god, the Philistines would not step on the threshold of Dagon's house, for it was still holy to them.

Read verses 6-12

6. Then the Lord put His hand down heavily on the city of Ashdod. The troubles that came to Ashdod were wonders, as the plagues in Egypt were. If we read these verses carefully, we find probably as many as three plagues.

339

a.   The hand of the Lord was heavy on them (verse 6) and He smote them (verse 9), probably with a quick-killing plague.

b.   He sent them emerods (hemorrhoids), which were bowel problems.

c.   And because the Philistines sent back golden mice (chapter 6:4), there must have been a plague of field mice which destroyed their crops.

7.   They knew Jehovah was destroying them, but their hearts were hard. They asked, "What shall we do now?" The question has a very easy answer: "Return the ark to Israel." But then they would have to say that Jehovah is the God of heaven and earth, and that they were in His power. They would not do that!

8.   So they brought the ark to Gath; and the Lord destroyed the people there.

9.   Without asking, the men of Gath brought the ark to Ekron. The rulers of Ekron would not accept it. But before they could gather to decide what to do, the plagues had begun.

DO NOT FORGET that in our world today, the ungodly are still like the Philistines. They will worship any god but Jehovah and believe anything except His Word. Thank God that He gave you faith to believe in Him.

WORD STUDIES

smitten — to be destroyed by blows or disaster

LESSON 96
Ebenezer
I Samuel 6, 7

BEFORE WE BEGIN, we should know that the ark of the Lord was in the land of the Philistines seven months; and their country was being ruined. Before they were totally destroyed, they knew they must think of a way to return the ark they had stolen from the land of Israel.

Read I Samuel 6:1-9

LESSON OUTLINE

A. The Philistines Make Preparations

1. The rulers of the Philistines asked the heathen priests and diviners in their land for a solution to their problem. It was not easy, after they had stolen the ark in the first place, to be humbled before the Israelites and admit that Dagon was not a god. They must protect the honor of their idol. The priests suggested a double plan. The first part was to send a trespass* offering.

   a. They sent five golden mice, to match the five large cities in the land of the Philistines. We learn in verse 18 that in their heathen superstition they sent many more mice.

   b. They sent five golden emerods (golden boils or tumors) which caused some of the plagues and sickness in the land.

   c. These were just outward gifts to Israel. The Philistines did not repent for their terrible sin. Their motive was to protect themselves and their god Dagon.

   d. They would not admit, either, that Jehovah brought the plagues. In verse 5 they said "peradventure." Maybe, perhaps, the Lord brought the plagues, and will lighten His hand. They left the opening that it was not Jehovah at all Who had brought the plagues, but just "a chance that happened to us," (the last part of verse 9).

   e. We do not know whether or when Jehovah stopped the plagues. Our Lord does not stoop to the superstitons of the heathen, and stop His plagues just because they make golden offerings. Remember, too, that it was Jehovah, not the Philistines, Who brought back the ark to Israel, for He rules over all men and their plans.

2. The second part of the advice of the priests was a clever plan.

a. The Philistines themselves would not take back the ark, but they would put the ark on a new cart drawn by two cows who had been separated from their calves, and see what the cows would do. It would be the instinct of the mother cows to go back to their babies, of course.

b. The Philistines were looking out for themselves. If Jehovah had sent the plagues, He would see to it that the ark was returned to Israel. The Philistines still were not ready to admit that the awful plagues came from Jehovah.

c. It was natural for the cows to turn back to their calves. The Philistines probably expected them to go back. They thought they were letting the cows decide. But God was deciding. He used their plan to bring His ark back, and to teach the Philistines and us that He is Lord of all.

Read verses 12-21

B. To Bethshemesh

1. The Philistines put the cows and the cart on the road to Bethshemesh, a priests' city, on the border of Judah and Dan. Find it on your map. The cows went lowing down the road, but did not turn aside to their calves. Jehovah directed them to go to Israel. The five lords of the Philistines followed them.

2. They arrived at Bethshemesh at the time of wheat harvest. The reapers rejoiced to see the ark, and the Bethshemites made a fire with the wood of the cart and offered the animals as a sacrifice. The Levites put the ark and the golden jewels on a large stone, and the lords of the Philistines returned home.

3. The men of Bethshemesh looked at (or into) the ark with curious, staring, unholy eyes. These men stood in their unholiness before Jehovah. They forgot that sinners cannot come into the presence of the Holy God without preparing themselves. The Lord killed seventy men there (the number in the King James Version is most likely an error in copying). And those who lived asked, "Who is able to stand before this holy Lord God?"

Discuss in class how God's children
prepare to come to their holy God.

4. The fearful men of Bethshemesh sent the ark to Kirjath-jearim, the nearest city on the road to Shiloh, where the tabernacle was. Find it on your map. The Bible does not tell us why they did not take the ark back to Shiloh: possibly because of all the wickedness at Shiloh, or because they were waiting

342

for a command from Jehovah. They brought the ark to the house of Abinadab, very likely a Levite, and he consecrated his son to take care of the ark.

Read chapter 7:1-12

C. Ebenezer

1. The most holy place in the tabernacle stood empty, and the ark was in prison in the house of Abinadab. Verse 2 tells us the ark stayed there for twenty years. That was only one period of its stay. The ark was still there eighty years later when David was king, and the ark was never again returned to the tabernacle.

2. These were strange days, when the people were afraid of the ark and afraid of God; and the tabernacle at Shiloh was an empty shell without the ark. During this period Samuel was prophet and judge.

3. Remember, Samuel was a Nazarite judge. He was called by God to be separate. He also called Israel to separate themselves from all their idols and turn to Jehovah, verse 3. The people listened to him and obeyed.

4. Samuel was a different kind of judge. When the people put away their idols, he told them to gather at Mizpeh (find it on your map). He did not say, "I will gather an army," or "I will lead you in battle against the Philistines." He said, "I will pray for you," verse 5. Samuel was not a man of battle, but a prophet and a priest.

5. When Samuel prayed for them, the people poured out water, a symbol of pouring out their hearts in sorrow for their sins. They also fasted, a symbol of being so sad inside that they could not eat.

6. The Philistines heard that they were at Mizpeh, and thought the Israelites were getting ready for battle. When their enemies came with their army, the Israelites were afraid. Do not forget that the Lord sent the Philistines there, to show His people that when they were faithful to Him, He would give them the victory.

7. Samuel prepared for battle in a strange way: he offered a burnt offering. When the Philistines came near, the Lord thundered, not with ordinary thunder, but with a wonder, as He had done once before, to the five kings of the south in Joshua's time. Israel chased the Philistines, and Jehovah gave them the victory, and they took back their cities from the Philistines.

8. As the Israelites were pursuing, between Mizpeh and Shen, Samuel took a stone and called it Ebenezer.

343

DO NOT FORGET what Ebenezer means: a stone of help; and Samuel said to Israel, "Hitherto hath the Lord helped us." Up to this time, the Lord had helped them. In fact, up to this time it was all God's work. And because Jehovah never changes, He will go on helping His people forever. Ebenezer is a stone of thankful remembrance and of glad hope — for us, too.

WORD STUDIES

trespass — a sin, or a wrong act accompanied by force

LESSON 97
A King for Israel
I Samuel 8, 9

BEFORE WE BEGIN, in chapter 7:16 and 17, we learn that each year Samuel traveled a circuit. Circuit comes from the word circle. The cities of Bethel, Gilgal, Mizpeh, and Samuel's home town of Ramah were in the circuit, in the southern part of Canaan. Find the cities on your map.

Read I Samuel 8:1-6

LESSON OUTLINE

A. Israel Asks for a King

1. In verse 1 we suddenly find out that Samuel is an old man. He was about forty years old at Ebenezer. Twenty or more years must have passed, and he was sixty or older.

2. Samuel made his sons, Joel and Abiah, judges over Israel. But they were not faithful, obedient sons, who served the Lord. They were interested in money and in taking bribes, but not in justice for the people. The Israelites did not want Samuel's sons to rule them. They asked for a king.

3. Israel's asking for a king probably did not surprise Samuel. The people's wish did not come suddenly. Do you remember that they had already wanted to make Gideon and Jephthah kings?

4. Was it wrong for Israel to ask for a king? No.

   a. God's law allowed a king. He even told His people what kind of king He would choose, Deuteronomy 17:15.

   b. God had promised a king when He said, "a Sceptre shall rise out of Israel," in Numbers 24:17. Israel's kings were to be types of the great King, Jesus Christ, Who was coming.

5. There was a reason why the people asked for a king. During the period of the judges, Israel was never brought together as a nation. We often read in Judges: "There was no king in Israel. . . ," no king to rule and no king to unite them.

6. But this request of the elders of Israel at this time was wrong, and Samuel had reason to be displeased with them. Why?

   a. By asking for a king, the elders were rejecting Samuel as judge. They rejected a judge who had called the people back to the service of Jehovah.

   b. The elders wanted a king as all the nations had. They wanted to be like the heathen nations.

345

7. Samuel went to the Lord in prayer to ask for His answer.

Read verses 7-9

B. God's Answer

1. God told Samuel to listen to the people, not because Jehovah thought it was a good request. He did not approve of the people's attitude: to be like the heathen nations. He gave them their wish so they would learn some hard lessons from all the troubles which would soon come upon them.

2. Then the Lord explained to Samuel that when they rejected him, it was not Samuel they rejected, but Samuel's God. They did not want God. They wanted to be like all the other nations and worship idols. Read verse 8 once more. They rejected Samuel because he was Jehovah's prophet.

Read verses 10-18

3. Although God told Samuel to give the people their wish, Samuel warned them about the rights a king has. A king has the right to demand their animals and crops for food for his table, and he has the right to treat his people as slaves.

Discuss in class whether you would want a king.

4. Samuel's protest to the people made them more certain they wanted a king. Read verse 19. After Samuel heard their words, he was short with them and sent them home, without telling them yes or no.

5. Remember, Jehovah was ruling over these happenings. He had planned them from eternity.

6. Most of the people came to Samuel with evil motives. But God had His own little flock in Israel. He kept them safe, so that the nation of Israel would continue until Jesus came. God tells us about it in chapter 9:16: "for I have looked upon my people, because their cry is come unto me."

Read chapter 9:1-4

C. Saul Loses His Asses

1. In this chapter, the Lord brings to Samuel the man who will soon be the first king of Israel. His name is Saul, the son of Kish, from the city of Gibeah in the tribe of Benjamin. God brought Samuel and Saul together through a simple problem. Saul's father's asses were lost; and his father Kish sent Saul and a servant to look for them.

2. When we do our map work, we will find the places they searched for the lost asses, verse 4.

Read verses 5-14

3. Saul was ready to go home without the asses. He was afraid his father was worrying. But the servant suggested that they go to the man of God who was in the city. Notice that Saul did not think about the man of God. He did not seem to know about Samuel and his works. Notice, too, that the servant called him "a man of God," and "an honorable man" in verse 6, and "the seer" in verse 11; but not by his name Samuel. Saul and his servant also had the idea that they could not go to the seer without a gift; and the servant furnished a gift of the fourth part of a shekel of silver.

4. As they went to the hill in the city, the high place where the altar was, Saul and his servant met maidens who told them to hurry, for the seer was ready to offer the sacrifice. This was the place God chose to have Samuel and Saul meet.

Read verses 17-27

D. Saul Meets Samuel

1. A day earlier, God had told Samuel that tomorrow he would meet and anoint the first king of Israel. He was a man from the tribe of Benjamin. Do you think Samuel was surprised to hear that the Lord chose a man from Benjamin? Hadn't God promised a king from the tribe of Judah? See Genesis 49:10. Samuel said nothing about this mystery.

2. When Samuel met Saul, what kind of man did he see? A choice and goodly man (verse 2) a head taller than most men. Saul was a handsome, intelligent young man.

3. Saul must have been overwhelmed by the next words of Samuel.

    a. You will eat with me today.

    b. Tomorrow I will tell you all that is in your heart.

    c. The asses that were lost three days ago have been found.

    d. On whom is all the desire of Israel?

4. Saul understood that God was speaking to him through Samuel's words. He could figure out that the desire of all Israel was to have a king. Read Saul's answer in verse 21.

5. At the feast, Saul sat in the place of honor. Afterward Samuel and Saul talked privately, verse 25. What do you think they talked about?

DO NOT FORGET that nothing, small or great, in our lives just happens. Jehovah has planned it all, down to things such as lost asses and meeting God's prophet. God has planned the small details in our lives, too. For us, His children, He plans every detail for our good and for our salvation.

LESSON 98
Saul Becomes King
I Samuel 10, 11

BEFORE WE BEGIN, in the last three verses of chapter 9, we can sense the excitement of Samuel and Saul. They talked together during the evening, and were up at daybreak. Samuel was in a hurry to have Saul leave. Our lesson will tell us why.

Read I Samuel 9:27-10:16

LESSON OUTLINE

A. Saul is Anointed

1. As Samuel and Saul walked to the end of the city (many Bible students think it was Bethlehem), they told the servant to go on ahead; for Samuel was ready to show Saul the Word of God.

2. Samuel wanted this early morning meeting to be private. He poured oil over Saul's head and kissed him. By pouring the oil, Samuel showed Saul that the Lord anointed him to be king.

3. Saul was to be captain over God's inheritance, verse 1. God's inheritance was God's people; and God's people are called a theocracy: a people ruled by God. Ever since the Israelites became a nation, they were a theocracy, a nation ruled by God. In all the history we have already studied, God ruled His people. Now, for the first time, Jehovah gave His people a theocratic king, a king who ruled under Him. Saul was the first king. Not all the kings of Israel ruled under God in righteousness. Some were disobedient, but all the kings were called to rule righteously under God. This is very important for us to understand before we study the kings.

4. Samuel then gave Saul three signs.

a. He would meet two men at Rachel's grave, which was just north of Bethlehem, at Ramah. Their message would be that the asses were found and that Saul's father was worried.

b. Next he would meet three men going north to Bethel, one carrying three young goats, another three loaves of bread, and the third a bottle of wine. They would give Saul two loaves of bread.

c. At the hill near to his own city of Gibeah, where a garrison* of Philistines was stationed, he would meet a company of prophets, with

348

musical instruments, verse 5. On our worksheets we will follow Saul's route, and also learn more about the musical instruments.

Discuss in class how you would feel
if you could join these prophets of Jehovah.

5. Notice the careful details of Samuel's instructions. When the words of Samuel's prophecy came true, Saul would know that Samuel spoke with authority from God.

6. In verse 6, Samuel told Saul that the Spirit of the Lord would come upon him — not the Spirit of the Lord Who gives His people new hearts of obedience and love for God. The Lord gives only His people new hearts. Saul was not one of God's children. He lived only for the things of this world. What, then, was this Spirit of the Lord? It gave Saul the talents and ability to be able to rule God's people. For even though Saul did not care about serving Jehovah, and later was very disobedient, Jehovah used him to rule His people.

7. When it was time for Saul to leave Samuel, the Lord gave him another heart, a heart which could serve as king under God, a heart which would make him outwardly religious and obedient, at least in the first part of his rule. He would appear to be a king under God.

8. After Saul left Samuel, he joined a company of prophets and prophesied. The people who knew him were surprised, and asked, "Is Saul also among the prophets?" They knew that Saul did not care about the things of God's kingdom.

Read verses 17-27

B. Saul's Inauguration*

1. Samuel called the people together at Mizpeh, for it was necessary that Jehovah show publicly, to the whole nation, whom He had chosen as king. As yet no one knew, except Samuel and Saul, not even Saul's nosey uncle! (verses 15 and 16)

2. Once more, Samuel spoke the Lord's words of scolding in verses 18 and 19, for Israel still wanted a king like the heathen nations had.

3. Because all of Israel must know that God was doing the choosing, the Lord chose Saul publicly, by lot.

4. After Saul was chosen, he disappeared. Why?

    a. He knew how difficult it would be to rule over Israel.

    b. He knew that he was called to be a king who trusted in Jehovah and who ruled under Jehovah.

    c. He knew he could not lean on Jehovah. He would have to rule in his own strength; and he must have hidden in a moment of panic, because he was afraid.

5. The Lord showed them where Saul had hidden, and all the people shouted, "Let the king live!"

Read I Samuel 11

C. Saul's First Battle

1. Saul went home to Gibeah and farmed while he waited for the right time to take over the rule of the people of Israel.

2. Meanwhile, on the other side of the Jordan, Nahash, king of the Ammonites, attacked Jabesh-Gilead. Find it on your map. Nahash had bothered them for some time already. See chapter 12:12.

3. The people of Jabesh-Gilead surrendered to Ammon. There was no one in Israel to help them. They told Nahash to withdraw his army, and they would be his servants.

4. The wicked Nahash knew that Israel would not come and fight him. He made a devilish condition to the agreement with the men of Jabesh-Gilead: He would withdraw his troops only if he put out the right eyes of every man. Why did he do that?

    a. To disgrace Israel before the other nations.

    b. To blaspheme* Israel's God.

    c. To lay it for a reproach (or scorn) on God's people (verse 2).

5. The elders of Jabesh-Gilead asked for seven days' time to send for help. Nahash agreed. He was sure there would be no one to rescue them in seven days.

6. When the messengers from Jabesh came to Gibeah, the people wept when they heard the awful tidings. Saul, coming from the field, asked about the weeping people.

7. When they told him the sad news, the Spirit of the Lord came upon him, the Spirit Who made him able to act as a theocratic king. The Spirit also gave him the anger of a king who rules under God. Saul's anger made him act.

    a. He cut his oxen in pieces,

    b. and sent the pieces through all Israel, with the threat that their oxen would be cut up, too, if they did not respond to the call for help.

8. The terror of Jehovah came upon the men of Israel, and 330,000 men came together for battle. Saul sent messengers telling Jabesh they would

350

have help tomorrow. The men of Jabesh told the Ammonites an untruth, verse 10, so that Saul's men would come upon them unexpectedly. And the next day Israel won a great victory over the Ammonites.

DO NOT FORGET that the victory was a wonder which God gave to His people because He loved them; and **DO NOT FORGET**, either, that Saul, who was the leader of this wondrous victory, could not love and praise the Lord Who gave that victory, for he was not God's child. It is a terrible thing to see God's wonders in unbelief.

WORD STUDIES
1. garrison — military troops stationed in a town
2. inauguration — a ceremony to put someone in office
3. blaspheme — to speak ill of God or sacred things

LESSON 99
Saul's Disobedience
I Samuel 12, 13

BEFORE WE BEGIN, we will go back to Mizpeh where Saul was inaugurated as king. Not everyone at Mizpeh received him as king. The men of Belial said, "How can this man save us?" (chapter 10:27) Now, after the victory at Jabesh-Gilead, Samuel called the people to renew the kingdom.

Read I Samuel 11:15

LESSON OUTLINE

A. The Renewal of the Kingdom

   1. Samuel called the people to Gilgal. We do not know which Gilgal it was: the one near the Jordan River or the one near the center of Canaan.

   2. At Mizpeh, where Saul was inaugurated, the people had shouted only: "Let the king live!" This time they made Saul king before Jehovah. They sacrificed burnt offerings and peace offerings (or thank offerings).

   3. Here at Gilgal, the nation of Israel was ready to be a theocratic kingdom, with Saul as a theocratic king, who would rule them under God.

   4. Then Samuel gave his farewell speech to Israel (in chapter 12). We will not study it in detail, but will notice three things:

      a. Samuel reminded them that he had been a godly judge.

      b. Samuel reminded them of all the wonders Jehovah had done for their fathers ever since they were in Egypt.

      c. Samuel reminded them once more of their sin of asking for a king as the heathen nations had; for Jehovah is their king. And Samuel warned them not to rebel against the commandments of the Lord.

   5. To show the people that their wickedness was great, verse 17, Samuel asked Jehovah for a striking sign. It was the time of wheat harvest (our months of May and June), and the land did not have rain in these months. But Samuel asked the Lord for a thunderstorm. Thunder is the voice of God's wrath. The people were frightened by the severe storm and confessed their sin of asking for a king; and they asked Samuel to pray for them, verse 19.

Read I Samuel 13:1-7

B. Saul Goes to Gilgal

   1. The events in this chapter took place soon after the renewing of the

kingdom in Gilgal. In verse 2 we read that from the people who were at Gilgal, Saul chose a standing army of 3,000 soldiers; 2,000 were stationed with Saul at Michmash, and 1,000 with Jonathan in Gibeah. He sent the rest of the people home. Find Michmash and Gibeah on your map, and Geba, where the Philistine garrison was stationed.

2. We meet Jonathan for the first time in this history. He must have been at least twenty years old already, if he was leading a part of Israel's army. That means that Saul was at least forty years old when he was made king.

3. Jonathan and his soldiers attacked the Philistine garrison. We do not know whether his father Saul knew about it or not. He smote the garrison, verse 3. Again, the Bible does not tell us how many Philistines were killed. The importance of this battle is that in these days of fear in Israel, such bravery as Jonathan had was an unheard of thing! King Saul broadcast the good news, saying, "Let the Hebrews hear!" (verse 3)

4. The Philistines were angry. Israel was "had in abomination." It means that they "stank" before the Philistines. The Philistines gathered a large army: 30,000 chariots, 6,000 soldiers on horseback, and foot soldiers as the sand of the sea: and they camped at Michmash.

Read verses 8-14

C. Saul Waits for Samuel

1. Saul called the men of Israel to Gilgal near the Jordan River. Find it once more on your map, and notice that it was not near the area of the battlefield at Michmash. Why did Saul go to Gilgal? He remembered Samuel's prophecy (in chapter 10:8). He waited there seven days, as Samuel had said.

2. These were seven hard days for Saul, a time of stress and tension. Why?

   a. He knew he had to fight a large, well-equipped army.

   b. Saul's men were "much distressed," and they deserted him, verse 6. Some even went over the Jordan to the area of Gilead.

   c. He had only 600 men left, verse 15.

3. Saul waited the seven days, until it was probably late in the seventh day, for Samuel to come to offer the sacrifice before the battle.

Discuss in class what Saul should have done now.

4. Saul said, "Bring hither a burnt offering to me, and a peace offering." As soon as he had finished offering the burnt sacrifice, Samuel came.

5. Saul acted as if nothing were wrong and went to meet him. Samuel had a short question to ask: "What hast thou done?" Read Saul's hopeless

answer in verses 11 and 12. He said, "I forced myself." It was the desperate act of a man without trust in God, who leaned on his own strength.

6. Samuel's answer was, "Thou hast done foolishly." From a natural point of view, he had done foolishly:

a. he had waited too long — he waited until he had only 600 men left;

b. he did not wait long enough, for he sacrificed too soon; Samuel came when he was finished sacrificing.

7. Saul did foolishly from a spiritual point of view:

a. he did not obey God's command which Samuel had given him, to wait seven days;

b. his sin was so serious that God would take the kingdom from him.

8. There are three parts to remember about Saul's disobedience.

a. Remember that a burnt offering was an act of consecration, an offering of oneself to the Lord and to His service with all one's heart. Saul did not do that. He only went through the motions. Therefore, his sacrifice was a lie.

b. Remember, too, that in chapter 10:8 Samuel told Saul to wait "till I come to thee, and show thee what thou shalt do." Samuel would show him the Word of the Lord. Saul needed battle instructions from the Lord, for the Lord would give the victory by a wonder.

c. Remember, finally, that Saul refused to act as a theocratic king, as a king under God. He went his own way.

Read verses 15-23

D. The Sad Ending

1. Samuel left Saul and went to Gibeah. Saul soon followed with his small army. What had begun as the gathering of an army for a great victory ended in failure. The Philistines still ruled, and Saul had just 600 soldiers left.

2. There were no swords or spears in Israel except with Saul and Jonathan, and no blacksmiths. The Israelites even had to go to the Philistines to sharpen their farm implements.

3. Saul and Jonathan and their soldiers were stationed at Gibeah, near to the Philistines at Michmash.

4. The Philistines did as they pleased. They sent out spoilers (thieves) to rob the land, in three directions: northeast, southeast, and west, verse 17. Saul and Jonathan and their armies were stationed to the southwest.

DO NOT FORGET that Saul was in a sad and hopeless position. He did not know what to do, not because he was stupid, but because he was unbelieving. Thank God that He made us His children and gave us the gift of faith. We can read Psalm 118:1-17 and understand what it means to trust in the Lord. See the Idea Corner on your worksheet.

Victory by Faith
I Samuel 14:1-46

BEFORE WE BEGIN, we will find Saul and Jonathan still stationed at Gibeah with their very small army of 600 men. Saul did nothing. He did not try to fight the Philistines, not because he was a coward, but because he had no faith. He did not believe in Jehovah's wonders. If he had believed, he would have remembered Gideon's wonderful victory with only 300 men.

Read I Samuel 14:1-10

LESSON OUTLINE

A. Two Opposites

  1. Saul

    a. Saul the king, the leader, sat still, doing nothing, under a pomegranate tree near Gibeah.

    b. With him was Ahiah the priest, the great-grandson of Eli. Ahiah wore an ephod out there on the battlefield. Remember that though Saul was an unbeliever, he did not worship idols. He was a "religious" man — outwardly. He knew the laws of Moses, and obeyed them — outwardly. He had a priest. He went through the motions of being religious.

    c. The 600 soldiers who were with Saul may have been a small remnant of believers. But they could not go to battle under the leadership of a king who would do nothing.

  2. Jonathan

    a. Jonathan said to his armorbearer, "Let us go over to the Philistines' garrison," verse 1. In verse 6 he called them "the garrison of these uncircumcised." He meant that the Philistines were outside of God's covenant, that they were blasphemers of God, and spoilers of His people. Jonathan did not tell his plans to his father, for he knew his father would forbid him to go.

    b. Jonathan had strong faith in Jehovah, and he showed it by his words and actions. He told his armorbearer that the Lord can work with many men or a few men, and that the victory for His people is always the Lord's. In verse 6 he said, "It may be that the Lord will work for us." Jonathan did not doubt whether or not the Lord would help them; but he said it humbly, for he and his armorbearer were sinful men, living in a sinful nation who did not really want Jehovah to rule over them.

    c.   Jonathan suggested a sign, and his armorbearer agreed with him.

        1) They would make themselves known to the Philistines.

        2) The Philistines could have two reactions: they could say, "Stay where you are and we will come to fight you;" or, "Come up unto us."

    d.   Jonathan was not tempting the Lord by giving this sign, but was showing his faith that God would save His people. This sign was a test which meant to show whether the Philistines were afraid or not.

Read verses 11-15

B. The Test

    1. At this time the Philistines occupied the heights of Michmash. There was a passage to go up to the top of the mountain, and on each side was a high rock, like a tooth, jutting up. The rock on the north was called Bozez, "the shining one," and the one on the south Seneh, "the tooth." Just below this steep passage was a thick forest.

    2. The Philistines at the point of the rock Seneh could look down and see Jonathan, and probably his armorbearer behind him. But they could not tell how many soldiers might be hiding in the thick forest below, ready to attack. The Philistines would never imagine that just two men came to challenge them.

    3. Jonathan had a purpose with his test:

    a.   If the Philistines said, "Stay there until we come to you," they were brave and ready to fight.

    b.   If they said: "Come up to us," they were afraid, and dared not attack Jonathan and his armorbearer.

    4. When they showed themselves, the Philistines said, "The Hebrews come forth out of the holes where they had hid themselves," verse 11. They were afraid! In the next breath they said, with a bravado* they did not feel, "Come up to us, and we will show you a thing."

    5. The Lord used Jonathan's test to terrify the Philistines. Jonathan knew that Jehovah had delivered them into the hands of Israel, verse 12. It was a sign of God's salvation for His people.

    6. Jonathan and his armorbearer went into action. They climbed with their hands and feet up the steep side of Bozez. No one can get ready for battle

357

by climbing the sheer cliff of a rock, single file. Anyone on top of the rock could kill him as he reached the top.

7. But Jonathan and his armorbearer climbed by faith. And by a wonder of Jehovah, the Philistines were paralyzed with fear. Quickly, Jonathan and his armorbearer killed twenty men in about a half-acre of ground.

8. Fear is contagious. The Lord made this special fear to spread through the Philistine army. The closest soldiers trembled, and then the whole army trembled. Jehovah made the fear worse by sending an earthquake. The whole Philistine army was wild with fear because of two brave men, whom God used to save His people.

Read verses 16-23

C. The Battle

1. Saul's watchmen saw the army of soldiers melting away. Saul ordered the soldiers to be numbered. He probably already suspected who was missing, for he must have known of Jonathan's strong faith in Jehovah.

2. We would guess that Saul's reaction would be to give orders to gather the army and pursue in haste. He didn't. He called for Ahiah the priest to bring the ephod so he could tell Saul what the will of the Lord was.

3. But Saul could see the will of God.

    a. He saw the Philistines fleeing.

    b. He saw (and felt?) God's earthquake.

    c. He knew that Jonathan and his armorbearer, who started it, were men of faith.

    d. He saw the wonder of Jehovah's victory, and closed his eyes to it.

4. The noise of the Philistines was so great that Saul stopped the priest (verse 19) and called the people to battle. Those who had hidden came back to fight, and Jehovah saved Israel that day, verse 23.

Read verses 24-32

D. Saul's Foolish Command

1. With a kind of religious piety, Saul uttered a curse. Read it in verse 24. No one dared disobey his order. His command had a selfish motive: "that I may be avenged of my enemies."

2. The soldiers needed food. There was no reason why they could not eat while they were pursuing. When they came to a woods with honey, no one dared eat it.

3. Jonathan was not present, of course, when Saul uttered his curse. He

358

ate the honey and was refreshed.

Discuss in class what Jonathan meant by saying
"My father hath troubled the land," verse 29.

4. The result was that at the end of the day, the people were so hungry they disobeyed God's law, verse 33.

5. When Ahiah asked God whether they should pursue the Philistines that night, He did not answer. Saul concluded that someone must have sinned. He must have suspected Jonathan, for he put Jonathan and himself on one side and his army on the other; and Jonathan was taken. Read Jonathan's answer in verse 43. Saul answered, "Thou shall surely die, Jonathan." In unbelief, Saul was ready to have his son, who saved Israel, put to death.

DO NOT FORGET that God's people saw that Jonathan was a man of faith, and that through him God brought the victory and salvation to Israel that day. They rescued Jonathan from his father. And Saul once again failed. He did not finish the battle.

WORD STUDIES

bravado — a boastful pretending to be brave

LESSON 101
Saul's Rebellion
I Samuel 15

BEFORE WE BEGIN, although Saul could not fight the wars of the wonders of Jehovah, for he did not believe in wonders, he did lead Israel with well-organized armies against many enemies. With his natural courage and ability to lead an army, he was popular with the people of Israel. Chapter 14:47-52 tells us about his victories and about his family. We will not study it in detail.

Read I Samuel 15:1-7

LESSON OUTLINE

A. The Battle With Amalek

1. Samuel came to Saul, verse 1. He reminded Saul that he came with authority from Jehovah, and that he was a true prophet of the Lord, who had anointed Saul to be a theocratic king to rule God's people under Him.

2. Samuel came to Saul with the words of verse 1 because he had an important message: the Lord had given a command to destroy Amalek. Samuel reminded Saul of the history of the Amalekites:

    a. what they had done to Israel at Rephidim (Lesson 49).

    b. that Jehovah would have war with Amalek from generation to generation, Exodus 17:16.

3. Through the years Amalek had bothered Israel. Now it was time to destroy Amalek completely. Read verse 3 carefully. God told Saul and his soldiers to leave nothing; for Amalek was under God's ban, God's curse, just as Jericho had been. All the Amalekites and everything they had must be devoted to the Lord, for it all belonged to Him in His judgment of this wicked tribe. Amalek could not be saved.

4. Saul gathered an army: 200,000 men from Israel, and 10,000 from Judah. Because Saul could not trust in Jehovah, he put his trust in numbers — a large army.

5. The Amalekites, you remember, were a wild, warlike tribe, with no fixed home. They wandered, usually in deserts. At this time the Amalekites were wandering to the south of Israel. Saul went to Telaim (find it on your map) and made an ambush against a city there.

6. He first warned the Kenites, who lived in that area, to leave the scene of

danger. The Kenites came from Jethro; and Hobab, one of the Kenites, went to Canaan with Israel. Do you remember?

7. Saul's army won a great victory and chased the Amalekites far west, to Shur, near Egypt. We do not know just where this place was.

Read verses 8-12

B. Saul's Disobedience

1. Saul and his soldiers destroyed all the people except Agag, which was a name for all the kings of Amalek.

2. Saul and his soldiers destroyed all the animals except the best of the sheep and oxen. Although Saul did not keep the same treasures as Achan did in Jericho, his sin was the same as Achan's sin. Why did Saul disobey?

a. He said, in verse 21, that the animals were for sacrifices. Verse 19 tells us that the people were greedy. They flew upon the spoil, and did not even think about sacrifices.

b. Saul's reason for saving Agag was probably pride. He could show off to the whole nation the king whom he had conquered.

3. Jehovah came to Samuel in the night, and told him that he rejected Saul. He was no more fit to be a theocratic king; and his sons would not rule after him. Why was this such a terrible sin?

a. It was God's will that Israel shall "blot out the remembrance of Amalek from under heaven," Deuteronomy 25:19. God's command was the same as He had given at Jericho: to destroy the city completely, for it was cursed by Jehovah. The Israelites were called to devote everything to God. (See Lesson 70.)

b. Saul and the people wanted the spoils of Amalek more than obedience to God's commands, just what Achan had wanted at Jericho. Therefore, Saul was no more fit to be a theocratic king, to be a ruler under God.

4. Samuel was sad and cried to the Lord all through the night, verse 11. In the morning he went to find Saul. You would think that Saul would have come to report to Samuel. But Saul would not be comfortable with God's prophet now.

5. Saul went to Carmel (find it on your map) and set up a monument to draw the attention of all Israel to his victory. Then he went to Gilgal, the place where Israel had camped just after they had crossed the Jordan. Find it on your map. Samuel followed Saul from Carmel to Gilgal.

Read verses 13-23

C. God Rejects Saul

1. With a guilty conscience and with forced friendliness, Saul greeted Samuel, in verse 13. Before Samuel could ask, Saul told him he had obeyed the commands he had not obeyed.

2. Samuel challenged his words and asked, "What meaneth this bleating of the sheep in mine ears?" Saul explained it this way:

   a. He blamed the soldiers: "They have brought them," and the people: "They spared the best of the sheep," verse 15.

   b. He explained that the people wanted to sacrifice the animals, even though they knew that the devoted things already belonged to Jehovah. They could not be offered to Him, for they had been cursed by Him.

3. Verse 9 tells us the truth: "But Saul and the people spared Agag, and the best of the sheep." Saul was to blame, too.

4. Read the scolding of Samuel in verse 17. Saul had never known how to be humble before Jehovah. Once he had hidden behind the baggage because he was afraid, but he soon learned that he was an able leader of his army. He won victories. He could do without God now.

5. Saul answered, "I have obeyed the voice of the Lord," verse 20. He blamed the people for the sin. But Samuel told him what his sin was: "to obey is better than sacrifice. . ." verse 22. This does not mean that sacrifices are useless, but they may not take the place of obedience. Obedience comes first, and sacrifices of praise and thanksgiving follow.

Discuss in class why God wants obedience first in our lives, too, and then thankfulness and praise.

6. Saul's sin was rebellion against God. Instead of offering himself to God, he made himself his own god. That is why verse 23 calls his sin idolatry — worship of himself, and witchcraft — through the power of the devil.

Read verses 24-35

7. At last Saul said the words of verse 24. He should have put a period after "words," but he added, "because I feared the people." He made his sin seem as small as possible. He blamed the people and did not really confess his sin.

8. After Saul heard that the Lord had rejected him, he must have been surprised and afraid.

   a. He still wanted Samuel to worship the Lord with him. Samuel's answer was no.

   b. Saul grasped the skirt of his robe as he was leaving, and it ripped.

Samuel explained that it was a sign of God ripping the kingdom from Saul.

c. Then the real reason why Saul wanted Samuel to worship with him came out: he wanted to be honored before the elders of Israel, verse 30.

9. Samuel turned and went with Saul. He had one more duty: to kill Agag. He had to finish the command of God and carry out the curse on Amalek.

DO NOT FORGET that when Samuel first met Saul, he said, "On whom is all the desire of Israel?" Now Jehovah rejected Saul as the theocratic king. It is no wonder that Samuel mourned. He was sad because Saul could not be king, and he was more sad that Saul was not one of God's children.

LESSON 102

David is Anointed King

I Samuel 16

BEFORE WE BEGIN, in this last lesson for the year we will end with God's choosing a new king for Israel, a king from the tribe of Judah, a man after God's own heart, and a man who was one of the ancestors of Jesus the King.

Read I Samuel 16:1-5

LESSON OUTLINE

A. The Lord Sends Samuel to Bethlehem

1. Saul had been rejected as king, but he was not immediately put out of office. He remained king of Israel for several years; for the Lord had a use for this wicked king for a time, as you will learn in your lessons next year.

2. The Lord asked Samuel in verse 1, "How long wilt thou mourn for Saul?" It would not be right for Samuel to continue to mourn, even though he grieved for Saul. For Jehovah had plans for His people. He called Samuel to work out those plans. He told Samuel:

   a. go to Jesse, who lives in Bethlehem, and take anointing oil with you;

   b. the king I have chosen is there; he is one of Jesse's sons.

3. Samuel was afraid.

   a. He lived in difficult and dangerous times. However, before this time we have never read that he was afraid when Jehovah called him to a hard task.

   b. He said, "If Saul hear it, he will kill me." This was the reason for his fear.

   c. Samuel seemed sure that Saul would kill him, probably because Saul was already under the influence of the evil spirit mentioned in verse 14.

4. But God would not let Samuel be killed. He had work for him to do. The Lord's answer made it easier for Samuel to go to Bethlehem. He said, "Say, I am come to sacrifice to the Lord," verse 2. Was that a lie? No, for Samuel did sacrifice at Bethlehem. Besides, it was God's command to keep the main reason private for the time being.

Discuss whether we as God's children
must always tell the whole truth.

5. It had been Samuel's custom to travel a circuit and visit various places in

364

Israel, to sacrifice and to teach the people. Remember: the ark of Jehovah was not in the tabernacle; and without the ark, the tabernacle was an empty shell. The Israelites' only place of worship was gone. On his travels, God's prophet taught the people, scolded them for their sins, called them to repentance, and sacrificed. In this way, the fear of Jehovah was kept alive in Israel.

6. The men of Bethlehem were afraid. They asked, "Comest thou peaceably?" They may have been afraid of being confronted with their sins.

7. Samuel's answer calmed their fears. He said, "Peaceably," and he called them to come with him to the sacrifice, the symbol of the taking away of their sins by Jesus' blood. First they must sanctify (or purify) themselves by washing themselves and by putting on clean clothes. It was a sign of getting their souls ready to meet Jesus, Who would wash away their sins. At the end of verse 5 we read specifically that he sanctified Jesse and his sons, and called them to the sacrifice.

Read verses 6-13

B. David Is Anointed

1. It is likely that Samuel went to the house of Jesse afterward for the sacrificial meal. There he met Jesse's family. Remember that Jesse was a descendant of Boaz and Ruth (Ruth 4:22) and in the line of the ancestors of Jesus.

2. Before Samuel sat down to eat, he took care of Jehovah's business. He called the sons of Jesse, one by one, to pass before him. To Samuel, Eliab the oldest son looked like the man chosen by Jehovah. Read the Lord's answer in verse 7. The verse in the Hebrew language says, "man looks at the eyes," for the eyes are the outward part of a man. God looks on the heart, the inner part of a man.

3. Abinadab, Shammah, and four more sons passed before Samuel. He must have told father Jesse why he had come, for each time he said, "Neither has the Lord chosen this."

4. He asked, "Are here all thy children?" Samuel would not sit down to eat until the youngest, who kept the sheep, appeared.

5. The Lord gives us a description of David. He was ruddy. This refers to his hair. It was reddish or auburn. Most of the people in the area of Canaan had black hair. David had beautiful eyes and was a handsome young man.

6. Samuel anointed him in the presence of his brothers. Samuel must have

been happy, for he anointed a man from the tribe of Judah, a fulfillment of the prophecy in Genesis 49:10. The Spirit of Jehovah came upon David. And Samuel returned to Ramah.

Read verses 14-23

C. David Plays for Saul

    1. After Saul was rejected, the Spirit of the Lord left him and the Lord sent an evil spirit, the spirit of a devil, to trouble him. From what we read about Saul later we know that this spirit gave him no peace of mind, but only thoughts of evil, even driving him at times to madness (insanity).

    2. When Saul's servants suggested soothing music to calm Saul's troubled spirit, they thought of David and his harp. They knew he was an expert harpist, whose music would have a soothing effect on Saul.

    3. They knew that he was a "mighty man and a man of war." The Bible does not tell us where David had fought. In fact, the Bible, especially in the days of Saul and David, does not make clear the exact order in which the events took place.

    4. David took with him the simple gifts from a farm home in the country, verse 20, and Saul loved him greatly and made David his armorbearer. In the house of the king whom Jehovah had rejected, God was preparing David for his calling to be a true theocratic king over His covenant people.

DO NOT FORGET that in all our lessons this year we have been following the line of God's covenant people, the people with whom He had a relationship of friendship. We also followed a special line in the covenant, from Adam, through Noah, to Abraham and his seed, up to David. Now David, the ancestor of Jesus and the first obedient theocratic king in Israel, has been anointed to be king. David looked forward to his Savior's first coming, as we look forward to our Savior's final coming.